DATE DUE

MAY 26. 1995			
AUG. 04. 1995			
SEP. 16. 1995			
OCT. 12. 1995			
MAY 07. 1996			
JUL. 24. 1996			
FEB 18. 1997			
3/22			
9/19			

Demco, Inc. 38-293

A SMALL COUNTRY LIVING GOES ON

Also by Jeanine McMullen

My Small Country Living
Wind in the Ash Tree

A SMALL COUNTRY LIVING GOES ON

Jeanine McMullen

Illustrations by Trudi Finch

W · W · NORTON & COMPANY
New York   *London*

Aknowledgments

The author would like to thank the copyright holders for their kind permission in
allowing quotations to be reproduced in this book:

Medieval English Lyrics, 'Daffyd Nanmor's poem to Gwen O'r Dhol, Joseph P. Clancy,
Gomer Press, 1961.

The Children of Green Knowe, Lucy M. Boston, Faber and Faber, 1954.

The Swan in the Evening, Collins, 1967, with the permission of the Society of Authors on
behalf of the estate of Rosamond Lehmann.

The Collected Poems, 'Stupidity Street,' Ralph Hodgson, Macmillan, 1965.

Hogmanay and Tiffany, Gillian Edwards, Geoffrey Bles, 1970.

Printed in the United States of America.
Manufacturing by Arcata Graphics/Halliday.

Library of Congress Cataloging-in-Publication Data

McMullen, Jeanine.
A small country living goes on / Jeanine McMullen; illustrations
by Trudi Finch.
p.   cm.
1. Farm life—Wales. 2. McMullen, Jeanine. 3. Small country
living (Radio program) 4. Radio broadcasters—Great Britain—
—Biography. I. Title.
S522.G7M355   1991
630'.92—dc20
91–17151

ISBN 0-393-03039-3

W. W. Norton & Company, Inc., 500 Fifth Avenue, New York, N.Y. 10110
W. W. Norton & Company, Ltd., 10 Coptic Street, London WCIA 1PU

1 2 3 4 5 6 7 8 9 0

To everyone who took part in *A Small Country Living*, to all of you in Bristol who helped to get it ready for transmission and, most of all, to those of you who listened.
With my thanks.

A SMALL COUNTRY LIVING GOES ON

Chapter 1

The stars were brilliant that night.

One speared light so sharply through the branches of the trees at the top of the hill that for a moment I thought it was a poacher's torch and started forward, territorial instincts screaming. A light breeze twitched the trees into a curtsy and the star bobbed with them, flickered blue and green, and settled back into a piercing crystal.

They're always making fools of me, those stars. In a valley like this, with the hills forming the rim of a great bowl, perspectives changing like a kaleidoscope, and the air above so clear you want to drink it, the stars have a life of their own and many disguises. I actually reported one to the police for being a satellite someone or other had lost, so large and close it had been, in its dance of many colours, as it hovered over the edge of one of the twin peaks of the Fans. My old friend, playing at torches, had been getting a rise out of me for years, especially on nights like this, with my mind tunnelled into the possibilities of what was happening in the lambing shed, and no time to admire the dazzlement of idle stars.

Lambing itself was over. The night before had been full of drama, with a final surge of twins and triplets arriving simultaneously and their bewildered mothers needing extra pens, or a few quick lessons in motherhood if it was their first time round. They'd been recovering all day, but by evening the ewes were busy re-establishing their places in the hierarchy or creating small circles of intimacy with their lambs at the centre.

The shearlings who, until yesterday, had still been dizzy young things, in spite of their lamb-heavy bulk, had now assumed a look of deep responsibility and sheer adoration as they beheld their tiny

1

reasons for living; but one or two had murder in their eyes when they beheld someone else's. The first lamb of the season is loved by all the flock, but once their own lambs arrive it had better watch out.

Which was why I was on my way out to the shed. To a young lamb an udder is an udder, never mind who it's attached to, and unless their own mother is particularly protective and sure of her own offspring, at the beginning there were often cases of mistaken identity. One of the homicidal maniacs in the flock was quite capable of battering an intruder to death against the wall of the shed. Of course all the newest arrivals were in special pens, but lambs can find the smallest hole to get through and into trouble. They can do this from the moment they're born, trying, I'm sure, to get back into that warm dark place they've come from.

Part of the trouble is that, much to the ewes' disgust, I keep the whole flock in much longer than I should. No matter that all around me I see the tiny bodies of newborn lambs braving rain, sleet, snow, crows and foxes, mine must have every protection I can offer them for as long as possible. And that protection means a constant check on who's doing what to whom or whose, and making sure one of those inviting holes hasn't become a lamb death-trap. So that night the stars beckoned and flirted with me in vain.

Another puff of the breeze rustled a strand of ivy in the hedge as I picked my way down the slope of the yard, which was dry, for a change, but still treacherous enough if I trod on one of the smooth stones hidden in the grass. Too lazy to open the gate, I climbed over the fence, swore as a hole in my jeans caught on a loose piece of wire, and the wavering torch caught the dull gold gleam of straw. Not a sheep moved, so used are they to the sight and sound of me stuck on the fence and swearing. Even the lambs did nothing but open a speculative eye before settling back against the plush flanks of their mothers. All was quiet, each small group in its own place, invisible barriers fought for and conceded earlier and now making a world of its own round each family; like refugees on the deck of a ship, within a crowded space creating their temporary home with nothing but patient endurance and a few belongings.

The shed itself was once the hay-barn, teetering on the edge of the field directly above the steep winding lane. It still teeters, but now three sides have been filled in against the wind and the fourth, facing the north-west, from which direction the wind roars overhead but leaves us alone, is gated and wired.

The hay itself now fills half of the big stone barn. There's no longer any need to leave it out with little more than a roof to cover it, so that it can be well aired and allowed to 'make' properly, because these days it's not cut at home. With nearly everyone round here making silage now instead of hay, the balers have been sold and the tractors are too big and too busy to cope with my steep little fields. So gone is the terror and the joy of haymaking and instead the endless searching phone calls and the disillusion (or just sometimes the elation) of getting hay from 'up country', and someone else's weather and weeds to worry about and a big hole in the bank balance every autumn. But it does mean the sheep can have the hay-shed for lambing.

Nowadays I do not have to hunt the fields for lambs arriving or departing this life but can sit, on a night like this one, quietly in the shed listening to the tiny rustles of movement, the peaceful breathing of the flock, and, if all is well, gaze up at the sharp clarity of the stars.

The first spark came quite alone, dancing gaily across the opening of the shed and for a moment, lost in peace, I thought it was another star trick. A shower of red lights came twirling and rollicking behind it and began to float down, within feet of the great beds of straw.

And then I remembered Cliff's fire.

I'd been nagging and worrying about that fire all day. It was a very dry spring, so dry that the warnings on the radio about lighting fires in the open had been repeated constantly. The trouble with warnings on the radio is that a surprising number of people don't hear them, not if they've been out since dawn lambing, as Cliff had been, and then decided to stay out and put a match to the pile of hedge trimmings he'd cut in the autumn.

Chances are, he may not have taken much notice anyway. It's amazing the number of bonfires that get lit round here almost as soon as the warnings go out, as if they've merely reminded the farmers of a job they'd meant to do before. And if I dance about

3

with rage and fright while the smoke drifts and curls (often towards my farm) I try to remind myself that one of the reasons I'm supposed to like country people is that they don't take a damn bit of notice of anyone if they can help it. There was even a time when I thought they knew exactly what they were doing.

So, although I kept an anxious eye on Cliff that day and hovered about while he piled more and more branches onto his fire, muttering sometimes about the radio warnings and pointing out that there was only the lane between the leaping blaze and my sheep shed, I did believe him when he assured me impatiently that he'd have it all damped down and safe before he went back to his other farm, eight miles away. As soon as I was sure he'd gone, I went to check and found nothing but a neat pile of ashes. Not so much as a wisp of smoke remained from all that crackling, roaring destruction.

The snipey little east wind must have been playing round the fields for quite a while that night. It had found the mound of ashes and gleefully stirred them into life again. Now, as I sat, for once at peace, with my animals in the shed and took time to enjoy them and the stars, the wind had begun to send the sparks over the hedge to the very place where they could do the most damage.

Back over the fence I went, swore as I caught my jeans on the same piece of wire, and lumbered out of the yard and across the lane to Cliff's fields.

The ashes were now a living, breathing, seething mass of red.

I suppose it was silly to try and put it out with a few buckets of water – running from the field, across the lane, up the steep yard, pleading with the tap to run faster, down the treacherous yard with slopping buckets, out of the gate, across the lane, and then throwing two pathetic splashes onto the monster, which simply writhed and spat and seemed to grow.

I kept it up for half an hour and the sparks flew wildly round me as I ran. I stopped once to try and shoo the sheep out of the shed. They doubled back on me and claimed their places again. I could imagine them then, sleeping while the shed went up in flames and the flames spread to the rest of the buildings and finally the house. The house . . . Oh my God. The house, with Mrs P sitting snoozing in her armchair, cats on her knee, chihuahua at her back and whippets on her feet.

She looked up as I came flying through the door and gasped out the possibility of us being burnt to the ground.

'Well, ring the Fire Brigade,' she said coolly.

'The Fire Brigade?'

'Yes,' she said, yawning. 'That's what they're for. Putting fires out.'

'I can't call them all the way out here!' I cried.

'Well, if you're too shy to call them and let yourself get burnt to the ground, then I think I'll be on my way. I suppose I could just get down to the river if I took it easily.'

I rang 999. When they put me through to the Fire Service, I began to think that perhaps I'd exaggerated the danger. After all, we hadn't caught fire yet. I glanced over at Mrs P, who gave me a beady look and set her jaw.

'Well, actually,' I said falteringly to the girl on the other end of the line, 'it's not really a fire yet. It's sort of a heap of ashes that's come to life and I'm a bit afraid the sparks will drift over and set my buildings alight. But I was thinking perhaps you have a little van with a squirter of foam or something, just to smother it . . . or something.'

'I'll send the Fire Brigade out,' she announced cheerily.

'You mean the big red one with the bells and ladders and things?' I muttered, 'just for a heap of ashes?'

'No trouble, dear. It'll put your mind at rest anyway. Just tell me where you are exactly again.'

I gave her the instructions and she said, 'Now don't worry. They'll be there in about twenty minutes. Let's hope it'll be all right till then.'

'But what happens if someone in town has a big house fire?' I said. 'Are you sure a little van with a squirter or something . . .'

'Oh do stop that!' said Mrs P. 'Let them send the big one.'

'I feel a fool,' I said to my mother as I replaced the receiver. She turned to the dogs and remarked acidly that I'd rather we were all burnt out any day than look a fool.

But I couldn't help it. I am a bit of a panic merchant, the curse of having too much imagination (but not enough for it to do me any good), and now I could see the breeze dying down, and the ashes going grey and quiet again by the time the fire engine arrived. So there I'd be, apologizing and trying to prove that there *had* been a real danger, while all the firemen got that 'fool woman' look on their faces and they'd check back with the police who'd tell them all about the time I reported the missing satellite that wasn't. Suddenly, the pulsating dragon, snorting sparks and threatening all I love, shrank in my mind to a few pathetic embers.

Sure enough, when I went back to check, the sparks had stopped drifting across the hedge and the mound, though still red and heaving, lacked the depth of movement, the menace, the malignity of half an hour ago.

The breeze, which had begun it all, had dropped a bit and was now just a delicate flutter of dry branches somewhere. Apart from that, there was, at that midnight hour, complete silence. Not even the odd grunt of a ewe in labour, nor the panic-stricken bleat of a lost lamb, came from the fields around. Not an owl hooted nor a fox barked; even the river seemed to be on mute for once. Above, the stars still sparked, and across the valley there was the odd stutter of lights from the big lambing sheds of the two farms, but for the rest there was a thick, rich darkness over the valley. And into all this peace I had summoned a great, noisy, brightly lit fire engine, which would creak and crash its way down the steep, narrow lane and everyone would know about me and my latest panic.

'Dear God,' I prayed, 'Please don't let them have their siren on and if you could turn their big lights off that would be perfect.'

I peered over the gate at the mound of ashes. It looked remarkably innocent.

'Damn you!' I yelled at it. 'Now where are your sparks? Now where's all that heaving and spitting! Go on . . . blaze!'

A faint creaking and groaning came from the top of the hill and a fierce, bright, spinning light flickered over the trees. Remorselessly the light span brighter and the sound of brakes and gears grew louder and there it was in all its hugeness, an enormous fire engine which filled the world and blotted out the stars.

I gave an apologetic grin as the door burst open and out they came, a gang of men laughing, chatting, collars undone, helmets on the back of their heads and the air ringing with jokes. Out they came and each one grinned merrily at me as if they were arriving for a picnic, and I remembered that this was Wales, where even a fire can have its funny side and you don't have to apologize for being alive.

There was a slight pause before the last man climbed down, looking more at ease than the rest. There was something familiar about him as he greeted me and stood, hands on hips, and peered around him. He frowned and I waited for him to accuse me of bringing the gang out unnecessarily.

Instead, 'Where's the microphone then?' he demanded.

It was Brian Butler, who's been delivering my coal for years; delivering it and being interviewed about it, obligingly panting with the seeming effort of heaving the big sacks up my pathway, and then tipping the coal out carefully while I recorded the sound.

It's part of the nightmare of delivering anything here: getting stuff down the steep lane, through the narrow gate, around the muddy yard and then being pounced on to talk on tape about the job. One of the postmen even had to sing. So, if I thought humping coal or feed sacks or piles of mail interesting enough for the radio, what was I likely to do when a whole fire-fighting team arrived? Brian had been briefing them on how to conduct themselves in front of the microphone.

'Been getting our speeches ready,' said one of the men as they started unwinding hoses and looking around for the fire. And, of course, instead of twitching about, I *should* have been ready with the tape-recorder to get the whole glorious, noisy scene on tape. Now it was no use rushing inside to collect the equipment, which was lying as limp and uncharged as I was feeling right then.

The mound of ashes made a lovely hissing and spitting sound as the jets of water hit it; in one last agony, it writhed and twisted and spat sparks high into the air and then it was quite dead.

'Could have been very nasty, that could,' said one of Brian's mates as he doused it once more. 'We've been out all day fighting some terrible grass fires. Just needs a spark to send the whole mountain up. And once it gets into the peat . . . well, it goes on forever.'

7

And all of them agreed, and said I'd done the right thing to call them out, and that was what they were there for and they'd only been having a quick one in the pub anyway, it being Saturday night, and they'd know where I was next time, wouldn't they?

So I stopped apologizing at last and they all came into the cottage and perched everywhere, while Mrs P made them coffee laced with something a bit stronger (all except the driver, who had tea) and entertained them with a few of her naughtier stories, and then they were all leaping back onto the fire engine and calling out goodbyes and all the noise and colour faded into the distance and I was alone once more with my slumbering sheep and the stars.

At last I wandered back into the house, where Mrs P had left a note.

'Winston and I have gone to bed. Fresh tea in the pot. Still some whisky left in the bottle.'

I had both, sitting in the deep armchair by the dying fire, staring at the pool of lamplight shining on the deep-green curtains and listening to the quiet breathing of the dogs as they slept, curled round on themselves, as longdogs do.

I closed my eyes. So many panics dissolved in so much good humour over the years. I was losing count of both the panics and the years since I'd stood on that autumn hill and gazed down on the little farm with its great ash tree, fallen in love with it, and persuaded Cliff and his wife Kathleen to let me have the house and buildings and a few acres, while he kept the rest of the land for grazing. Sometimes when we meet, as he goes round his flock or scares me to death with his bonfire, we make a tally of the years and both of us get a shock.

But not much has changed since that autumn day so long ago when I rushed through the gate, breathless with wonder. The little farm looks much the same as it did then. The great ash tree still stands guardian over the cottage, defying the gales; the barns still gleam with whitewash in the morning sun or their blue slate roofs glisten subtly in the rain, Doli the big draught horse still demands attention over the gate; there are still ginger and tortoiseshell cats hunting rats in the hedge; chickens of many breeds still scratch and quarrel round the yard; whippets and lurchers still leap and race across the fields; the hedge, which Cliff's wife planted, still curves around the garden; a gander still screams defiance at the gate; I'm still nagging Cliff to sell me another field, and his sheep still find their way onto my land and my goats onto his.

No, not much has changed, but a great deal has happened.

Chapter 2

I t's post-natal depression,' I told Bertie Ellis as we strode towards the loose-boxes from whence came a blistering, reverberating, mind-wrenching scream that petered out into a deep, mournful boom, and began all over again.

Bertie looked at me over the top of his granny-specs.

'Goats,' he said severely, 'do *not* get post-natal depression.'

'Probably not. But Mrs P reckons Gorgeous has got it,' and we both winced as Bertie opened a door and the sound exploded out.

The big gold and lilac goat rushed towards us, paused, and then, sniffing deeply, raised her top lip and held it, quivering, up into the air. At her feet two tiny kids, momentarily released from the awful blast of sound, got up and tottered about drunkenly before settling down to pee. The movement caught their mother's attention and she swung round bellowing protectively, trying at the same time to wash their little behinds. The kids ducked quickly down into the straw again.

'You could gag her,' said Bertie thoughtfully. 'Or a bullet between the ears might work wonders. How long has she been yelling like this?'

'A week,' I sighed. 'It's driving everything mad. I think those kids'll be deaf when they grow up.'

He shut the loose-box door as Gorgeous went into full voice again.

'This the first time she's kidded?' he asked.

'Not *really*,' I said slowly, 'although I don't think she remembers much about last time. I do, though, vividly.'

One does tend to remember every last moment of anything to do with Gorgeous. If I'd known what a complete pain in the neck she was to become I'd most likely have asked Bertie to knock her on the head that time when he'd groped deep inside her mother, Dolores, to find the tiny remnant of a dramatic and almost fatal delivery. Instead, at the time, I'd been so enchanted with this last one of the triplets, so delicate in form and colour, that all I could say was 'It's *gorgeous!*', and thought her the loveliest thing I'd ever seen.

Even Mrs P agreed with me that this animal was unique, at least in beauty, with a mother-of-pearl shimmer of delicate golds and blues and creamy white over her coat, and a lilac stripe down her back.

Her own mother didn't like her, though, and, being a very wise goat, I should have taken her advice, for Gorgeous was the soul of ingratitude and dizzy with it. Most kids, given extra bottle feeds and brought into the house and handled frequently, tend to fixate on people, but all that loving care went straight in one side and out the other of Gorgeous's black heart.

Gorgeous, it has to be said, is very thick. But, as is so often the way with the less aware of this life, she is always the cool, uncaring centre of controversy. For instance, somewhere out there, in a small Welsh village, is a man whose social expectations have probably never been quite the same since the day he met Gorgeous. Not face to face, as you might say, but he certainly met her. Just mention 'The man in the hat and Gorgeous' to Gwynneth Griffiths and that usually calm, self-contained lady will start hooting and giggling and generally give way to ribald mirth. It was all a matter of timing, you understand – as the best comedy usually is.

For many years, every autumn, getting the goats served by a worthy male has been a big problem and, more often than not, given the slightly loony character of both goats and self and the lack of our own proper transport, the whole business has ranged from pure nightmare to low, slapstick farce. Until that year, my friend Christine Palmer had been the ringmaster of our annual circus but her stud males were now too closely related to be used again on my goats, with the exception of her champion Toggenberg, Celtic Crusader, and he was on loan to someone else. I had already been to him that year with Dolores's older daughter, Minnie, and that had been silly enough.

Myrddin Parry, another neighbour who, along with Gwynneth herself, had done much on behalf of me and my animals over the years, had offered to take us. He didn't mention, however, that his Land-Rover was temporarily out of action and he arrived in his beautifully kept, gleaming Alfa Romeo.

The boot of that car was amazing and, although I dithered and worried about the ethics of transporting a large, very rampant goat in it, he calmly packed it with straw, settled Minnie down with a swatch of hay, waved aside my squeals of anguish, commanded me into the front of the car and drove us speedily and silently to our destination.

The lady who came to greet us was cool, efficient and obviously expecting another vehicle to follow us into her yard. We all made polite conversation for a while until she thought to ask us directly where the goat was.

With a flourish, Myrddin opened the boot of his car and Minnie, who'd been having a quiet cud on the way, stepped out of it with as much aplomb as any star attending a first night. I could almost see the cameras popping. It wasn't until she caught the penetrating aroma of virile male goat, drifting faintly but languorously towards her, that she forgot her airs and graces and reverted into the little tramp she is normally. Crusader's guardian was transfixed.

A few days later, two of the other goats began calling and rushing about with their tails whipping from side to side and this time I asked Gwynneth, who lived across the valley, if her old van could manage to get us to yet another male with a fancy pedigree.

'You'll never find this place,' his owner had warned me. 'I suggest you come to the village and give me a ring from there. I'll pop down in my car and guide you in.'

Gwynneth's little blue van groaned a bit as the two goats hopped into it enthusiastically.

'These the last ones, then?' asked Gwynneth, as we tied them up securely so that they couldn't leap over and join us in the front seats.

'No, dammit!' I said. 'There's still Gorgeous to go yet. I thought she had a funny look in her eye this morning, but being her she probably won't come in properly till we get back.'

'Well, we could always take her too, just in case,' said Gwynneth, and she grinned at me. 'The sight of the others enjoying themselves might get her going.'

And so we loaded Gorgeous up with the others and set off on that warm sunny morning without a care in the world, except that Gorgeous managed to turn herself round and stand with her behind resting on my shoulder.

'I'll kill her if she does anything,' I said grimly.

Gwynneth giggled. 'Well, it's only pellets. Not as if it was a cow, now, is it?'

I looked at her sourly and gave the big rump by my ear a shove. It wiggled happily and settled back again.

'Bloody goat,' I said and then let the loveliness of the green unfolding hills, with their neat, white farmhouses tucked into the hollows, work their usual magic as we sped on. An ancient ash tree scattered leaves of clear gold over us as we passed, and the autumn sun sent long shadows running along the hedges.

When we arrived at the village where I'd been told to wait, Gwynneth drew up beside the phone box, switched off the engine and sighed happily.

'I can just do with this, a little sit in the sun,' she said and, shaking her long blonde hair over the back of the seat, she closed her eyes.

I got out of the van and went to phone the owner of the stud.

'Be with you in ten minutes,' she cried and I rang off and strolled back to the van. I glanced idly down the long steep street of the village, and vaguely noticed a group of three people chatting animatedly outside a hardware shop. There were two women and a small dapper gentleman in a neat suit with a tweed hat perched jauntily at an angle on his head.

I opened the van door, got in and settled back in my seat. Gwynneth smiled but didn't open her eyes.

'I hope she takes her time,' she murmured when I told her our guide was on the way. 'It's so lovely and warm here.'

'I can't lean back because of this horrible goat which won't sit down,' I replied, and began instead to watch the street behind through the rear-view mirror. I could see that the conversation outside the hardware shop was nearing its end. The two women began to move away, and the dapper gentleman raised his hat with a flourish and inclined his head as they said their goodbyes. He turned and began to trot jauntily up the street towards us. I saw him notice the van, and see through the large back-window that it contained a head of long blonde hair. He wouldn't have seen the goats from that angle because two of them were sitting down, and Gorgeous was pressed against the side of the van, lost in a dream. Just at that moment she gave a little cry and backed her behind against me.

'You know,' I said to Gwynneth, 'I think she *is* in season,' and I lifted her tail and peered under it. Gwynneth opened her eyes and peered with me.

At that precise moment, the gallant cavalier in the tweed hat doffed it and thrust his smiling, inquisitive face through the open window. I noticed fleetingly that he had a long sharp nose, just before that nose connected violently with the wonder and glory of a goat's pink, quivering vulva.

Gorgeous gave a happy little bleat but Mr Tweed Hat let out a scream of horror and Gwynneth's wild, high shriek of laughter sent him scattering and scampering and shaking his head from side to side, clutching his little hat and reeling away out of sight. He turned his head back just the once and the look on his face sent Gwynneth off again and she was still doubled up when our guide's car came skidding alongside. We had to wait for quite a while before Gwynneth was fit to drive again.

'Teach him to shove his head in strange cars,' she moaned at last. 'I do like taking your goats to the billy. Something awful always happens, but that was the best yet.'

Next spring, one bright clear morning, I checked on all the goats feeding at their buckets, before running back to the ones which were kidding or the sheep which were lambing. Gorgeous, not due to kid for five more days, was, I noticed distractedly, eating a hearty breakfast.

I was in the big stable next door to the goat-shed when I heard a small, strangled bleat but then nothing more than the sound of steady munching. A few minutes later, back in the goat-shed, there was Gorgeous still standing, happily engrossed in her bucket, while behind her a large kid was struggling to fight its way out of its birth slime. Gorgeous obviously hadn't noticed a thing and subsequently never admitted responsibility.

'Was it wearing a hat?' asked Gwynneth when I told her about the kid.

Now, another autumn mating and another winter had gone by and here I was telling this unsavoury story to Bertie outside the loose-box where Gorgeous, far from ignoring the fact that she had given birth to two kids, had been shrieking the news abroad day and night.

'Can't you,' I pleaded, 'do something about it? Please!'

'Yes,' Bertie nodded, 'she is a bit loud, isn't she? Probably hormonal. You sometimes get it when it's their first time round, but we decided long ago that this goat isn't quite normal, didn't we? Like me to remove her voice box?'

I looked at him happily.

'Only joking!' he said quickly. 'I'll give her an injection and see if it shuts her up. It should sort her insides out. Otherwise there's the good old humane killer. Who do you want it for, her or you?'

'Me if she doesn't stop that noise,' I said bitterly.

Bertie pursed his lips and frowned.

'Are you going to stop here for ever?' he asked slowly.

'I don't know. Why?'

'Well, you'll only get older and poorer if you do,' he said.

'I'll get older wherever I am. Poorer too, given my talent for collecting animals that actually enjoy ill health. At least the view's good here . . . and don't say it, I know you can't live on a view but it helps. And not all the animals are awful. Look at young Sophie there. A wonderful mother, quiet, loads of milk and charming with it.'

'That's the one that keeps hopping over the fence, isn't it?' said Bertie innocently.

'OK, OK,' I said and paused before taking careful aim, 'but, if you're so worried about me getting poorer, how about knocking something off the bills? You could start by fixing Gorgeous for nothing.'

Bertie stared at me as if this time I really had gone over the edge and stumped off to his car to get the hormone injection for Gorgeous.

When he'd gone I escaped to get some peace and a cup of tea in the kitchen.

'I can't bear that noise,' I told Mrs P, who was taking a large bowl of milk out of the fridge. 'I nearly picked up a hammer and brained Gorgeous just before Bertie got here. It's such an awful, despairing and yet demanding sound.'

'I told you, it's post-natal depression. Lots of women get it.'

Mrs P is a trained midwife (amongst other things) and, in spite of many arguments about it, still calmly maintained that goats and horses and sheep were just the same as humans when it came to birth.

'Bertie said goats don't get it,' I replied. 'Actually, he just thought I was nuts.'

Mrs P snorted and began to ladle thick, rich cream off the milk.

'This,' she said, 'is Sophie's milk. It's always the best!'

As soon as I bring the milk in each day, it's strained into big wide bowls which have been keeping cold in a special fridge overnight. Twenty-four hours later, a thick rind of cream has risen to the top. In spite of all their traumas and nonsense, my goats have lovely rich milk and, as Mrs P had said, Sophie's is the best of all. Even today, when she is, frankly, getting on a bit and has milked through for three years without having a kid, still the rich creamy milk keeps flowing.

Sophie is not a beautiful goat exactly, being short of leg and dark and hairy of body, but she is one of those animals which, though they may never win a prize for looks them-selves, can nevertheless produce the ones that do. Strangers who come to see the goats may ooh and aah over the others (for they are a good-looking bunch on the whole) but it's not till little Sophie turns her back and they see her mas-sive udder that she gets their attention. Sophie is a pearl of a goat.

She knows it, mind you. Mrs P said it was because Sophie spent the first moments after her conception riding in an Alfa Romeo.

16

Sophie and her sister Phoebe were the result of Minnie's mating by Crusader.

When they were born, Phoebe came bursting out first, complaining as soon as the air hit her, and was one of those boring little beasts who haven't got a clue how to suckle and think you're trying to murder them when you show them how. Sophie, on the other hand, had a very difficult birth and an umbilical hernia of the variety where the navel comes out and, unless you're careful, the insides of the animal follow it. It had happened to a kid once before and I was too appalled to save it in time, but when Sophie was born I had lint and strapping ready and was able to swaddle her up quickly. For the first few weeks of her life she looked like a tiny Belted Galloway and submitted to all the changes of the dressing with perfect calm, even snuggling up against my shoulder as I treated her.

The little kid was also a good 'doer', suckling calmly and steadily and ignoring her mother's Victorian attitude to her children. Minnie always thoroughly enjoys conceiving them but, if she'd been human, her babies would have been bundled off to a wet nurse as soon as they were born and later she'd have had a nanny or an au pair and never seen them more than she had to. She reminds me of quite a few women I know.

Of course, a lot of goat-keepers prefer to bottle-feed the kids or put them on a self-feeding unit, selling the goat's milk itself, but I only need enough for our own use and have no longer the time to bottle-feed, so the goats have to get on with it themselves. Minnie did so most reluctantly. That year her daughter Phoebe annoyed her more than usual and spent the rest of the time bullying Sophie.

Which is why, although Phoebe was a much more beautiful animal, it was she who went elsewhere and Sophie who stayed and if, with her stubby little legs, she has a bit more bounce for popping over fences, she can also find her own way back, unlike some goats, which can go one way but never remember how they did it.

Sophie was blissfully circumspect when it came to her own time to be mated, bore her eventual kidding with much grace and patience and treated her babies with gentleness and concern.

They were lovely ones too, but she was to do even better next time and eventually give me one of the proudest days of my life. Meanwhile she had put up with the appalling noise coming from Gorgeous in the next loose-box with her usual stoicism, although once or twice I caught her giving her aunt a filthy look over the half-door.

In spite of Bertie's injection, still Gorgeous moaned and screamed and sobbed until at last I put her mother, Dolores, in with her. Dolores sniffed carefully at the kids, ate all the hay that was left and looked at her hysterical daughter long and hard. She then gave her the hiding of her life and finally Gorgeous shut up.

'I told you so,' said Mrs P smugly. 'Some women really do have a genuine reason for feeling awful after they've given birth, but there are others who just play up and a good telling off snaps them out of it. And don't say goats are different. Why shouldn't they get post-natal depression like anyone else?'

Why not indeed? A few of mine have had it since and sometimes the hormone injection works and sometimes it doesn't. And the last time I rang Bertie's surgery to ask for help with a screeching goat, his young female assistant coolly informed me, 'It's nothing really. Just a form of post-natal depression goats get, you know.'

'I do know, dear,' I said tartly. 'One of my goats invented it.'

Chapter 3

'**A** nd *what*,' cried the Customs Lady triumphantly, 'have we *here*?'

She'd gone bright red with excitement and it looked as if the neck of her uniform would choke her, as she stared at the twenty-four HP7 batteries nestling coyly amongst the knickers and bras.

'What do you want those for?' I said crossly to my companion. 'I told you I've got my own rechargeable battery units.'

'Ah,' she said, 'but you never know, in the country, whether you'll be able to charge them. They might have old-fashioned plugs.'

I stared at her with contempt. 'I always bring every kind of adaptor,' I said loftily and turned back to the Customs Lady, who was now beckoning wildly to one of the men at the next counter. It had just occurred to her that catching terrorists red-handed could get very nasty, even if she had been waiting for this moment all her career.

'I'm sure you've been notified that we'll be passing through with a lot of equipment, if you'd just care to check,' I said wearily. I knew that I'd supplied exhaustive lists and details of where we'd be going in Northern Ireland to the BBC to pass on to Whoever Needed To Know. I presumed their concern began at Bristol Airport. Frantic whispering in my ear informed me that this had not been the case.

'You sort it out then,' I said crossly and limped painfully over to a chair and sat down.

Carrying bales of hay and straw, and buckets of feed and water, shifting tons of muck and wood, lambing and kidding, and hours of sitting at a desk finishing off a book, had finally done for me and I was in agony with a really crippling attack of sciatica. Which was why I hadn't protested too loudly when Mary Price insisted on coming to Ireland with me. For once, I knew that driving for miles and heaving tape-recorders across fields would not be so easy but neither was having a producer along on the trip going to be easy either, especially one I'd never worked with before and was deeply suspicious of anyway.

Long before I'd met her I'd made up my mind to dislike her, had even told the Radio Network Editor in Bristol that I'd rather not do another series of *A Small Country Living* with this new producer, thank you very much. For Mary's reputation had gone before her and one of the members of the board which had appointed her to her new job had told me gleefully, 'You won't get too much of your own way with this one.' Which was a death knell as far as I was concerned. It's a fault, but working on my own is the only way I can operate creatively, which is why I've never been too beloved of producers. Producers like to produce – or at least be seen to.

I still had my toes dug in firmly when Mary Price rang to ask if she could come and see me at the farm but she disarmed me a bit when she cheerfully told me, 'Actually I've got a face like a friendly horse.'

Nevertheless, when she did come (bearing a couple of bottles of Guinness because it was St Patrick's Day), she infuriated Mrs P by insisting on coming into the hallowed mess of the kitchen and, as we discussed the programme, we clashed swords, wills and anything else we could find – in the nicest possible way, of course. In an unguarded moment, however, I'd mentioned something about doing some interviews in Northern Ireland and the Republic if possible. Mary had pounced on that, being Irish herself, and before I knew where I was I'd committed myself definitely to going – and she was coming with me.

'All right then,' I'd conceded after a stiff argument, 'I'll set up the interviews and you just clear the way for us'.

And now here we were at the airport, setting off for Belfast and giving the Customs Lady the thrill of her life, when she found enough batteries to set off an arsenal of home-made bombs. I sat on my chair and glared at the excitement going on over at the counter. Identity cards were being flashed about, phone calls were made and after, much waving of hands and consultations with this one and that, I was beckoned over to have my own baggage cleared.

The Customs Lady made a grab at a fat brown holdall and I snatched it back. A nerve twitched in her cheek as she demanded to see it again.

'You just be careful,' I told her. 'That's Gert in there and she's utterly irreplaceable.'

'Gert' is a full-track Uher tape-recorder, of blessedly simple operation, which records and plays back superbly. She was one of ten, ordered specially, with modifications, by a film company which then went bust and had to cancel. I was lucky enough to be offered one at a very good price. To replace her would cost the earth, even if I could find one exactly the same. Gert is my second skin: we hear and think alike.

'Well, you'll have to put that bag in the luggage hold anyway,' I was told acidly.

'Oh, no!' I cried. 'Gert comes with me.' And then Mary showed her true worth. Somehow she managed to arrange for us to keep Gert and the Dilly Bag with us, even if it meant sitting right up at the front of the little plane, almost in the cockpit, with our knees up round our ears. I began to see the advantages of having a tough producer firmly on my side.

As we waited for the plane to take off, Mary said, 'I can understand about Gert, but this Dilly Bag thing – was that really necessary?'

'You just wait till we're stuck out in the back of beyond and not a hope of tea or coffee or anything, then you'll see why. The Dilly Bag might be our lifeline, and they could smash it to bits in the luggage hold.'

The true Dilly Bag is the pouch which aboriginal women carried at their waists to collect roots and seeds and grubs in, but now, in Australia, it also has the same meaning as a Tucker Box and no rural traveller ever moves without one. My Dilly Bag, which is now very old, is made of blue and red canvas and carries everything from tea and coffee to cough mixture and whisky in it. It goes with me everywhere.

After a long, weary stop at Cardiff, when we had to carry Gert and the Dilly Bag over to the airport lounge while they searched the plane again in case a departing passenger had left something explosive behind, we finally headed towards the Irish Sea, and at last I forgot how uncomfortable I was and that I didn't like having a producer with me and began to feel as if I was going home for the holidays.

Ireland! The last time I'd been there I lived in a dream for months afterwards, deeply homesick. I'd been in Europe for a few years then, but, although I knew that the illness I suffered in the Australian heat had to keep me living in a much cooler climate, I was still vaguely miserable, trying to put down roots but always feeling alien at heart. For, if my body thrived in the cooler climate, my heart and mind couldn't quite get to grips with the cooler English temperament.

Neither could I really finally settle down to being a teacher and at last decided to catch up on my childhood ambition to be a broadcaster. Intensely literal at all times, I'd taken it seriously when some wit at a party told me to go and learn how to interview first, and somehow or other got myself taken on by a market research firm as a 'depth interviewer'. This meant getting all sorts of subliminal reactions to a product without people really knowing what you were after. On the basis of that, they make up all those questionnaires people wave at you in the street.

Perhaps it was my neutral Australian background which made the firm send me to the Republic, to do some research on baler twine, of all things. They flew me over on Aer Lingus, gave me a little green car to call my own, a cosy hotel in Dublin (the sort where they put hot-water bottles in the bed) to lay my head down in, a lecture on Irish politics so I didn't tread on any patriotic toes, and two weeks of pure joy.

The only time the political lecture came in useful was to give some explanation as to why two brothers in Cork began smashing up their living room around me as I dived under the sofa. Nothing to do with me, just the usual end to their political discussions, they assured me, with infinite politeness, as they dusted me off and plied me with vast mugs of really strong tea – or would I prefer a Guinness, or a whiskey even? For the rest, the little green car and I picked up merry old ladies hitching a lift to town and got all the local gossip in return, or we strayed into seemingly deserted villages and came away hours later, full of food and laughter, escorted by everyone to see us on our way to the Dublin road. And back in Dublin it was one long party till I was on a high I thought could go no higher. But it did, just two days before I left.

'Of course it's all changed since then,' said Mary Price rather primly when I tried to put all that wild, wonderful fortnight into words, as the little plane flew steadily on and the pain in my back got worse and I began to regret my determination to keep Gert and the Dilly Bag so close.

'Yes,' I sighed, 'I suppose it has changed, what with the business in Northern Ireland going on and on, and the Republic being in the EEC.'

'And lots more,' said Mary. 'Anyway, your little old ladies are probably batting into town on mopeds these days. But what happened just before you left?'

'It's a long, long story,' I murmured slowly.

Mary glanced down at the last few miles of the Welsh coastline disappearing below and the sea coming up ahead.

'We've got time,' she said briskly. 'How's your back, by the way?'

'Awful,' I winced.

'Well, come on, tell me. It'll take your mind off the pain.'

'You know,' I began tentatively, 'about the Children of Lir?'

Mary smiled and said softly, 'Yes of course I do. It's one of our loveliest folk tales.'

'Well, I came upon them for the first time when I was a student teacher in Sydney, and it was because of them, I suppose, that I went on teaching for longer than I meant to and eventually came to London. So it wasn't surprising really that they later led me straight into the Fairy Hill – or what seemed like it at the time. Let's just say that I know how people feel when they declare that they were bewitched. Anyway, I found the Children of Lir in a book. It was called *Something Particular* and a friend gave it to me for Christmas.'

And Mary had been right. I forgot the pain and the drone of

the engines and the vague panic I always feel when setting off on a long interviewing trip, wondering if I'll get to all the places and if the material will be any good anyway, and this time we were, after all, going to Northern Ireland, where there were a lot of other things to worry about as well. Now all that melted away and I was standing in a cool, open-plan house on Sydney's North Shore, picking at the wrapping paper and ribbon, while Toto jiggled impatiently and watched me anxiously as I drew the big book out and exclaimed over its delicate watercolours of children.

'I knew you'd like it,' cried Toto gleefully.

I looked at her doubtfully. Toto was an art student, so I supposed she'd liked the pictures in the book, but they *were* of children and I wasn't too sure I liked children very much at that point in time. I'd just started my probationary years as a teacher, in one of the outer suburbs, and they had given me a class nobody else could or would teach.

They were a pretty tough little bunch and the only slight chink in their armour of indifference had opened a short while before when we'd put on a small dance and mime performance for the school assembly. Every class had to take its turn every morning at entertaining the rest of the school on the theme of National Bird Week. Achingly bored (ever since I'd been a child myself) with ersatz Kookaburras and Willy Wagtails strutting around woodenly and preaching at us about being kind to birds, I'd unearthed that little poem of Ralph Hodgson 'Stupidity Street':

> I saw with open eyes
> Singing birds sweet
> Sold in the shops
> For the people to eat,
> Sold in the shops of
>   Stupidity Street.
>
> I saw in vision
> The worm in the wheat,
> And in the shops nothing
> For people to eat;
> Nothing for sale in
>   Stupidity Street.

I dressed the children in a weird motley of colours with a faint medieval look and taught them to mime and dance the poem to Respighi's 'Fountains of Rome'. Dance wasn't too common in Australian primary schools then and it caused a sensation. For the first time in their school lives, my sad little band felt important and clever. They were reverting rapidly, however, and I was wondering what to do with them next.

Toto took the book from me and began showing me the pages properly.

'It's about dancing and mime,' she explained. 'I thought it might give you some ideas for those kids.'

It did more than that. It opened up a whole new world. All the way home in the train to the other side of Sydney, I was lost in the dusk of an English winter and a large room where, once, a small boy called William and a group of his friends listened to stories and music and made up their own dances and mimes.

I don't know if it was the fact that Toto had spent a large chunk of the money she'd earned slaving over a counter at David Jones's for the Christmas rush on the book, or the beauty of the drawings in it, or my own faint stirrings of a realization that teaching (until then embarked on only grudgingly) might be more exciting than I'd supposed, or even the fact that it was nearly Christmas and soon I'd be going home to the country, but to this day that book has about it a lingering drift of excitement and wonder whenever I come upon it buried on my shelves. And still as I pick it up the pages fall open at the story of the Children of Lir, and I can hear the beat of the marching music as Queen Aifa (second wife of King Lir) and her four stepchildren, Fionula, Conn, Fiachra and Hugh, come onto the stage escorted by the soldiers taking them to the court of their neighbour King Bov .... ('I'd rather be a swan Miss Mac,' said Fat Annette. 'Annette, my love, anyone can be a swan, not everyone's tall enough to be a soldier. No, I don't think on your knees would work, Annette. But you can be the soldier who tells King Bov what the wicked Queen did to the children. And later on you can be a Sorrowful Peasant. And that is really difficult because you have to be struck with Wonder and Amazement right at the end. 'OoohAAAA,' breathed Annette, and suddenly everyone wanted to be a Sorrowful Peasant, Struck with Wonder and Amazement. Echoes and echoes ....)

They used a pretty ending for the story, in the book. We didn't, and the children had a lot of fun crumbling into dust – as well they might after nine hundred years singing and drifting on the Irish loughs after their stepmother turned them into swans. Stupid woman, she cast her spell right in front of the soldiers and they, of course, told King Bov. He was quite good at that sort of thing himself and turned Aifa into a spirit of the air, wandering and homeless. But he couldn't undo the enchantment on Fionula and her brothers and they had to spend three hundred years on Lough Derry, three hundred years on the Mull of Kintyre and three hundred years on Erris Bay. Only when a Woman of the South married a Man of the North would their enchantment end.

When the nine hundred years were up, a Prince of the North fell in love with a Princess of the South, who asked him to capture the singing swans of Erris. He did and led them, in their golden chains, to a priest who baptised them and – well they were nine hundred years old and I suppose they were luckier than Queen Aifa, who is still, they say, wandering and drifting about sighing on windy nights. ('I'm very good at sighing,' said Annette.)

'And that was what got you really interested in Modern Dance,' said Mary Price, and brought me, aching back, cramped legs and droning plane, throbbing back to the present.

'Mmmm. We went from strength to strength. The kids discovered all sorts of other talents – even Annette. Well, perhaps Annette not *quite* so much, but I remember her best of all. And then I got sick and had to go home to the mountains and the children in *that* school were just the opposite. Very bright and very bored. So it all sort of worked in reverse and we did some marvellous dances. At last I got so interested I wanted to find out more, so I upped and came to England and went to study at the Laban Art of Movement Centre in Surrey. And then I taught Dance in a secondary school for two years.'

Mary glanced out of the window again.

'We're nearly there,' she said. 'But what's all that got to do with the last time you were in Ireland?'

'Well, to cut an even longer story very much shorter, when I left teaching and the market research firm sent me to Ireland on this baler twine lark, I landed up in a little market town talking to an agricultural merchant and very boring he was too – although it's surprising how high feelings run on the pros and cons of various makes of baler twine. Anyway, we weren't all that far from one of the loughs where the Swan children spent three hundred years and I happened to ask him about it. It was incredible. He suddenly threw off his staid merchant disguise and turned into an ardent folklorist. He was still telling me little local embellishments to the story an hour later and insisted on taking me to the lough to see it for myself, and finally he showed me the Dublin road, and off he went.'

'And then?' asked Mary, hunting round for her seat belt as the plane began to descend.

'I honestly don't know what then,' I said. 'I think that's my seat belt you've got, by the way. I set off on the Dublin road and I saw this cairn of stones on a little hill. My friend had told me look out for it – one of those stories about a witch dropping rocks from her apron when she was flying overhead. Anyway, I stopped the car and climbed up to see it. I can remember standing on the cairn and suddenly feeling absolutely wonderful, and not at all alone. I can't remember going back to the car, I just knew I was driving along experiencing this incredible wild joy, unlike anything I'd ever felt before. Everything was so crystal clear and sharp. I *was* every blade of grass and every cloud and every tree, and all the time it was as if there was this great crowd of wonderfully beautiful, laughing, benevolent people around me, sort of racing with the car. I couldn't see them, just felt them there.' I gave Mary a sideways glance as the plane began circling the airport.

'Sounds mad, I know. But I've read of other people having the same sort of experience.'

'Go on,' said Mary.

'Well, that's all really, except that eventually I ended up in this old churchyard standing in front of a big Celtic cross. And the weather had gone very foggy. You know, I'm terrified of driving in the fog, but I didn't mind a bit. Heaven knows where I was, but I drove back to Dublin and straight to my hotel without a wrong turn. And I felt that laughing, friendly crowd with me all the way.'

'Not,' grinned Mary, 'Sorrowful Peasants struck by Wonder and Amazement?'

'Definitely not,' I said and went on, as the plane taxied to a halt. 'I took a friend back with me the next day to see where I'd been. We couldn't find the churchyard or anything other than a bright spring day full of blossom and a lot of crumbling ruins with nothing more than sheep wandering in and out of them. It was like being shut out of heaven – or the Fairy Hill, if you like. I've never forgotten it and for weeks after I was utterly distracted, but happy too, if you see what I mean.'

'What happened to William?' asked Mary as we began queueing up to leave the plane.

'William?'

'The little boy the book was written about.' Mary has two small boys herself and tends to be a bit broody when you mention children.

'Oh, him! Well he grew up to be a prince too. William, Duke of Gloucester.'

Mary gave me a hunted look.

'It's all right. This is Belfast, not Dublin,' I said.

'That's what I'm worried about,' she said and smiled bleakly at the air hostess as we said goodbye.

'We've got a hire car waiting for us in the car park,' said Mary as we walked across the tarmac. 'We should be in good time for this interview of yours. What are we going to see this man about?'

'Greyhound Pigs,' I said sweetly and gestured towards the Customs. 'And now, will you explain about those batteries this time, or shall I?'

'I will,' said Mary firmly. 'You'll probably tell them we've come to see a Greyhound Pig and they'll lock us both up. In the bin!'

Chapter 4

Actually, there was such an animal as an Irish Greyhound Pig. In most books about the history of the pig, you'll find a picture of one as drawn by Richardson in 1850. It's not a very lovely beast – thin and humpbacked and bristly, with wattles hanging down under its chin, floppy ears, a long snout and a tail like a rope. And legs like a greyhound.

At the Ulster Folk and Transport Museum at Holywood, Co. Down, they knew all about the Greyhound Pig. Mervyn Watson even dredged up the information that the last recorded ones were kept by an Irishman in Liverpool during the Second World War. They apparently eked out a living on the civic rubbish dump, but 'did not flourish'. This was strange because they'd thrived in similar conditions in Ireland for ages and, until the late eighteenth century, were allowed to wander the streets of Dublin unhindered.

Now, although I've seen the Irish Greyhound Pig dismissed by at least one historian as mere 'swine' (there are, it seems, social strata in the pig world too), I've always had a fancy for one. It could be the name, but I don't know. In Richardson's drawing, it has a keen, knowing eye and I doubt if anyone would ever have dared to chain it up in a pig crate. It looks as elemental as the hills it came from.

'Yes, it was,' agreed Mervyn Watson, as we dodged and darted to avoid the crowds conscientiously milling about the lovely old country cottages which had been re-erected in the grounds of the museum. 'It was a bit hard to keep them at home at all, actually. They say a Greyhound Pig could run ten miles in an hour and jump a five-barred gate. That's probably how it got its name.'

'And you're sure there are none left?'

'Well, not as far as we know. If there *are* any out there, they're keeping very quiet about it.'

'Excuse me,' interrupted a small boy, 'is this the way to the lavatories?' It's a question people frequently ask me whenever I'm in a public place. Expecting the usual queue of seekers after this vital information to form at any moment, I wound up the microphone lead and humped Gert a bit higher on my hip.

'I think,' I told Mervyn, 'that I'll go and find Jonathan and ask him about peat digging, the old way. Mary Price will be devastated. She had high hopes of finding the last remaining Irish Greyhound Pig and making me keep it on the farm. Might have been fun to race it with the whippets!'

'If I hear of one, you'll be the first to know,' grinned Mervyn and turned to give the small boy, who was jiggling up and down by now, the directions he needed.

Mary was sitting in the car listening intently to some deep political discussion on the radio. I always say she must have had a radio with her in the womb and certainly she'd as soon go naked as move without one today. When I banged on the window she jumped nervously.

'No Irish Greyhound Pigs left,' I said as she wound down the window. 'And the place is crawling with people. Doing an interview without assorted irreverent remarks in the background is not easy.'

'Do you want me to come and shoo them away?' she offered.

'Yes please! But remember, you stay out of earshot!' For, if I had given in about her coming with me, one thing I'd made clear was that there was to be No Interference. It was something I was very twitchy about, having had a few good interviews ruined in the past by a producer glaring over my shoulder at the interviewee and turning us both into nervous wrecks, interrupting with some abstruse question just when I'd got the golden stream of words finally flowing, and once actually stopping the flow completely by pointing at my victim and saying, 'Try not to "um" so much, would you.' I don't mind how much people 'um', as long as what they say in between is good – or can be made good with a razor blade and splicing tape. Also, people are much more relaxed speaking to one person rather than two.

'You won't even know I'm there,' Mary promised as she hopped out of the car.

I did, though. For the next half-hour, I was conscious of her lurking and creeping in the background, waving disgruntled tourists away from the tiny traditional walled fields where Jonathan Bell (who went under the grand title of Assistant Keeper, Department of Material Culture) and I wandered about discussing peat digging and why the new, modern machines were likely to ruin the beds for ever, dry-stone walling methods in Ireland (north and south), and fairy thorns.

'We actually *planted* that one,' said Jonathan, pointing to the middle of a field where a single graceful hawthorn tree stood, lightly touched with the first buds of spring, 'but, do you know, when the men come to plough this field they leave a huge circle around it. I mean, it's not as if it grew there of its own accord.'

'People still really believe that the fairies will wreak a terrible vengeance on them if they interfere with a single hawthorn tree?'

'Oh, I can tell you tales about fairy thorns. There's even a story that they re-routed a motorway round one because the locals were so upset about it. And I suspect the men making the motorway weren't too happy about it either.'

'Good grief!' I said. 'I had a letter from a man once who said he'd had to leave his wife because she was threatening to cut down the fairy thorn in their garden and he didn't want to stay around to take the consequences. I thought it was a bit extreme at the time, but perhaps not. I'd better stop tying the washing line onto mine.'

'Have you got one, then?'

'Several,' I replied. 'The most beautiful one is right by the back of the cottage and it's very old. The others are all in rather awkward spots and, as they've forgotten about the old superstition in my part of Wales, kindly men are always offering to cut them down for me. They think I'm cuckoo when I tell them the trees belong to the Tyleth Teg, the Welsh fairies. Anyway, perhaps we'd better do an interview about the Irish fairy thorns, so that I'll have a good excuse to leave mine where they are because, superstition aside, I really think they are exquisitely beautiful trees.'

'Is that a fact?' smiled Jonathan. 'You're not *really* superstitious about hawthorn?'

'Well, a bit. I won't let anyone bring the blossom into the house. They say that really is dangerous.'

Neither will I burn elder logs on the fire. The old country belief is that if you do, 'the devil will come down the chimney.' I defied this warning once when an old elder tree fell down and a helpful friend chopped it up and brought it in for the fire. That night, coincidentally, the most appalling sequence of disasters followed one after the other, and I've never dared risk it since. But, although all these taboos can be a great bore sometimes, I suspect that the origins of them had a lot to do with common sense. Elder logs spit sparks, and hawthorn blossom, whilst lovely when fresh, makes an awful mess in the house when it starts falling – as lasting and invasive as confetti. Perhaps the fairy thorn legend was started by some prehistoric tree lover trying to warn off the axe-happy locals.

'Well, I hope you've got what you came for,' said Jonathan after we'd finished our interviews. He cast a furtive glance towards a distant skirmish between Mary and a particularly truculent party of sightseers. 'I think we'd better let the public through again, or there could be bloodshed. Where are you off to next?'

'To your flax mill,' I said.

'Ah. Now that is something really special,' said Jonathan, who'd been helping me for weeks to find everything from this traditional flax mill to Moiled Cattle. I'd spent hours on the phone to him and if he didn't know the answer to one of my more bizarre requests he found someone who did.

We began to walk slowly back towards Mary, who had won her battle and was staring triumphantly at the indignant retreat of her adversaries.

'Oh well,' sighed Jonathan, 'it's nearly closing time anyway. You're going to be rather late at the flax mill.'

And we *were* late, very late, in spite of Mary taking corners on two wheels and rushing us through the gorse-scented lanes, till we drove down the lonely farm track towards the tall mill chimney which pointed forlornly at the darkening sky. Breathlessly, we raged in upon the McConvilles, who were just finishing supper, and everything went very slowly again. In that stark kitchen where three generations sat around the table, time became quite irrelevant.

I still have the bunch of dried stalks and flowers of flax, and the hank of fibres, which Eugene McConville presented to me later as if they had been a spray of rare orchids.

'That's the first flax that's been grown and scutched locally for twenty-seven years,' he said, beaming at me.

'Scutched?' I said.

'That means breaking down the fibres in the stalks of flax so that it can be spun. This is a *scutching* mill. Then it went off to the spinning mill.'

There is still a faint scent clinging to the flax and it brings it all back – those strange scenes at the moonlit, owl-haunted farm. The great water-wheel in its cavernous shed, turned slowly at first, as the water thrashed it into life, till it was vibrating the whole building and all the pulleys and belts began thudding and booming in the scutching room, which was lined by golden wooden racks piled high with oatmeal-coloured flax. The smell of the newly scutched flax, a blend of new hay and sweet oil, sent us wild, so that Mary and I had to go out of the door again and come in to catch it once more in its full intensity. And all the while Eugene, his face lit by love of his subject, explained how once the whole of that part of Ireland was full of flax fields and the blue flowers gloried the landscape, and how the flax was harvested and soaked in great ponds and pits and finally brought to the scutching mills, piled on carts, to be made ready for spinning into real home-grown Irish linen. It may still be spun in Ireland, but most of the flax itself came from abroad; the little farm-based mills have turned to ruins, and cows and sheep graze the old flax fields. But there was a gradual revival of interest in flax growing and, due to their own enthusiasm, the mill on the McConvilles' farm had been kept in good working order and soon they hoped to open it to the public.

We stayed and we stayed. Gert ran out of juice and, with no time to recharge, Mary, vindicated at last, produced the torch batteries to keep going. We recorded the water-wheel churning and splashing, the pulleys vibrating, Eugene scutching the flax in the old machines, the owls hooting, dogs barking and all the old stories, over and over again. At last, when even the moon and the

33

owls had gone, we drove reluctantly away, found our neat, new hotel and sank into oblivion. But just to make sure we went back the next morning and recorded it all over again. Which made us late for the Moiled Cattle.

If the Irish Greyhound Pig has galloped off to extinction, the Irish Moiled Cattle are just about hanging on. The name comes from the old Gaelic work *mael* meaning 'hornless', and bones of these naturally polled cattle have been found on ancient Irish archaeological sites.

'Cattle, of course,' said Mary as we drove, 'were the reason for the great raid of the armies of Connaught on Ulster. Might have been Moiled Cattle.' And she began to drive rather more erratically as she gave me a wild and potted version of the Irish saga *The Tain*. Finally, while Cuchailan was still holding up his enemies, single-handed, at the ford, we skidded into the farm belonging to the secretary of the newly re-formed Irish Moiled Cattle Society.

'They've got red ears,' I said.

'What's that got to do with it?' Mary growled.

'Cattle with red ears were supposed either to be fairy women in disguise, or at least to belong to the fairies, and if one of their bulls got into your herd it was the greatest luck because their offspring would be beautiful and prolific. But if you annoyed the fairies the whole herd would disappear overnight.'

'Oh no! Not more fairies!' Mary exploded.

'Well, come on. Maeve and her hosts and Cuchailan himself weren't exactly your ordinary average types, were they? And what about the talking head that roused the hosts of Ulster to go and defend their lands? Or the red bull himself who was warned to take his herd out of danger? Anyway, I think he had horns, that bull, so it can't have been a Moiled, now can it?'

Mary raised her eyes to heaven as she leant on the doorbell.

Phoebe Warnock was extremely enthusiastic about her cows. Listening to her talk to them and extolling their ability to do well on poor ground, the quality of their milk and their fine calves, I could quite see why the old farmers had claimed fairy origins for them. She actually had one which was white with red ears. When she spoke to it, it murmured back confidentially at her.

Irish Moiled Cattle are still on the critical list of the Rare Breeds

Survival Trust. Their journal, *The Ark*, printed the following description of them in December 1988:

> The preferred colour is rich red with a white line down the full length of the back, white tail, white underline and white udder. Yellow, dun or plum-coloured animals are acceptable, as are white animals with red ears, with or without some red, dun or plum colour on their sides, but in all cases the back, tail underline and udder should be white . . . . The head should be naturally polled, prominently domed with no trace of horn.

As we drove away, I pointed at the fields full of black-and-white Friesians. 'Just think,' I said, 'once they'd all have been Moiled Cattle probably, or little Kerry cattle, or Dexters.'

'Or goats,' said Mary darkly. 'Look here, you're supposed to be doing a programme about making a country living. All this business of Greyhound Pigs and fairy thorns and ancient cattle is all very well, but what about the practical side of it?'

'Not just making a living, but living itself,' I retorted. 'Understanding the past might give us a clue to surviving the present. Anyway, at the next farm there are Moiled Cattle being used as part of a big commercial herd. This time it's strictly business.'

But it wasn't entirely. Roderick Swann, whose uncle had done much to preserve the breed, tried to be terribly modern and 'viable' in his attitude to the Irish Moiled Cattle in his herd, but it was clear that he was just plain fond of them, particularly Fred the bull, who was a friendly lad and insisted on having his poll scratched before he'd move away.

By the time Mary and I had reached the little town of Cushendall, with its soft green slopes and trees bursting into leaf, and the sea, distant and blue and still, like a painting, Mary had given up trying to be practical. She was more excited than I was when we collected Patrick McCambridge from his shop and followed him up into the hills to cut peat (or turf, as the Irish call it) from the beds leased by his family. It was Mary who leapt down to collect the soft, black blocks of peat and stack them, as Mr McCambridge sliced them from the bank with the long peat shovel; it was Mary who wanted to know more and more about the old days, when whole families picnicked at the site and found strange things, like old sword hilts and perfectly preserved butter, as they collected the fuel supply for winter. It was Mary who had to be chivvied away from the raw wind cutting through the grass and the lambs crying and Patrick McCambridge's endless patience, for we had one more call to make that day.

This is not a textbook, so I will leave the full history of the Cushendall ponies to someone else. What with the peat cutting and the endless miles of road and tape we had covered that day, I was a little hazy when we got to the Cullens' farm. I remember a beautiful mare called Lily and the story (so often produced to explain a rare quality in a breed, be it horse, cattle or sheep) of a stallion swimming ashore from the Spanish Armada and serving the local ponies to produce the sturdy Cushendall with a sharp turn of speed in it. But it was the Cullens themselves who distracted me with their kindness, their big family, the massive tea and the personal history lesson they gave me on the McMullens. They then sent us along the road to find rooms in a guest house owned by a friend of theirs.

'You realize what you've done,' said Mary as we sat on the floor after dinner, she with her shoes kicked off and I trying in vain to get some relief for my back. 'What you've done, according to this schedule of yours, is to dot us about between Protestant and Catholic.'

'So?' I said.

'This is Northern Ireland,' Mary said and then she giggled. 'If anyone is trailing us they'll be in fits. Talk about fools rush in . . .'

'Nonsense. They'll just see us getting a lot of country stories together. No one but an idiot could think we had any political motives. Anyway, why would anyone want to trail us?'

But, the next day, where we were and who we were dealing with was made very clear.

Still like a pair of kids on holiday, we rose early so that we could go along the coast road and look at the Giant's Causeway, where we sat on the cliffs and delved into the Dilly Bag and smelt the salt air before going on to see the one group of people Mary had found. It was a small rural co-operative which had, as one of its activities, the knitting and sale of traditional Aran sweaters. Of course I had to buy one, which was why, having interviewed the manager of the co-op about the rest of their business and gone to see two of the farmers' wives who did the hand-knitting, we ended up in a little shop.

The ladies in the shop had all the time in the world to help me choose my sweater and they then sat us down and gave us coffee and, for a while, allowed the phone in the background to ring on and on. At last, with many apologies, the manageress went to answer it. For a bit longer we chatted on, but the rest of the ladies went rather quiet and still until their friend came back. She coughed politely and drew us to one side.

'It seems it would be advisable,' she said in a low voice, 'not to use the main road to the town. I will show you on a map the best way to go.'

Mary shot a warning look at me, too late.

'Why?' I asked gaily. 'Bombs?'

Mary flinched and the manageress glanced around her.

'I have just been told that it would be better for you on this other road,' she said quietly. 'Now, it's quite a pretty way to go' – and she began ushering us firmly towards the door. The rest of the ladies were suddenly very busy re-folding all the sweaters and cardigans. They smiled at us as we left but there was a new tension about them. As if a hawk had flown over a flock of hens.

'Now I know,' I murmured to Mary, 'why you wanted that list for Those Who Needed To Know.'

She looked at me grimly. 'That phone call was nothing to do with *them*.'

'Well,' I said as we waved our goodbyes, 'somebody loves us. At least they don't wish us any harm. Unless, of course, it's all a plot and they've sent us this way on purpose to blow us up.'

'Don't joke about it,' said Mary, frowning at the road ahead. 'I do hate these little roads. I mean, it only takes a sniper in the bushes. They wouldn't find us for days.'

'But you said they never attack reporters,' I reminded her.

'There is always a first time. And you have not been behaving like a normal reporter.'

'Rubbish,' I said, but my feet had gone all tingly as they do when I'm scared stiff. I began scanning the passing hedges for snipers.

'Oh, look,' I cried a few miles on.

Mary didn't swerve the car, but she said afterwards that all her hair stood straight up on end. 'We *mustn't* stop,' she said with a shrill edge of panic in her voice.

'Well, look at it in your rear-view mirror,' I said. 'That's the biggest pair of ears I've ever seen on a sheep'.

Mary glanced up, stopped the car and reversed it.

The sheep with the outsize ears was still standing by the hedge. It was not so much a sheep with ears, as a pair of ears with a sheep.

'Someone,' I said, 'has been using a very smart Border Leicester ram.'

The ears semaphored back and forth at us, a mad little breeze came flittering along the hedge, innocent of snipers, and we collapsed against the car and armoured our fears in laughter. We kept it buckled around us all day and, if the laughter was a trifle hysterical at times, it got us safely through the next few hours and a warning, less kindly given, from the other side.

We had no trouble finding our way to the address we needed in the town. The centre was ominously deserted and our mirth subsided as we passed the grim barricades soaring round some of the buildings. Until that moment the cheerful hospitality and interest of the country people we'd met had glossed over the bitter reality of what was going on around them.

We were still rather jumpy after we had left the town and were hunting around the lanes for the next farm on my list, and a shadow over the sun made the flat landscape bleak enough to fit our thoughts. There was something vague and distracted about the people we accosted for directions, so that we back-tracked and cruised around between the low hedges in an aimless way that did nothing to help their opinion of us as we passed them again and again.

'I can't stand any more of this,' I said at last. 'If that's not the place we're looking for down this track, let's hightail it for the Northern Goat Club and then we can make a dash for Dublin and a really good dinner.'

Mary looked at me in disgust. 'You think we're going to be able to make a dash?' she exclaimed. 'Take no notice of these well-made roads we've been on so far. After we cross the border . . . Oh well, you'll see! Now, is this is the place we want or not?'

It was and I'm glad we didn't miss it or the man we'd come to see. Let's call him Joe, because he didn't want his real name used. Joe had found a nice little earner clearing out the local rabbits, which had returned in plague proportions, and then freezing them and selling them to the Arabs. He was also a very keen gardener and grew prize-winning vegetables of every exotic kind in the big walled garden behind the farmhouse.

Joe had no legs. He cultivated the garden by flying around it on his hands (the crutches delayed him, he said) and he did his rabbiting by going out into the fields in his little car, followed by his labrador, Rex. Joe shot the rabbits through the window of the car and Rex collected them and stowed them carefully behind the seats. I could not get any specific details of how the trade with the Arabs was conducted.

Gert and I spent a long time out in the fields recording Joe and Rex as they tried to pot rabbits, so long that I forgot to get the Thermos in the Dilly Bag topped up, what with Mary pointing to her watch and sourly reminding me that what looked like not so very far on the map was a good many miles away yet.

Joe and Rex and the non-existent rabbits had cleared my nerves, but Mary was muttering about getting to the border in the dark.

'Well, I've only got to see the Secretary of the Northern Goat Club,' I said soothingly. 'I had hoped to see a smallholder who breeds greyhounds. One of his dogs is fancied for this year's Greyhound Derby.'

Mary gave me a sharp glance. 'Why aren't we going to see him, then?' she demanded, all thoughts of those nocturnal dangers lurking by the border gone. A good story always comes first.

'I'm not sure,' I said. 'He was very keen to see me at first when I rang, but when I got in touch again to make a definite time he was a bit sniffy. Said something about "being advised not to talk to me".' I suspect it's just the usual caginess of the racing bunch, though, nothing more sinister. Anyway, I couldn't shift him. And I *did* try. It was one interview I really wanted. But

I suppose if I owned a Derby fancy I might be a bit wary about talking to some fool reporter. D'you know, we've had nothing to eat since breakfast except a packet of crisps and some biscuits. I need a gallon of coffee and a hot meal.'

'So do I,' said Mary. 'Keep your eyes peeled and we'll have a quick bite somewhere.'

But peel them as I might, my eyes failed to see anything at all resembling a café, and the few pubs we passed had a remote, unfriendly look to them and we knew, without stopping to ask, that coffee and a hot meal would not be forthcoming there. The very landscape, although open and rolling away to the distant hills, seemed introverted and turned in on itself. For the first time on Irish soil I began to feel unwelcome.

'Beautiful, isn't it?' said Mary, waving a hand at the countryside around us.

'No,' I said, 'there's a cold despair out there somewhere and it's infected the very earth.'

It was a very subjective feeling, although there was a pale, shadowless light that evening which robbed everything of depth. For some time we'd been passing the tattered remains of wind-ripped flags hanging like corpses in the tallest of the trees. I have a horror of things hanging in trees, the left-overs of two nightmares which haunted me as a child. The most frequent and terrifying was of a man hanging from a burning parachute caught in the branches of a tree. Although his body was covered in flames, as he hung there he smiled and beckoned to me until I awoke, screaming. Mrs P always said it was because when I was a small baby she'd had to flee with me through a bush fire, with trees crashing behind our car as the driver twisted and turned it, yards ahead of the flames. But in my dream there was no noise and no hurry and the ghastliness of it centred on the smiling face of the man in his burning parachute. To this day, even an abandoned kite hanging in a tree brings out that cold sense of sickly sweet dread. The flags hanging in the trees began to work their horror, sounds faded and the road became a tunnel leading inexorably to disaster. Mary's voice yanked me back to sanity.

'Oh, good! A town coming up,' she cried. 'If there's nothing open there, it's the Dilly Bag again.'

'I'm afraid there's only enough water for half a cup of coffee each,' I said. 'We could try knocking on a door for some boiling water, though.'

'I'm not knocking on any doors round here,' said Mary. 'Have you noticed that all the pavements are painted red, white and blue?'

I had noticed and, after the flags, this arrogant patriotism made me long to get well away, but ahead of us, on the right, I saw a consoling sight. A large, elegant Georgian building declared itself open for hot meals, coffee and bar. Everything swung back into normality and, smiling with relief, we hunted for a parking spot on the crowded street, locked the doors of the car and marched hopefully towards the colonnaded doorway.

It was warm, it had good clean loos, tatters of faded grandeur and echoes of long-gone house parties and balls, and a comfortable restaurant where a small, friendly waitress promised us toasted sandwiches and proper percolated coffee. The other customers gave us quick smiles and nods of welcome and we settled back against the thick velvet seats and relaxed.

'It's obviously been quite a grand house at one time,' said Mary as she read about its architectural features and a brief history from the back of the menu. 'There's an impressive stable block out the back and an old ruin in the landscaped garden.'

Our waitress interrupted her with a large pot of coffee and the news that the sandwich machine was giving trouble and the chef was having to make ours under the grill and she hoped we wouldn't mind waiting a bit longer.

Mary jumped to her feet. 'While we're waiting, I think I'll just get on to that hotel and tell them we might be pretty late tonight.'

'The phone's down there in the bar,' smiled our waitress and bustled back to the kitchen.

The bar was an extension of the restaurant and the man looking after it paused in his conversation with a group of quiet, earnest men, to explain to Mary how to work the phone and that she'd have to go through to the exchange. There was no direct dialling from here.

Mary glanced over at me and shrugged and then announced

into the phone that she needed a Dublin number. It seemed that not only was it not possible to dial direct but the person on the exchange had a serious hearing defect, because Mary had to repeat her request in ever-increasing tones for the next minute. She was then disconnected and had to start all over again.

A curious hush had descended on both bar and restaurant. At first I thought it was merely because Mary's shrill demands were making other conversation impossible but, as I watched, several of the men by the bar got up and casually drifted outside. The noisy family party at the table opposite to ours glanced furtively at each other and then they too seemed suddenly to have finished their meal and were leaving. And still Mary, her back turned, was indignantly demanding of the operator where his brains had been left. In vain I tried to catch her attention.

Three large men walked quietly through the door and took the place just vacated by the family. They nodded to the waitress, who had been hovering anxiously nearby. She dumped our sandwiches on the table and retreated to the kitchen once more. I glanced at the bar and noticed that another group of men had installed themselves in the seats a little closer to where Mary, with one hand over her left ear, was now loudly inquiring if she was indeed speaking to the hotel near Dublin at last. Reassured, she outlined our requirements for the night, our estimated time of arrival and the chances of some kind of food and drink at that early hour of the morning. She also became very matey with whoever was promising her the fulfilment of these demands, quips were exchanged, inquiries made as to present weather conditions and how the recent horse sales had gone at Goff's. And all the while at least ten pairs of eyes drilled holes in her back. The tension was appalling and it grew worse when Mary began to berate the obstinate operator who had cut her off from Dublin in mid-sentence. The ten pairs of eyes swivelled round and stared at me.

Giving a sickly grin of helplessness and mustering up my faded Australian vowels, I raised my voice, and called out to Mary to hurry up or her sandwiches would be cold. The atmosphere relaxed slightly. Neutral territory again.

We chatted brightly in our best Barnum and Bailey manner while we munched our sandwiches and drank our coffee. As she'd turned away from the phone, Mary had instantly noticed the changed clientele and my own fixed grin and caught the cue I flung her. This was strictly clown time. Innocently we paid our bill, still gaily trilling at each other and the waitress, bid everyone a cheery goodbye and fell out into the corridor.

'Keep walking and keep talking,' I said to Mary through clenched teeth, 'and don't look back!'

We both breathed deeply as we hit the fresh air and then stopped quite still. The long main street with its painted kerbs stretched away before us, completely deserted of people and cars. Except, that is, for a bright-red car with its cargo of Aran sweaters, hanks of flax and a handful of torch batteries prominently displayed on the back shelf. It still stood at an angle to the kerb where Mary had had trouble squeezing it into the narrow space. Now it had all the space in the world.

'Oh my God!' breathed Mary, and we began to walk very slowly and very stiffly towards it.

Chapter 5

We came face to face under the car.

'Do you know what we're supposed to look for?' I asked Mary.

'Um . . . I suppose a sort of unidentified lump, or something,' she said. We peered up at the mass of pipes and metal above us.

'They're all unidentified as far as I'm concerned,' I mumbled, bewildered.

We edged out backwards on our knees, stood up and met again over the roof of the car.

'Well, how about peculiar-looking wires hanging down?' said Mary and vanished under the car again.

'Actually,' I said as I joined her, 'in all the films they look under the bonnet. Except that sometimes when they lift it up the whole thing explodes.'

'In real life,' said Mary, 'they get the bomb squad to have a look. We could go and ask the police.'

'I suspect the police are watching from a distance and laughing their heads off,' I replied. 'Someone's probably been making fools of us.'

'Yes,' said Mary tersely. And there it was again – both of us would rather get blown up than look like fools. That decision made, we crept into the car and closed our eyes as Mary turned the ignition key gently.

The car purred innocently into life.

'Sometimes,' I said gloomily, 'the bang doesn't come till they've driven a few yards.'

'Wonderful!' Mary shouted, and she slammed in the gear lever viciously and plunged her foot on the accelerator. Neither of us spoke for a long while.

We passed by more flag-hung trees and through towns with their centres barricaded in steel, and somewhere behind one of them we found Eunice and her owners. Eunice was a prize-winning British Toggenberg and, the moment I saw her and the rest of the herd of goats, our recent terrors seemed just plain silly.

There are times, many times, when I cry to heaven and wonder why I keep animals (especially goats) and yet, when I meet others, elsewhere, I feel an instant sense of identity and belonging, like seeing again members of a well loved family. Domestic animals (and their keepers) share a universal language. That's not to say that there isn't a difference between one goat's voice and another's, and I can identify all my sheep individually by listening to them, not to mention the other animals I know well, but the basic sounds are the same. So now the voluble Eunice and the rest of the goats were the night-light on our recent fears. We need not, in fact, have stopped at the restaurant for food at all. A massive tea had been prepared for us by the Pattersons, and by the time we left their smallholding we were reeling with good things.

Certainly we felt restored enough to treat with withering scorn the menacing group of boys loitering with obvious intent as we drove through Newry at about eleven o'clock. Neither did we take much notice of the soldiers hurrying round a corner towards us, but drove straight on till we reached the border, where a notice commanded us to Stop and Declare.

So stop we did, once again preparing to explain batteries, machines, flax and Dilly Bag, but there was no sign of anyone. Mary marched into the customs shed and brought back a rather sleepy woman in uniform who looked at us wonderingly.   'And what would you be wanting me to do for you?' she yawned.

'We have Stopped and we have Declared,' said Mary.

'Oh good!' said the woman and sauntered back to the customs shed.

'I don't suppose they mind bombs going out – just bombs coming in,' I said, and settled back with a contented sigh as we left the border lights and surged into the darkness ahead. The next moment, seat-belt notwithstanding, my head made violent contact with the dashboard as we hit the mother and father of a pot-hole.

'Welcome to the Republic,' cried Mary and threw back her head and laughed.

'Oh, very funny,' I said, but I remembered that the little green car and I had had some alarming experiences on the Irish roads. Once, bowling merrily along a little country lane, suddenly, with no warning sign, we shot straight across the main road, narrowly missing at least three cars, and landed with a bump in the muddy entrance to a farmyard, where two old men glanced at our sudden arrival and continued their conversation as calmly as before.

Therefore, on that midnight dash to Dublin and beyond, I was very grateful that Mary was driving, knowing as she did the Irish roads so well and the habit of her countrymen of driving with their lights on full beam at all times. I was glad, too, that she was familiar with the practice of using painted tar barrels to indicate road-works, and had had a lot of practice at avoiding the ones that had rolled over into our path. After a while, I didn't look but said my prayers instead.

We span through Dublin itself in style, and arrived in a flurry of gravel at the hotel just before one o'clock in the morning. It looked completely deserted and the big studded door was firmly closed against us.

'I knew it,' I moaned in despair.

'Relax, we're home now,' grinned Mary and began hauling bags out of the car. 'Ring the bell,' she commanded and I tottered up the steps and did so.

It rang, mournfully, somewhere deep within, but not a lot else happened.

'I feel like Rat and Mole trying to rouse Badger in midwinter,' I whispered to Mary as she joined me, laden with bags. 'Only there are no shuffling footsteps made by someone wearing outsize slippers coming to rescue us.'

Mary raised a fist and knocked on the door loudly.

'And there you are,' she said, 'shuffling footsteps, right on cue.'

The big door opened a crack and a smiling face, dimly lit from behind, inquired our business. We were just about to explain it when the door shut in our faces again. It swung back almost immediately and it was clear that welcoming lights had been switched on and the porter had taken a moment to button up his jacket and acquire a more official air.

As we stepped over the threshold, a voice from somewhere off left assured us indignantly that there'd be no sense at all in putting money on the big colt if the little mare was in the race. Our guide grimaced sheepishly and disappeared. The faint chink of glasses and much invective followed, while Mary and I gazed round the hall. It had something vaguely familiar about it.

'It's supposed to remind you of stables,' Mary whispered, 'because of being so near to Goff's, you know. This is where a lot of the buyers stay for the horse sales. It hasn't been built very long. I've been wanting to see it.'

Our porter returned and waved apologetically towards the side room, which was now silent.

'Just a friend,' he said, 'popped in to keep me company for a little while.'

'It'll be the little mare, I tell you,' declared the voice from within.

'Meanwhile,' I laughed, 'is there any chance of a hot drink?'

'Just tell me what you'd like and I'll bring it up to you,' promised the porter and, our luggage collected, our names sketchily registered and much debate as to the relative merits of hot milk, tea or whiskey, we all tiptoed up the wide staircase and along the dim corridors, where the entrances to the rooms were cunningly designed to look like stable doors and adorned with horseshoes. The theme was carried through inside, where cupboards and shelves resembled mangers and the hooks and handles were standard equipment in a tack room. I don't think I'd have cared by then if the bed had been made of straw, but both it and the bathroom were designed for the comfort of rich horse-dealers. Except that, as I was having a shower, three of the wall tiles fell off and hit me on the head.

A knock on the door announced the porter with my whiskey and a hot-water bottle filled to bursting, in spite of the central heating.

The next knock came from Mary at some hideous hour in the morning and, as she hurried me along, she complained that she'd waited for over an hour for the hot milk she'd primly asked for.

'Serves you right,' I said as we hastened below for a quick breakfast.

We didn't get it, of course – well, not quickly, anyway. Certainly Mary had plenty of time to pop in and out of the dining room, making her inevitable phone calls, in between courses which were brought to us by a young waitress with much charm and solicitude, who was also in great demand as a conversationalist by our fellow guests. I could have sat and listened to them for ever.

It was Mary who finally dragged me forth into the rain, pouring down steadily. It didn't seem to matter, somehow. From the moment we'd got to the hotel the feeling of holiday had come back, and now we were on our way to see a real Irish Draught at a real Irish stud farm.

I'd always wanted to see a good Irish Draught because for years people had been telling me that my old mare Doli was one.

'No,' I would correct them, 'she's a draught horse from Ireland. There's a big difference.' But when they asked me exactly what that difference was I'd dodged the question, never having met a real Irish Draught in the flesh.

Doli herself is built like a tank, with huge feathered feet, and, I believe, came over with a job lot of horses from Ireland when she was a youngster. Although I always maintain that she was conceived when a Clydesdale mare was minding her own business on one side of a fence, and was suddenly surprised and delighted by the attentions of a thoroughbred stallion who just happened to have hopped over that fence (thoroughbred because there is some quality of hot blood in Doli which has no right to be there in one of her looks and conformation), I would never dream of confusing her with the actual breed known as the Irish Draught. So here we were approaching the stud, run by Mary McCann, where we'd see the real thing.

We found it in the person of a stallion called Sea Crest, a tall grey with a knowing air and one eye on the thoroughbred mare gazing winsomely at him from her box across the yard.

'People mostly try to produce the show jumpers by putting a thoroughbred stallion on an Irish Draught mare,' explained Mary McCann, 'but some of us think it would work better the other way, so Cresty's booked up this season.' And she led me into his box and told me all about the Irish Draught, while Cresty stood perfectly still in spite of Gert and the microphone. He didn't look a bit like Doli, although probably horses of her type did play a part in the evolution of the Irish Draught, which came into being from the desire of Irish farmers to have a horse that could pull a plough one day and ride to hounds the next. There's a dash of thoroughbred, a dash of Connemara and perhaps a dash of something stronger in the Irish Draught, which had got enough jump in it to produce show jumpers like the fabled Ryan's Son.

At last we left Sea Crest (much to his disgust) and walked the fields in the wind and the rain, terriers at our heels, to see that year's crop of foals and hear Mary McCann's hopes and plans for them. We got back just in time to watch her Connemara stallion serve a little pony mare, while Sea Crest shouted his frustation in the background. And still the rain poured down and still we talked horses and, to complicate matters, the two Marys (who had found they were old friends) began to reminisce and inquire after acquaintances until conscience smote us and we bundled ourselves and Gert up into the car and fled around the waterlogged lanes to find more goats. Eventually Mary obeyed the instructions I was reading out to 'turn right onto a tiny road up a hill, past a silver birch forest till you come to two cottages. Both are dilapidated but the Rowsomes' shows some sign of life.'

'But I know her,' shrieked Mary as one sign of life appeared in the doorway of the cottage under renovation. And then I did abandon all hope of making up the time we'd lost at the hotel and stud farm, for Mary Price and Deirdre Rowsome fell on each other's necks with wild cries of delight. Twice now, in a weird sort of jackpot, I'd organised an interview with someone from Mary's past, both of them disguised by married names.

It was a long time before Gert could be unearthed and Deirdre and her husband led me to the goat house to do their interviews about the present status of goats in the Republic, and to meet the first offspring of their imported Toggenberg, a chubby pair of kids called Palestrina and Monteverdi. The Rowsomes and a few like-minded people were desperately trying to upgrade the goats in the Republic and to organize properly run breed shows, as they were already doing in the North.

We went back to the house and still the rain drummed down and fog began to drift malevolently across the fields, obscuring the view of lake and hills which I'd been admiring so steadfastly while waiting for Mary and Deirdre to finish taking addresses down and exchanging girlish notes on their history.

'Where are you going to next?' Deirdre asked finally.

'To see the Misses Baker,' I muttered as the fog swirled round the yard and almost blotted our car from view. 'But I'm wondering if perhaps we shouldn't ring and cancel. It's getting so late and we still have to drive back to Belfast tonight.' Why we had to go all the way back to Belfast just to catch a plane the next morning was a matter Mary and I had been arguing about. It was all something vaguely mysterious about BBC policy, and hire cars and plane tickets being easier to organize, but it remained a sore point.

'No!' cried Deirdre now. 'You *must* go and see the Bakers. The Bakers are unique.'

And so we went and so we got to heaven. Or at least to that seeming paradise that every latterday self-sufficer dreams about and is so often disappointed in.

Of the outside of the house or of the actual smallholding itself, I have little knowledge, except for a dim vision of sloping fields smeared with fog and rain. But the cowshed was full of the rich breath of sleek black Kerry Cattle, another Irish breed which, along with the little Dexter, at one time almost disappeared. It was very rare to see a complete herd which could trace its ownership and pedigree back for so long. For Freda and Connie Baker had never given in to fashion. Ever since they were children and their parents had given them a goat, they had pursued their own sweet way, as true individuals do. Later they had set up their tiny farm, bred the animals they preferred, grown the things they wanted to, and made their living out of their yogurt and home-produced cheese and organic vegetables, long before any of those things had been appreciated as they are now. Without the current obsession with healthy food to bring customers to their gate, the Bakers had had to rely on people coming back for the sheer quality and taste of what they had for sale.

As the rain racketed on the roof of the cowshed, and I dodged about behind the stalled cattle while Mary shouted warnings at me from the door as to which one was about to let fly a rich stream of dung, these two enchanting Quaker ladies explained their loyalty to their good Irish Kerry cows and called each one by name and told me exactly what she had given in milk. From that milk they made butter. For the yogurt they relied on the milk from the Anglo-Nubian goats next door.

They're marvellous-looking animals, Anglo-Nubians, with their long floppy ears, which should meet at the end of their high, aristocratic, Roman noses, and their wonderful haphazard colouring. I've often been tempted towards them, but stories of their more possessive and neurotic temperament have put me off. My own Dolores had a dash of Anglo-Nubian in her and I've always suspected that it was because of that dash that scatty animals like Gorgeous appeared in the herd from time to time. But all that was forgotten when I saw the Baker Anglo-Nubians for, like their owners, they were perfect ladies, every one. If the cattle had been disturbed slightly by the sound of rushing gutters of water outside, the goats were in a state of absolute calm as they sat dreamily cudding on their thick beds of straw. Only as we paused at each stall to hear her history and her powers of production did each goat get to her feet and nuzzle her owners or mutter quietly back as her name was mentioned. It was a world away from the constant dramas of my own goat-shed, where I sometimes feel more like the headmistress of a girls' school along the St Trinian's line, than a simple goat-keeper.

Perhaps, I thought, as we stood there amongst these beautifully behaved Anglo-Nubians with their coats of many colours (dotted and dashed and eel-striped, deep mahoganies and browns, pale golds and creams and fawns), goats, like any other animals, are simply reflecting the inward state of the people who look after them. Given the steadying influence of the Bakers, my own British Toggenbergs might become models of rectitude; given my usually manic state of mind pervading their lives, the Baker Anglo-Nubians might turn into raging delinquents. I sighed and tried to be more basic in my questioning.

'I know their milk is the richest of all the breeds,' I said to Connie Baker, 'but Anglo-Nubians are not very good at milking through the winter, are they?'

'Well, we've never had any trouble over that,' she replied. 'That one there hasn't had a kid since last year and she's still giving a good gallon. But why don't you come and taste the yogurt?'

I can still taste it. It was the most wonderful yogurt I've ever eaten, or rather devoured, because both Mary and I dipped our spoons in again and again. We had it plain and we had it fancy, rich with home-grown blackcurrants.

'We do a strawberry, too, later in the season,' we were told. 'The blackcurrants, of course, we can keep in the freezer. Now, why don't you have some of the soft cheese. We can give you a plain one or there's one covered in raisins and nuts. We have to say that of course the raisins and nuts aren't home-grown. They're the only things we have to buy in.'

We tried the cheese and we went mad. We bought pounds of it between us, but the yogurt we left regretfully, thinking of the long flight to England and the possibility of it oozing over our luggage.

Ever since, I've been trying to find yogurt like the Bakers'. I've tasted and tried and bullied Mrs P into creating it, and never ever found it again. The nearest is a certain brand of Greek yogurt (and, flavoured with home-made lemon curd, that can be made remarkable too), but somehow there is still something missing. The Bakers gave me the actual recipe, but I think it had nothing to do with methods of making, but all to do with the actual milk their cows and goats gave. No wonder the Bakers had survived the era of junk food and all the mass-produced stuff on the supermarket shelves. Once you'd tasted their butter, cheese and yogurt, it was worth the trip out from Dublin to keep on tasting it.

At last Connie, like an indulgent nanny, detached us from our bowls of nectar and led us gently forth into the big dining room where Freda had laid out tea. Full as we were, we fell victim to the home-made bread and jam, the slices of floating sponge cake thick with cream, and the soft lilting voices telling us about their years of growing and making and marketing. The Bakers were enthusiastically trying to cultivate a new type of wheat designed to grow in damp climates. Already they had some of the ground flour from their first crop to show us.

I looked round the neat room, deep in warm colours and glowing lamps, and compared it with the chaos I so often found when I went to see the present-day self-sufficing community, some of whom gloried in the ramshackle mess of their farms, loud in self-congratulation and with an overbearing contempt for any other way of living. I suddenly wanted to parcel them all up and force-march them to the Wicklow Mountains and give them a good strong dose of the Baker way.

A light scratching at the door distracted us and a tiny Manchester terrier was admitted, her little black-and-tan face adorned with a toothy smile.

'Vanessa,' said Freda Baker, 'has been sleeping off a mouse hunt. She's the best mouser in the world and the best smiler, aren't you Vanessa?' And Vanessa danced around and smiled and smiled.

'I don't know about being shut out of the fairy mound,' I said to Mary as we drove through the dark lanes in the ever-present rain, 'but it's a cold old world out here after that.'

'What I'm so sick about,' she said, as she guided us past the blinding lights of an oncoming car, 'is that I lived in Dublin all those years and never knew that that miracle of a yogurt and that cheese were just a few miles away.'

We stopped in Dublin briefly to see Mary's mother and dutifully ate the supper she had ready for us, although we were staggering with food, and then back we went to the North, avoiding the tar barrels and the pot-holes and the headlights blinding us through the rain-smeared windscreen. When we reached our hotel not far from Belfast, everything was modern, warm and very boring. I longed for imitation stable doors and falling bath tiles and wondered idly if the little mare had won her race.

We were very quiet on the flight back to England (partly through terror because when we looked out of the window bits seemed about to fall off the plane, and I was suddenly reminded of the time I came back from Paris on a charter flight in midwinter and they weighed the passengers as well as the luggage), but when we stormed into the BBC in Bristol everyone gave us startled looks.

'You two,' said Mary's secretary, 'look as if you've been on an almighty high'.

'That's right,' said Mary. 'We have.'

Chapter 6

E ven Mrs P was impressed with the cheese I'd brought back
from Ireland, and I regret to say we had something of an
orgy with it. A slow, calculated orgy, savouring every bite
but continuing on until there was nothing more than the memory
of a taste to haunt us. It haunts me still, along with a few other
ghostly tastes. There was, for instance, a small, light, fluffy chocolate cake filled with lemon cream which was the speciality of a shop
in the New South Wales town of Orange, when I was about five
years old; and there were the 'Dream Bars' which Mrs P used to
make when I was in my teens. I found the old recipe recently, but
they weren't exactly the same. Perhaps they needed the heat of an
Australian outback summer or just the sharper palate of youth.

Mrs P and I looked at each other sadly and guiltily as the last
piece of the Bakers' cheese dwindled to nothing.

'It's probably the McMahons, you know,' remarked my mother
thoughtfully.

'No, Baker is their name,' I said, puzzled.

'I mean the McMahons are probably the reason why you feel so
much at home when you go to Ireland,' said Mrs P impatiently.

'Sorry, you've lost me,' I said as I collected our plates.

'Your great-great-grandfather was a McMahon. He was the
one who ran off with the Spanish girl and they had your great
grandmother, Margaret. The one you look like. Except that she
was only half your size.'

'Ah. The one who hatched chickens out down her cleavage and
taught you to play poker.'

Mrs P gave me a sour look. 'Well, she was a lot more fun than
the English one, who lived till she was 104 and we all had to call her
Ma'am. She must have been as mad as anything when she woke

up dead. Nothing else ever got the better of her. Sometimes, when you're in one of your moods, I think you take after her in character. But you *look* like Margaret. And she was half a McMahon.'

I groaned. We have, as Mrs P is fond of reminding me, an ancestry like a patchwork quilt. Pure mongrel, born in Australia, is how I'd describe us and my own opinion about why Ireland felt so much like home is that a lot of the Irish character went into the makeup of the Australian one. And, although some freak of those ancient genes of ours has made it impossible for me to survive the Australian summer without being half-dead with asthma or hay fever, I do miss the country I was born and raised in, almost to desperation point sometimes. But that spring, when I came back with the warmth of the Irish hospitality still wrapping me round, it was to an entirely Australian household.

Although she'd been away from home for a couple of years by then, Jane Crawford still had that look of bounding health that means a childhood diet of sun and plenty of really fresh food. She was tall, with hair the colour of burnt honey, and blindingly efficient. For a while, she'd been Bertie Ellis's receptionist and veterinary nurse, and when she was there his practice went smoothly as never before, bills came in on time and, no matter how desperate your animal crisis, you came off the phone soothed and calmed, knowing that somehow Jane would get a vet to you, if it meant dragging them there in person. And then she left, as is the way with Australians seeing the world. When she came back to Wales at last, Bertie and Sara Ellis had filled her job and Jane was at a loose end. Hardly believing my luck, I put in a bid for her, in the hope of just once getting some help over the summer when I was working on the programme.

So, when I got back from Ireland, there were the goats and the sheep, neat as new pins and minding their manners like anything, the dogs had that contented, much-walked look and Mrs P was happily trotting out all her Australian sayings (knowing they'd be immediately understood) and reliving the good old, bad old days in the Sydney of her youth, while Jane brought her up to date on how things were now. For the first time I could come home from a trip without having to get straight back into the frantic rush to attend to the stock, continue the endless mucking out and somehow get the

55

next trip organized. I had a glorious vision of ending the summer relatively sane. Some hope!

Within a day of my return, Bertie and Sara remembered Jane's efficiency and rang to offer her a job. Unable to match their offer, I watched my happy summer go up in a puff of green smoke. But there were still a couple of weeks in hand before Jane left, so at least I could go off on another journey with a clear mind. Well, that was the general idea, until my bad back began playing up again and it looked as if I'd need a co-driver. So my neighbour Gwynneth agreed to do the stock, as she'd been doing them for years, and Mrs P would have to look after the house and dogs on her own. And, all the time away, I'd be worrying about her doing too much.

If I'd been afraid of being blown up when Mary and I were in Northern Ireland, Jane and I damn near were when we went to East Anglia. Violent thunderstorms seemed to pursue us personally, striking as we arrived and clearing as we left. All I can properly remember of the landscape was blinding rain and great sheets of water which we either plunged into, parting water on either side like cliffs, or planed across in terror. Except for that first evening, when we came to rest in a rich, full-blown garden somewhere near Cambridge, where Jane nodded off on the garden seat, hypnotized by the smell of freshly cut grass and the dying heat of the sun, while I trailed down to the end of the garden and fell in love with a fox.

Cailleach was small and fierce but she came at once when her owner called to her. Her russet elegance and fine black legs blurred into a speed shot when she saw the cat strolling along with us and she called a warning to her two cubs, who came rolling boisterously out of the den behind her. Cailleach (whose name in Gaelic means "old wife") belonged, if a fox can ever truly belong to anyone, to a young artist called Fiona Silver. Fiona was to illustrate my first book, but, faced with the living delight of Cailleach and her cubs, the book suddenly seemed very sterile and unimportant, although Cailleach played her part in that too, for her portrait appeared in one of the margins. The story of how she came to be living with Fiona is not mine to tell. I just have the lasting memory of that warm evening in late spring, with the little vixen fussing about while her two cubs rolled and darted around her; the cat, who was called Black Sod, keeping a safe distance and winding himself around our legs; Fiona's horses galloping and calling from the next paddock; and the sun taking forever to sink in glory from the flat Cambridgeshire horizon. It was a long time before I roused Jane from her slumbers and we went off into the quiet dusk.

It was cold in the big farmhouse where we spent the night. Next morning it was raining and icy winds swept down from the North Sea. All day I hauled my victims out into their fields and barns and gardens in between the showers, for sometimes the sun came out in blinding bursts, warming the red-brick cottages and turning the vast fields of oil-seed rape an even more bilious shade of yellow. We skirted around and through Essex and on into Suffolk, seeing publishers of country magazines, small home tanners, makers of jams and pickles, booksellers and fishermen.

On we went to Norfolk and a whole farm full of the old Norfolk Black turkeys, the chief stag drumming his wings and gobbling indignantly at us while his wives applauded, their backs covered with green cloth saddles to protect them from the stag's claws during mating. For the Norfolk Black, like all the other, smaller, older breeds of turkeys, can still do his own mating. In the huge commercial breeds, the stags are too big and cumbersome now and the females have to be impregnated artificially. The obscenity of what we do to animals!

As we drove to the next farm on our list, lightning shot viciously down through the trees and great reverberating shouts of thunder enclosed us. On an instant the roads became rivers and lakes and there was nothing to do but pray the Beetle wouldn't stop as the water rose around us. Only luck and blind instinct got us into the yard of the old farm, whose owners dashed out and rescued us into a warm, lived-in kitchen with steaming mugs of tea and mountains of fresh scones.

That farm was an island of sanity, after those awful, boring fields of rape and corn, devoid of any animals. Here there were pigs and cows and, above all, chickens – chickens of all kinds, like the dainty Buff-Laced Wyandottes or the big, heavily feathered, ponderous Orpingtons.

It was the Chapmans' son Paul we'd come to see because, as

well as helping on the farm, he painted chickens. He painted chickens instead of people, so that the gay Victorian picnic party, posed against a haymaking scene reminiscent of Stubbs, were all chickens. It was a wonderful mad world Paul had created and all over the walls of his attic studio the bright paintings showed chickens at the fair, Henry VIII (an Orpington of course) having dinner with all of his six wives (assorted breeds), chickens running a farm with a big cockerel blacksmith shoeing the Shire horse, chickens out boating and, most wonderful of all, chickens going fox hunting. To this day I curse myself for not buying that painting, for Paul had managed to give his hunting chickens all the arrogance and pomposity which so many humans assume the moment they hop on a horse and go chasing something. The fox, incidentally, was hiding in the base of a hollow tree, peering out gleefully as the hunt raged past. It could have been Cailleach herself.

Jane and I drank coffee in a stately home that evening, in company with a baby monkey having its bottle feed, and, in between the outbursts of torrential rain, I dashed outside with Lady Fisher to interview her about her herd of tiny Falabella horses. It was very late when we crossed back into Suffolk and the lovely old house in Brandon where we were putting up for the night. It was not only comfortable, warm, and beautifully furnished, but the owners didn't mind a bit when we showed up somewhere around midnight. But that was the last year I put up at bed-and-breakfast places. Apart from being cheaper, I'd always thought that I was likely to pick up more casual stories than I would at a hotel, as I did that night in Brandon. Don Arnold had invented a board game based on cricket and one of the reasons he and Christine had been up so late was that they were getting a rush order ready for dispatch. They also got a much-needed plug on the radio for their game and it proved to be extremely popular in cricket-mad Britain. So being kind to a couple of unknown, weary travellers paid off.

These days I go to hotels where they have a porter on duty all night. When you travel miles from one place to the other and when you have to take into consideration the uncertain weather, the determined silence of animals and the nerves of their owners when confronted with a microphone, and my own persistence in staying till I get the best I can out of everything and everyone, it's inclined to get later and later. Small bed-and-breakfast places do not appreciate the sight and sound of their guests arriving in the middle of the night. Some of them had, like the Arnolds, been very understanding, but the next night Jane and I found the joker in the pack.

It had been a hard day and we ended it somewhere north of Boston in Lincolnshire, hours behind schedule. Begging the use of a phone so that Jane could ring through and warn the bed-and-breakfast place that we'd be much later than expected, we then spent the next couple of hours amongst a superb collection of old hay carts and farm wagons, trying to ignore the long buildings outside which made up a massive turkey-rearing unit.

The carts and wagons, painted in all their regional colours and designs, were ranged round the side of a vast shed and their owner knew the history of every one of them. Gert gobbled up tape after tape as I egged him on, unable to miss one of his stories. At last I realized that I had enough to fill a couple of programmes on their own and began to put everything away.

The turkey farmer looked at us thoughtfully and then, coming to a decision, he said, 'Would you like to see something a bit special?'

'More special than these?' cried Jane, who'd been enthralled by everything.

'Much more special,' said the farmer and he led us to the end of the shed, where one section had been enclosed in wood to make a separate room.

He pulled a key from his pocket, unlocked the door, groped around the walls and switched on a blaze of lights. There, gleaming with black paint and highly polished brass fittings, stood a real stage coach. Jane gasped and the farmer smiled at us proudly.

'She was hardly ever used,' he said, running his hand fondly over the high wheel arches. 'It wasn't a proper stage coach, because it was ordered by a private family. They could take the servants and all in a coach like this, you see. It was probably one of the last ones made and it had been very well looked after. I just had to get the upholstery done and the paint touched up. Now I'm learning to drive it, and one day I shall go out of that gate with four horses in the shafts and blow the horn and go places in her.'

I looked at him wonderingly. Here was this man whose farm was extremely modern and part of it had been turned over to rearing huge turkeys intensively, who could love with all his heart this reminder of the past, when hens and cows and pigs and turkeys roamed free. I thought of the Chapmans, who had told me how their neighbours laughed at them for keeping the old breeds and how it was all a bit of a struggle to make ends meet, and yet remembered what a happy, if haphazard, place their farm had been. In spite of its affluence and the beauty of the gleaming coach and the carts, the turkey farm did not, somehow, have the same warmth.

'Are you going to come and sit inside?' called Jane from within the depths of the coach, and I shook off my churlish thoughts and climbed up to join her. As we sank into the rich-smelling studded leather of the seats, our farmer told us how the long-established firm which had made the coach, realizing that soon the car would put them out of business, decided to go out with a bang. They made a huge bonfire and burnt all their designs. And, sad though it was, that story cheered me up. It was a gesture of defiance at the coming age which would make not just stage coaches extinct, but breeds of farm animals like the Lincolnshire Curly Coated pig and the Suffolk Dun cow; would condemn battery hens to tiny cages, turkeys to a grossness that denied them their natural behaviour and create featureless prairies of rape and corn out of the fields and woods.

'The trouble with you,' said Jane as we left, 'is that you need a square meal.'

'A cup of hot tea might help,' I muttered. Not once all day had we been offered so much as a glass of water. At one very prosperous farm we'd been kept firmly outside, with the car as our only refuge when the rain got too much for me to risk Gert's health any longer. By now even the Dilly Bag had offered up its last and we drove to Boston hungry, tired and thirsty.

'Look!' cried Jane as we drove around the town. 'A Chinese restaurant.'

We ate well and drove out of Boston and on towards our

appointment with bed-and-breakfast with reasonable confidence. It faltered and faded as we beheld the mean little dwelling right beside a busy main road. It was in total darkness.

'I thought you said it was a farmhouse,' said Jane.

'That's what it said in the B & B book,' I replied. 'It also claimed various architectural delights of which I see none whatsoever.'

We drove into the narrow space beside the house and sat for a moment listening to the rain drumming on the roof of the Beetle.

'Well, here goes,' said Jane and she dashed through the rain and knocked on the door. It opened a crack and a face peered out suspiciously.

'You're late,' cried a shrill voice. I joined Jane at the door.

'I'm sorry, but we did ring to say we wouldn't be here before ten and it's just that now,' I tried to explain as the rain shot out of the guttering and down our backs.

'Can we just get the luggage out and then we won't disturb you?' asked Jane.

The small face nodded reluctantly.

A few moments later, we'd transferred our bags and Gert and the rest of the equipment into the small front room, which was dimly lit.

Our hostess returned from somewhere above and stopped to look in horror at our luggage.

'What do you want all that inside for?' she cried.

'I'm afraid I never leave my equipment in the car,' I explained. 'Especially not right by the road like this. We'll take it upstairs out of your way.'

'You won't get it into your room,' I was told.

'Well, even if they're small rooms, it will fit between the two of them,' said Jane.

'*One* room!'

'No, we booked two rooms,' I said.

'*One* room you booked.'

I glanced at Jane, who had her hands on her hips and was looking dangerous. She had heard me book two rooms for two women, quite clearly. I decided not to argue.

'Then you have another room spare?' I asked.

'I have but it's not convenient to get it ready.'

'Is it,' demanded Jane, 'convenient to have us at all?'

The woman stared up at her defiantly, tossed her head and said, 'Well there's no other accommodation round here. It's up to you!'

'Right,' said Jane, and she began to gather up our bags. As we left I glanced back at the woman who stood with her mouth open, aghast.

'Do you think,' I said, as we drove through the stormy night, ' that we were altogether wise?'

'It was worth it to see her face,' laughed Jane. 'One room, indeed!' All she had to do was fling us a couple of sheets and we'd have been fine. But she's right, there is nowhere else, it seems.'

We'd already been back to Boston and, as it was Saturday night, there was not even one room to be had. So we decided to keep driving and see what the gods could offer.

They offered nothing more substantial than a small signpost pointing left. I checked the name on the map by torchlight.

'It looks fairly main, this place,' I told Jane. 'Let's give it a try.' And she swung the car round and we entered upon a network of little roads that looked anything but main for a very long time. And then, appearing out of the rain like a mirage, was a whole town. It even had taxis cruising up the main street.

We pulled up outside a brightly lit hotel with thumping music blasting forth and Jane got out of the car and ran inside. She came back a few minutes later waving two keys at me happily and before long we were both steaming in front of a roaring fire and downing good stiff drinks.

The rooms weren't up to much. Someone had furnished them in the thirties and a commercial traveller of that time would have recognized them at once, along with the creaking bed springs and the solitary electric lights. But they were warm and dry and the people who owned them friendly and welcoming. I would have slept well except that the local rugby club was holding its annual do in the ballroom underneath. It was something like three in the morning when the music stopped, and a good hour after that before the cars and the noise went away. And then the thunder started again.

Next morning we were told by our hosts that they'd only just bought the hotel. The previous owners had not been so obliging.

'A few weeks ago and you'd have had to stay out in the rain, even if all the rooms were empty. You'd have never got in at that hour.' And they filled up our coffee cups and plied us with more food.

Things looked up after that. We went into Lincoln and saw a delightful couple who were breeding lobsters in their garage. Not exactly a country story, but they *were* hoping to move on to a farm.

We drove from Lincoln straight home to Wales and slept the clock round, while Mrs P and Gwynneth went on coping. A few day later Jane took up her job at Bertie's and, in the fullness of time, a clutch of Buff-Laced Wyandottes hatched out of the eggs the Chapmans had given me, with their blessing.

'More mouths to feed!' said Mrs P, but Great-Grandmother Margaret would have loved them.

Chapter 7

It wasn't the last trip I made that spring. One was a marathon which took me into Somerset, Dorset and Devon, from which I returned with the car smelling like Fortnum & Mason's. I had on board, for Mrs P's further delight, fresh trout, smoked trout pâté, a huge round of farmhouse cheddar laced with herbs, several lemon curd tarts baked to a special Devon recipe, pounds of home-made sausages of various flavours, and a pint of real clotted cream. But no goat harness.

The year before I had been to see Lady Betjeman, the wife of the poet, who, when she wasn't leading expeditions up the Himalayas, lived in the hills beyond Hay-on-Wye with no car and no telephone. Everywhere she went she went by pony and cart and, at the age of seventy ('I feel about forty, actually'), managed to make me feel twice her age. On the day I went, she was going to the local fête to take people for rides in her governess cart. While I was still trying to sort out tapes and microphones, she had the pony harnessed and ready and, before I knew what was happening, set off at a cracking pace along the road.

'Hop on,' she cried over her shoulder.

'Hopping on' to a governess cart is not so easy when it's standing still and you have the full use of both hands. When it's already bowling along and you have a fragile tape-recorder on one shoulder and a bag full of mikes and tapes on the other, it is impossible. So I just stood there feebly as it disappeared. It came back and I did finally manage to scramble up, but I was given to understand, by a contemptuous look, that in my place Penelope Betjeman would have had no trouble at all.

We had a stimulating afternoon at the fête and, although my score of Brownie points went down to minus a hundred when I refused to hold the pony (which had a look in its eye that said as plain as anything, 'Just wait till she's out of sight and then see what I'll do') and cart while she went into tea, I made up a few when I brought her out a plate piled high with cakes.

'Oh, goodie! Buns!' she cried and ate the lot. And that was when I decided I liked her very much indeed. I can't stand picky eaters.

Certainly things between us were amiable enough for me to be invited back to her cottage, wreathed in mist and smelling of woodsmoke. Somehow, in the course of conversation, photo albums were brought out.

'But that's a goat in harness there,' I said, as we turned the pages.

'Yes, that was during the war. I made the harness and the cart myself. Horrid beast! It used to lie down in the road if anyone came along.'

'What did you do?'

'Waited till they'd gone past and gave it a good whacking. But on the whole it was pretty good. They make useful draught animals if you're firm.'

I gazed at her joyfully. For a very long time I'd been trying to find someone who could remember using goats in harness. Often, as I was being towed unexpectedly across the yard by one of mine, I'd wondered why all that strength couldn't be put to good use. Hauling small loads of muck up my steep yard would have been a very suitable occupation for a large goat. But nobody seemed, at that time, to know much about draught goats. And now here was Penelope Betjeman holding forth.

So I'd broadcast not only our revels at the fête but also an interview about goats in harness pulling carts. First of all, though, I'd rung the local police station.

'Can you tell me,' I asked the constable on duty, 'if there are any laws about driving goats on a public highway?'

There was something of a pause.

'Could you repeat that, please, madam?' said the constable.

'Goats,' I said. 'Are there any laws about driving them on a public highway?'

There was quite a long pause this time.

'You did say *goats*, madam?'

I realized too late that once again I'd be classified as a raving nutter by the police. I hastened to explain.

'You see, I'm about to broadcast this interview about driving goats, and it suddenly occurred to me that I should warn people if there are any new laws against taking them out on the public highway.'

'Well now, I have to say that as far as I recollect there's nothing in the traffic laws about goats. Not goats!' I thought I detected a slight waver in the voice, which then went on more severely, 'Of course, if your animal causes an obstruction or an accident, you could then be liable.'

There was another pause. 'Do you actually keep goats, madam?'

'Er, yes,' I said slowly, wondering what other bye-law I might be cautioned with.

'I only ask because I'm looking for a good Saanen billy for my nanny goat.' And, for a while, the drive against crime in South Wales was pushed into the background whilst my policeman and I discussed the relative merits of our chosen breeds, the difficulty of finding the right sort of male within easy distance, milk production, kids, feeding mixtures and the usual deeply fascinating subjects that goat keepers everywhere gossip about endlessly.

As for the interview itself, everyone in the studio thought it was a joke and there was no response from the public, until a year afterwards I received a letter from a lady who lived in the New Forest. She enclosed photographs of her goat pulling an antique carriage. It was, as it turned out, a very special carriage, because it had belonged to Holmes Pegler.

To own a first edition of Holmes Pegler's *The Book of the Goat*, published in 1885, is, to a dedicated goatkeeper, a bit like having a first edition of the Ten Commandments. And in that book is a photograph of one of the great man's goats pulling a carriage. Jill Livock's goat was not pulling that particular one, but another he had owned. All of which is by the by. My main interest in going to see her was that Miss Livock had not only managed to train her goat to harness but had done a lot of research on the subject.

I can't say I was much more successful at driving her goat, Baby, than I was at jumping onto Penelope Betjeman's governess cart in full cry. In fact Baby took off, antique carriage and all. Not that I was in it, of course. It was made for a child and Jill Livock and her partner Peggy used it to carry home-made fudge and yogurt to sell at local events. Their current concern was to replace the carriage (which didn't belong to them) and to find some good strong, workaday harness. Having seen Baby in her carriage, my mind was now full of possibilities. Why not, one day, a four-in-hand of goats?

It was an idea many other people had too and now, just a few short years later, there is such an interest in the whole business of driving goats that there's a proper club and some very smart turn-outs appearing at all the big shows.

Meanwhile, at that time, goat harness was at a premium.

'But I'm going to see someone who markets pony and donkey harness,' I told Jill and Peggy. 'She might be able to help us. Mind you, she sounds a bit of a Tartar on the phone. Very no-nonsense. She might not approve of goats.'

Which just goes to prove how stupid I was. I should know by now that you can't judge people by their voice on the phone. It's like people who write a stunning letter (Paper Dolls, Mrs P calls them) and are very boring when you meet them. No, the voice is a lying cheat (and so are the tape-recorder and the camera; they either like you or they don't) and many times I've been beguiled or repulsed by it, only to find its owner completely different.

So, having heard her brusque voice on the phone, I was not looking forward to Meg Mason in person. I was late, for a start, having spent too long, as always, at one interview and stopping to squeeze in another on the way. I also got lost in spite of her precise instructions both as to directions and my estimated time of arrival.

'Oh well,' I muttered to myself as I made a final stab at the right lane, 'if they send me away, they do. They're so hard, these horsy types.'

They were waiting for me on the yard. As I drove in, the man started waving his arms. To send me back, I supposed. I wound down the window and tried to explain. The arms went on waving.

'Come on, then. Swing her left and park here. Tea's waiting.'

The voice was loud and cheerful and full of welcome and its owner guided me around till the car was neatly parked against the garden gate. He then helped me out as tenderly as if I was made of glass.

'But you're not well,' cried his wife as I tried to straighten my back, winced with the pain and felt myself go faint. 'Get back, Bones!' she shouted to a large bulldog, which was bouncing forward to add his welcome.

They helped me into the house and they sat me down in a cool room and they gave me strong tea and lace-thin slices of bread and butter (David Mason's speciality in spite of his big farmer's hands), rich, home-made cake and a deep sincere concern, which restored me more than anything. In vain I listened for those sharp, precise tones of Mrs Meg's, until the phone rang. And there it was, as she answered it. She grinned at me as she came back to the tea table.

'When you have anything to do with horses, you learn to get off the phone sharpish,' she said, 'otherwise you'll be there for ages. We don't answer the phone after half past eight at night now, because that's when people start ringing you up with darn-fool questions and keep you there till midnight. And if you've got to get up for milking in the morning, that's not funny.'

The Masons (who've remained great friends) had semi-retired from a larger farm where they'd run a dairy herd of Jersey cattle. They still had a few cows and their Highland ponies, which Mrs Meg had been breeding so successfully that she'd had quite a brisk export trade to Brittany.

'You see, Highland ponies are the nearest thing to their own native ponies, which are virtually extinct,' Mrs Meg explained. 'They were more or less the same colouring and size and they used to work them on the little farms there, much as the Highland was used on the crofts in Scotland. We use ours to cart wood and do some ploughing and harrowing as well as take us out driving. But it's hard to get proper working harness for ponies, so I designed a set and got a saddler to make it up for me. Anyway, it's pretty useful because when they come over from Brittany to buy Highland ponies, if I'm lucky I can flog them a set of working harness too.'

As she was speaking, a large cheerful face peered in at our

gathering. It was Bones the bulldog, banished to the garden, who'd perched himself up on the wooden seat under the window so that he could keep us in sight.

'Do you feel up to coming outside again?' asked Mrs Meg, pushing her chair back. 'I'll harness up one of the ponies for you and you can see how it works.'

The next half-hour was a bit on the technical side. I've been shown how to harness up everything from tiny Shetlands and donkeys to huge Shires and Clydesdales (not to mention Baby the goat) and I still get lost somewhere in the middle. I find my attention straying to the animals themselves and their reaction to all the straps and belts and buckles. And Bonny the Highland pony was worth looking at, with her lovely creamy coat, black mane and tail, dorsal stripe and eel markings on her legs. If she stood less stolidly than usual, it was entirely the fault of Aubrey, who insisted on making derisory guttural noises, over the fence, whenever we got to a tricky bit.

Aubrey was a very small donkey with a cynical look in his eye.

'Aubrey's a bit fed up,' said Mrs Meg. 'Aubrey used to go out hunting when we had children staying, but we were asked to keep him at home because he made the horses nervous. Whenever he got carried away with excitement he used to hee-haw at the top of his voice. Utter chaos!'

Aubrey rather put paid to our lesson and so, some time later in Berkshire, did Henry. Henry was a show stallion who'd learnt the trick of pulling the top off a ring-pull can and noisily siphoning lemonade out. I've met many another donkey with unexpected talents, but little Aubrey was my first love.

By now it was getting late and the Masons began a campaign to persuade me to stay with them that night, but I opted to spend it in a picturesque village some miles away. All visible TV aerials, telegraph poles and road markings had been forbidden and it was as near as you'll get to an original English village, mouldering thatched roofs and all. The pub was equally original in its gloomy lack of welcome, no telephone for the use of guests and an airy disregard for their welfare. I thought longingly of the Masons' cheerful farmhouse.

I thought about it all the next day as I interviewed thatchers, Mrs Meg's saddler and my old friend Charles Pinney, who was looking unusually solemn as he instructed a class how to harness up one of his massive Ardennes mares. I took him aside and he reverted to his natural irreverence and did a brilliant few minutes on why he thought the ultimate draught animal for a smallholder would be a pig. Logical, if you think about it.

From the ludicrous to the sublime was only a few miles. It looked as if it had rolled straight out of the nineteenth century, but in fact it had been made in the workshop across the yard. Ruth Salter was Mrs Meg's daughter and her husband, Rodney, had made the elegant landau from scratch. I'd heard about his carriages (one of which had recently been made for the Japanese government) from various people, had even seen a few on my travels and had no idea he was connected with the Masons. When Mrs Meg had mentioned casually that her son-in-law made driving vehicles, I'd really only gone to see him out of curiosity. It wasn't till I got to his yard that I realized just who he was.

The extraordinary part of the story was that until he met Ruth and her parents, Rodney hadn't even been able to ride. He was a graphic designer appalled at Ruth's attempts to make a donkey cart. So he designed one properly, found when he did get a leg over one of the Masons' horses that he was a natural rider and now here he was, an expert driver, a judge of hackney horses and the creator of superb carriages of all kinds. He also owned a beautiful hackney stallion which, when neither of them had anything better to do, played football with him. But there was an air of tragedy too, because, just the year before, his other hackney stallion had been killed by an idiot driver, refusing to slow down on a country lane as Rodney drove it out. It had been such a fearful accident that even the Masons themselves were now extremely wary of driving their ponies along the roads. The cruellest thing was that the driver, instead of being concerned about the beautiful animal dying in agony across the road, yelled at Rodney about the scratches on his old heap of a car, which wasn't even insured. I did a long interview about it, hoping that it might prevent another similar accident, but without much hope that it would. Yobs are yobs and always will be, I suppose.

As the sun began to wander towards the west I left the Salters and found my car, seemingly of its own accord, meandering along a familiar lane. When they saw me, David waved the car in, Aubrey hooted a greeting, Bones bustled round me and Mrs Meg put another spoonful of tea in the pot.

'I've made lots of inquiries about your goat harness,' she told me. 'I can't seem to get anyone interested in making it. But I'll keep trying. And now this time you *will* stay the night, won't you?'

But I didn't. On the way south, I'd stayed at a little bed-and-breakfast place which also ran a small café. It had been so comfortable and the setting by the river so pretty, that I'd booked in again to break the journey back to Wales. I felt that I really couldn't let them down by cancelling at such short notice. So, val-iantly, I crossed the motorway and headed for North Devon. Being tired, I didn't hurry because the café stayed open quite late and I'd been told that the owners would be expecting me at any time.

I crossed the river and drew up beside the café at about nine o'clock. It was completely shuttered, not a glimmer of light showed anywhere and no amount of knocking would open a door. Not so much as a curtain twitched or a dog barked. Where a few days before everything had been lights and music and the comings and goings of quite a large family, not to mention customers and guests, now there was silence and darkness.

'Like the *Marie Céleste*,' I thought and cursed myself again for not staying with the Masons.

The next hour was very demoralizing. I spent it driving up and down that long, tree-shadowed road begging a room at smart fishing hotels beside the river. One look at my dishevelled hair, red face and frantic eyes and their proprietors were immediately fully booked. I ended up with Caroline and Robin Boa at their trout farm, drifting to sleep in their lovely old mill-house with the sound of water chuckling below, marvelling once more at the tricks of fate, for the Boas had been one of my completely unscheduled interviews a couple of years before.

They'd been suggested by Anne Petch, who was an enthusiastic breeder of the rarer old varieties of pigs at a time when they were considered a complete waste of time. Anne and her husband lived in a very old farmhouse, full of panelling and hidden archways and corners. The stables next door were ranged with high wooden stalls and, with the golden Tamworths and Gloucester Old Spots and Berkshires lolling about in the straw and a wildly colourful bunch of bantams roosting above them, it was a living, breathing picture by Moorland or Herring. I went there several times, but the year I met the Boas was the last I was to see that stable.

After a long time, when the pigs barely paid their way, Anne decided to make sausages to old country recipes from her rare-breed pork, and to smoke bacon and ham the traditional way, slowly, over oak chips. I was invited to come and sample their first offerings. Later, they were a huge success and the next time I went to see the Petches the old stable had been replaced by a modern building full of stainless steel and white tiles, the pigs and bantams were in other housing and there was a queue of people who'd come from all over the country to buy sausages and ham.

But at the time of that original, tentative tasting, life at the Petches' still moved slowly and conversation was possible.

'You really ought,' said Anne as we drank our coffee outside, gazing across the fields, 'to go and see the Boas. They've just started a trout farm a few miles away.'

'So have a lot of other people,' I yawned, as the sun warmed me and the prototype sausages settled comfortably within.

'Ah, yes,' said Anne, 'but the Boas are different. It's a lovely spot anyway and we'll come with you.'

And so, not very thrilled at the prospect, I'd followed the Petches and gone to Head Mill Trout Farm. The result was one of the most evocative pieces I ever did for *A Small Country Living*.

It's all there on tape: the evening birdsong; Robin and Caroline Boa, still at the beginning stage of making a living from their dreams; the sound of trout leaping in the ponds; the goats wandering at will along the river and the ducks dithering amongst the reeds; Exmoor ponies in the stable with the creaking door; the great mill-wheel churning the water mixed with the theme music from *Tarka the Otter*, part of which was filmed beside the mill.

'Don't forget,' Caroline Boa had called as I left at last, 'if you're

72

ever this way again, there's always a bed here.' She never thought, poor lady, that a couple of years later I would remember and come knocking at the door in the middle of the night and, as she welcomed me inside and fed me and put me to bed, everything seemed much the same at Head Mill.

It wasn't, of course. The goats were gone and so were the ponies; the ducks were sadly depleted and the Boas themselves had fewer stars in their eyes. They had had to face competition from other trout farmers, floods, drought and rising prices. Determined not to be beaten, they had worked harder, were now smoking some of their trout, and Caroline was making trout pâté to sell on a stall in a nearby market town. The Mill, so lovingly restored, needed constant attention and, with boxes of fish being sent up country and a constant stream of customers at the door, the Boas had begun to run to keep standing. The idyllic dream was getting harder to maintain. These days, Head Mill fresh, smoked and potted trout go all over Britain, Caroline has opened a shop in Exeter to sell other farm produce from Devon and the Boas have set up a second fish farm. The small is disappearing from their country living.

The next morning I bought fresh trout and lots of the smoked and potted kind, waved goodbye to the fading ghost of Tarka and went to see someone who never seems to change. Her name is Hilary Charnley and she is unique.

Hilary is a cheese maker. Which is a shocking understatement. Hilary is a genius with cheese. She almost understands how it thinks. And, believe me, to make cheese well, you have to.

Hilary is a large lady. She moves slowly and soundlessly and, in her quiet voice, is as funny as a fit. The first time I saw her she was arrayed in a long Laura Ashley smock and strapped shoes ('I put them on especially for you to keep up the image,' she said later) and when I saw her my heart sank. I could not imagine this casually flippant person putting in the hours and effort that a good, steadily marketable cheese requires. It's touchy stuff is cheese, especially if it's made from unpasteurized milk, and if you go adding herbs and playing about with traditional recipes you have to know exactly what you're doing. Apart from anything, the milk itself changes from season to season.

A dark slim man hurried across the yard.

'That's Pete,' said Hilary, waving a vague hand in his direction. 'My husband. He looks after the cows and I do the goats. I make the cheese and he makes and mends the equipment.'

The cows were Jerseys and the goats were Toggenbergs and Anglo-Nubians. All of them looked wonderful. So did the white-washed, stone 'cave' where the big round cheeses matured in a carefully controlled atmosphere.

Until I met Hilary Charnley, cheese had been cheese and that was that. Oh, I enjoyed it in all its variety. I've even been known to wax passionate about it, as I did once in a market in Spain when an Australian woman I'd met asked me to show her round. I'd been living there for a while and knew most of the various types and qualities of the cheese laid out all around us. We wandered from stall to stall, we tasted, we discussed, we exclaimed and finally I asked my new friend which of the cheeses she wanted to buy. She looked at me in amazement. 'These? Oh, none of these!' she said. 'Kev (Kev was her husband), Kev only likes Kraft.'

But if I was a little bit further on than Kraft myself and had already suffered Mrs P's anguish as she made assorted soft cheeses, listening to Hilary Charnley was a whole new world of heights and depths and dramas and triumphs, with cheese at its centre. And somehow she also managed to make it sound extremely funny.

Like the Petches and the Boas, Hilary and Pete have come a long way since then. Their cheeses win awards, and Hilary herself has been acknowledged as the expert she is. But she never changes.

So now, as I left the Boas, I went to pick up a whole Devon Garland cheese from Hilary ('Are you sure you really want to do this? It's quite a lot of cheese,' she murmured), went east again to the Petch farm for sausages, stopped at a dairy farm to buy clotted cream and sped on home to Wales. Whenever I stopped the car to get petrol, everyone on the garage forecourt began sniffing as if they couldn't believe their noses.

I drove into my own yard triumphantly, but before I'd had a chance to tell my mother of the wondrous things I'd brought her, I was assailed by a long and convoluted tale of goat hooliganism. It seemed to involve feats of unparalleled strength, someone being dragged across the yard, fences breached and mayhem on the road.

74

'Mother,' I cried, stemming the flood, 'just look what I've brought you – sausages, trout, cheese, lemon curd tarts and clotted cream from Devon.'

Mrs P put her head through the car window and sniffed.

'Hmmm,' she said, 'I wish you'd told me. I bought some of the butcher's special home-made beef sausages that you like, and I've made you lots of my special herb cottage cheese and a big apple pie. And I've got pints of cream off the milk. What I want to know is, did you get any harness for those awful goats?'

At which point I sort of gave up.

Chapter 8

That was a vintage year for the series. At last I had a
producer with a sense of humour as silly as my own,
who allowed me to fool about with the endings of the
programme and juxtapose some solid country story with a bit
of pure nonsense. All the country programmes I'd heard over
the years were either deadly serious, or quaint, or, as a friend
of mine used to say, too 'God Wotted' ('A garden is a lovesome
thing, God wot!'). You were allowed to laugh at some dear 'old
gaffer' being wicked (and most of that was pure fantasy anyway)
or some poor benighted woman keeping goats. Now, although
the wickedest 'old gaffer' of them all was one of our regulars, and
my own attempts to make goat keeping as ordinary as any other
part of stock keeping had been somewhat foiled by the likes of
Gorgeous, I also wanted to go out with a bang each week.

On the whole I've found that country people have a greater
sense of the ridiculous than anyone. They have to, to stay sane.
When you spend part of your life shoving food into one end of
an animal and cleaning up what comes out the other end; when you
are constantly sorting out their mating problems and acting as midwife afterwards; when you have weather that is too hot, too cold,
too wet, too windy or just plain impossible, especially to foil your
attempts at producing a crop of some kind; when markets and politicians and the fickle public do everything to withhold any small
reward you may expect for these efforts; when the media and the
conservationist and the happy weekend wanderers blacken your
name whenever they can – well, you have to laugh, don't you?

So, when 'They' took away my signature tune in one of their
little purges, I wanted to leave the listeners not with a feeble 'Goodbye . . . be with you next week' but something that would leave

them laughing, crying or wondering if we'd all gone completely barmy.

I explained all this to Mary Price, who gulped a bit, but let me loose on the record library, and didn't bat an eye when I asked her to compile a special sound-effects tape of chickens hunting, to go with Paul Chapman's painting. We ended up with some pretty bizarre combinations: a simulated duet of a huge Lincoln Red bull and one of the tiny Falabella stallions singing 'Anything you can do, I can do better'; a full battle with clashing swords and horses neighing and dogs barking with extracts from the Irish saga, *The Tain*, to go with the Moiled Cattle; Johnny Ray 'Walking his Baby Back Home', complete with goat accompaniment; Henry the donkey stallion doing a fine rendition of the drinking song from *The Student Prince* as he guzzled out of his ring-pull can; and a truly poignant snatch from the song 'Jessie Come Home' to round off the mother and father of a dogfight between my big brindled lurcher Lily, and the last remaining Welsh Hillman, as the latter went yelping off into the distance.

Jess was a delightful little dog – fawn with a black saddle, a white flash on her face, white socks, brisket and tip to her tail. She had been rushed to see me by her owner, an artist called Anna Pugh, in the hopes that someone, somewhere, would recognize that description and realize that they had a Welsh sheep-dog with similar markings.

Anna was feeling very guilty. Jess had been spayed before Anna discovered that she was one of a very rare type of herding dog, probably descended from the ancient gellgi, owned by the Welsh nobility and even mentioned in the famous laws of Hywel Dda some time around AD 950. According to tradition, these dogs were later used to herd the flocks on the mountains, as well as to hunt game, and were eventually known as Welsh Hillmans. Jess had been one of a litter of pups on a Welsh farm where Anna had been staying, and she'd chosen her because of her unusual markings. They returned to Surrey, Anna had Jess spayed, and it wasn't until both of them were spectators at a sheep-dog trial, that the awful truth came out. The expert who recognized what Jess was, was appalled to know that this rare dog would never have pups.

So poor Anna, consumed with guilt, made it her life's work to find another Welsh Hillman, persuade its owner to breed from it and remove from her the burden of having made the breed extinct. She had written to me to ask if I could help and, one hot summer's day, she and Jess arrived at the farm.

I was a little worried about my own dogs, but they were the perfect hosts. They were terribly impressed when Jess flung herself into the river to cool off, lying there with her nose just above the water. The whippets (who don't like getting wet) stood around admiringly on the bank, but Lily plodded into the river and pretended to be looking for a really interesting stone or something on the bottom. Jess ignored her and went on with her bathe. When she came out, shaking silver drops lavishly from her thick coat, she barked at the whippets to stay clear. Lily watched her carefully and stayed by my heels. The whippets tried to interest Jess in a really good run, but got a sniff and a nose in the air for their trouble. Lily went on watching her, the little-town miss putting on airs for the country bumpkins.

For the rest of the day, Jess was queen. Her contempt for the whippets extended to Mrs P's chihuahua, Winston, much to his surprise, but they all adored her. Lily retreated to her bed and stayed very quiet, only her eyes following Jess wherever she pranced, completely conscious of her own rarity and beauty.

I suppose I should have seen it coming, but as usual I was too anxious to get a good recording.

'We must,' I told Anna, 'get Jess's voice. She is, after all, a very rare dog. It might be like having the last recording of a dodo.'

Jess stood by and wagged her feathery tail but remained quite silent.

'Perhaps if you bring one of the other dogs outside,' suggested Anna, 'she might bark at them.'

'Merlyn is the most vocal,' I said and went back inside to fetch him.

Jess was extremely nasty to Merlyn. She didn't bark, she just lifted her lip and threatened to bite him if he came any further. Merlyn barked back at her.

'That's no good. I don't want Merlyn's bark on its own,' I said, exasperated.

'Will anyone know the difference?' said Anna.

I stared at her, shocked. 'Probably not. But we will. And one day someone might want the last recording of a Welsh Hillman and all they'd hear is a whippet.'

'I see,' said Anna, and she looked around her apprehensively.

'I'll get Lily,' I said. 'She doesn't bark much and, being a bitch too, Jess might be a bit more vocal in warning her off.'

Lily was not anxious to leave her bed. She was waiting, she gave it to be understood, for That Woman to Go Away. I hauled her by force out into the yard where Jess and Anna were waiting.

Jess did bark at Lily. She barked her head off defiantly. I got a very good recording of the almost-extinct Welsh Hillman. I turned triumphantly towards Anna, my fingers hovering over the stop button on the tape-recorder. I saw a golden blur out of the corner of my eye and swung, too late. Lily, her patience tried beyond bearing, was noisily making sure of the immediate extinction of the Welsh Hillman.

I didn't have time to press the stop button so it was all there on record – all the barking and the growling and the shrieking voices of two hysterical women trying to separate their dogs, and the retreating sound of howling yelps as poor Jess ran into the distance, when we finally hauled Lily off. There was nothing in the least God Wotted about that tape, but the funny thing is that everyone thought I'd cooked it up.

Jess was all right except for a lot of injured pride. Lily's fights tend to be more noise than action and Anna very nobly said that Jess had had it coming. Just to show there were no hard feelings, Anna sent me a drawing of Jess encountering a long, curly-feathered Sebastopol goose, a breed I'd featured on the same programme with her. I still have it hanging on the wall.

Yes, it was a vintage year for the programme that year, but how I personally survived it I'm not sure. The thunderstorms Jane and I had finally escaped in East Anglia turned up exultantly in Wales. It was all Fiona Silver's fault, of course. She brought them with her from Cambridgeshire. She came, rattling and banging in an old car that had never known the indignity of a wash, nor the disturbance of its rich inner collection of debris.

'I might forget something if I clear it all out,' said Fiona, waving at the muddle.

'Do you need those redundant pony nuts?' I asked.

'Might do, you never know,' said Fiona as she rummaged about.

'You're terribly late,' I said accusingly. 'I thought you'd had an accident.'

'Ah,' said Fiona, emerging with a battered holdall and an immaculate art folder, 'that was because we had the most dreadful thunder and lightning. You've never heard anything like it. I just shot back under the bedclothes and prayed that my poor horses would be all right. I didn't dare go out.'

'Well, you'd have been all right in the car, driving along. They say that's the safest place in a thunderstorm – moving fast.'

'Not true,' said Fiona firmly. 'A friend of mine and I were hit by lightning in a car once.' She began walking towards the house.

I stood and gazed after her in horror.

'I don't believe you,' I called. 'That's the only thing that keeps me sane when I'm driving in a storm. The fact that you're safer to keep driving.'

'Well, it isn't, because the lightning struck the car and we bounced across the road and into a ditch.'

'Of course,' I said hopefully as I caught up with her, 'you were out in the Fen Country and it's so flat there, I suppose the car was the highest thing on the road.'

Fiona looked at me pityingly. 'Yes, we were on a Fen road, but it could have been a tree on any other road and then we'd have been squashed flat.'

Fiona does not dish out crumbs of comfort. In fact comfort of any kind doesn't seem to concern her.

'Anyway, it's a nice clear day here', she said as we got to the house.

I opened the door and ushered her into the front room, where Lily and the whippets twisted themselves into knots and grinned and generally made further conversation difficult. Mrs P and Winston came storming in from the kitchen.

'You're very late,' said Mrs P. 'She thought you'd had an accident. She always worries when people are late. Me, I only worry about the lunch. You'll have to have yours a bit burnt now.'

'Thunderstorms in Cambridgeshire,' I told my mother hastily to divert her from the burnt lunch theme, which tends to go on a bit, once started.

Mrs P looked at Fiona suspiciously. 'Mmmm. Well, I hope you didn't bring them with you. Burning the lunch is one thing. Burning the house is another.'

Mrs P can always find a connection to get her back on course if she's pursuing a theme.

Fiona grinned at her happily. 'Oh, no, Mrs P, no chance of that. I left them behind, I promise you!'

'Oh, yes?' said Mrs P. 'What's that, then?'

'That' was a resounding clap of thunder and, swiftly following it, a streaking flash that stopped even Fiona in her tracks, sent me into agonies of terror, the dogs under the table and the electricity off with a thump.

'Just as well I'd already boiled the kettle for your coffee,' said Mrs P above the din.

Gwynneth, who lived across the valley and had a panoramic view of my entire territory, told me afterwards that the lightning looked as if it was dotting my fields, and mine alone.

'I expected your house or the barns or the big ash tree to go at any minute,' she said, shaking her head. 'It was fantastic. We had a bolt go down the chimney once and it went straight across the room and out the door, but I've never seen the lightning so close to your place like that.'

It certainly felt and sounded close enough, but I took my chance and rushed outside to shoo the animals into shelter (I've had it on the best authority that they really *are* safer inside). Not that they needed too much persuasion, the goats in particular all getting jammed in their door together in their hurry, the sheep hurtling down the hill with their lambs to the hay-shed and the chickens cackling loudly for cover. Only one lone cockerel stayed out and defied the sky to fall on his head. I left him and flung back into the house to pull all the plugs out and shove the television aerial in an old rubber boot (I've been told that's useless, but it feels safer), covering the mirrors and promising God not to do whatever it was

I'd done, ever again. Mrs P and Fiona ignored all this activity and cheerfully exchanged horrendous stories of storm and flood and fire. I was surprised at Fiona after her experiences that morning, but I'm used to Mrs P, who has such faith in her prayers that, having offered up a quick one on our behalf all round, she just gets on with what she's doing and usually brings me down off the heights of screaming panic by making me blazing mad at her.

At last the gaps between thunder and lightning grew longer until only a deep growl came echoing back across the hills, a distant flickering shimmered the horizon and the rain fell steadily and silently and straight.

'You can't go outside in this,' I said to Fiona, who was itching to start her drawings for my book.

'Never mind. I'll just sit here and draw your little arrowhead. Any lights yet?'

I tried a switch and nothing happened. Fiona shrugged and began to set out her paper and pencils on the table by the window. I went upstairs to get the arrowhead. I keep it very close to my bedside and when things look very bad I take it out of its little case and hold it tight, trying to recapture the sense of wonder and renewed hope it gave me the first time I picked it up.

Not so very far from where I live is a lake with a powerful legend of an underwater kingdom and a fairy bride who came from there to marry a local farmer. I don't go to the lake very often. I suppose I don't want it to be a commonplace in my life and lose the magic I've always felt about it. Like the day, blazing with summer, when I was in such deep despair that only a miracle could have shaken me out of it. And I got one when I found the wet arrowhead newly flung from the lake which was lying drought-stricken and still before me. I told the story in full in the book Fiona was about to illustrate for me and, to tell the truth, I was a bit nervous about doing so. But it had been a vital turning-point in my life at the farm and, strange though the experience had been, I felt it had to go in. If anyone thought I was raving they've never said so to me, and even the most cynical of visitors ask tentatively if they can see it. And, just a few weeks ago, I found that I was not alone in the experience. It was in another book which I found on the library van.

Even in such a remote spot as this, we have a door-to-door library service which calls on the first Tuesday of every month. The big yellow van blunders and rolls its way down the steep little lane and announces its arrival with a series of loud hoots on the horn. And if, after all these years, I know almost every book on its shelves intimately, and often feel slightly seasick negotiating the floor of the van as it sits drunkenly on my uneven yard, I'd be devastated if it stopped coming.

For a start, the men in charge of the library van have never been of the usual librarian mould. In fact they've not been bookish men at all. Their talent has been for people, and certainly Mrs P regarded their coming as a social event. First there was Denzil, who ran a pub, looked just like the comedian Jimmy Edwards (handlebar moustache and all), and had a fund of rather naughty stories and lots of cuttings from the paper to amuse us with. He and his wife also had a chihuahua, so Mrs P and Winston spent a lot of time with Denzil discussing the care, feeding and general intelligence, adorability and guarding qualities of the breed. We were terribly upset when he retired, but his place has been taken, over the years, by two charming men who, if not quite so colourful, have been just as patient and obliging. Their most regular customers are the elderly, who can't get out to an ordinary library and to whom the yellow van is a brief dash of literary excitement out in the hills, so the character of the drivers is far more important than their knowledge of books. And just sometimes I find a book on the van which surprises and delights me. Like Rosamond Lehmann's *The Swan in the Evening*.

I thought it was one of her novels, but it is partly about her childhood and partly about the psychic phenomena she experienced after the death of her daughter. And it contained a passage which came very close to my experience in Ireland, by the cairn of stones, and on the day I found the arrowhead at the lake. Rosamond Lehmann describes how she was sitting in her house on the Isle of Wight:

> . . . watching a pair of woodpeckers in the garden and hoping for a glimpse of the red squirrels, when I felt suddenly *caught*, as if in a magnetic current. Such a strong sensation of *being*

watched assailed me that my skin crept. All my imagination, very likely; but I jumped up and almost ran through the french windows onto the lawn.

Whoever it was came with me, hurried hither and thither, as if I was expected to be searching. But what could I be looking for? Now my small garden seemed full of noiseless laughter, mischievous, non-human . . . swirling with it. Next moment I stooped and picked up from a corner of the rose bed a roughly heart-shaped stone object: a flint; an unusually pretty and delicately finished Stone Age implement with a pronounced cutting edge along its smoothly polished matrix. The back, which was uppermost when I first saw it, making it look like a tiny pale-shelled tortoise, was scored all over its surface with a faint but definite criss-cross pattern, and pierced round the perimeter by tiny holes, like pin holes.

When I showed it, shortly afterwards, to a guest, I could only insist, 'It wasn't there there before. It couldn't have been. I couldn't have missed it.' My guest did not contradict me, or mock me.

That is the unembroidered story of my flint. It is beside me now. I am no psychometrist, but I like to hold it.'

Like Rosamond Lehmann, I like to hold my little white flint and, frankly, I don't much like other people touching it. Afraid, I suppose, that they might wipe out whatever there is still left of the Stone Age person who last touched it, so many thousands of years ago.

'Well,' said Fiona impatiently, 'are you going to let me draw it or not?'

Slowly I placed the flint in front of her, stood anxiously as she arranged it to catch the rain-dimmed light in the window, peered fretfully over her shoulder as she began to sketch it and, as she inched her shoulder up and down as if to dislodge my gaze, finally sat down opposite her, frowning, as she worked. Which is possibly why, although she spent more time over it in relation to its size and significance, I think that was the least successful of the drawings Fiona did. It was the animals she caught to the life, so that even today sometimes as I look at the real thing I have this odd feeling that I'm seeing one of Fiona's drawings of them.

'It's a shame about Doli, though,' said Fiona as she left the next day, her bag full of film and her sketchbook covered with quick drawings to be worked on later.

'Yes,' I said, 'I'm sorry, but for Doli you'll just have to go by the old photographs.'

Doli the draught horse had featured a lot in the book. But Doli was no longer mine. I had sold her to a friend when it became apparent that Doli was lonely and heading towards a spectacular career as a hypochondriac to get attention. Sedley Sweeney had promised that he would give her enough work and the company of other horses to stop her pretending to be lame or have a raging dose of colic. But Fiona, who, along with her exquisite work as an artist, her university degree, her interest in foxes and other wildlife, also ran a small riding school and rode in three-day events, had been particularly keen to draw Doli.

'I don't mind using photographs to jog my memory,' said Fiona, 'but I do like to see and sketch the original. I'll leave her drawings till last. You never know what might happen.'

With which enigmatic remark she flung her much-tried little car at the hill and disappeared with a resounding bang from its exhaust.

It was quiet when Fiona had gone. She had rushed from one part of the farm to the other, flung off to see the lake, enthused over Mrs P's cooking and stories, left her drawing things all over the place and generally bubbled about till I felt a bit like a tired old draught horse myself, trying to keep up with a small, excitable and very energetic pony. Even Mrs P had enjoyed the whirl of Fiona.

She left us a legacy, however. The thunderstorms came back again and again that summer. And, every time they came back, the electricity went off.

Not that that would normally have bothered me so much. It was a bore having to get the Rayburn up to cooking heat in the humid weather and the cottage is very dark once the sun has swung round to the west, but by and large we can cope without electricity. Except when I have to edit ten sets of tapes and get them all reeled up and ready for a weekly programme. Then having no electricity is dreadful, especially when it stays off for forty-eight hours, as it did at least once that summer. That was the time I think the electricity people prayed that my phone would be cut off too.

I was reduced at last to getting out an old Uher, and editing tape on its tiny heads, by candlelight. But eventually the summer began to fade into autumn, the storms went away and, as I drove home from Bristol each week, I no longer saw the soft folds of the mountain as I left the main road, but had to guide myself in by the pin-points of light from the hidden farms.

'What are you going to do for the ending of the last programme?' asked Mary Price on the penultimate week.

'I don't know,' I said. 'I've used up all the really good pieces. Oh, I suppose something will turn up. It usually does somehow.'

What turned up was Doli. It was in that final week that Sedley Sweeney announced he was giving up the Smallholding Centre; it was in that final week that I was offered a small television job that would pay for Doli and her keep; it was in that final week that she came home and I interviewed Sedley Sweeney about her fate if I didn't buy her. 'The knacker's,' he said.

I put that rather stark interview a couple of places before the finale. I could almost hear the gasps from the listeners as I told him that the knacker's would probably be the kindest thing for her. I then went on to another story.

I finished the programme, thanked everybody and then told that audience, which I couldn't see, but could feel in their outrage and shock, that I'd have to hurry home to attend to those big feet thundering about my little fields.

'Oh, come on,' I said. 'You didn't *really* think I'd send her to the knacker's, did you?' And then they heard it: the Land-Rover and box creaking down the hill; Doli stamping impatiently as the box came to rest in the yard; her exit down the ramp; me greeting her with the words 'Hullo, you old sod!'; and Doli's wild neigh of recognition. They then heard a rousing chorus of 'Hello Dolly' with Aubrey and Henry, Jess and Lily, the Irish Moiled Cattle, the Falabella stallion, the Lincoln Red bull, the Sebastopol geese and any other animal that had been on the series that year. It was Aubrey, I think, who hit the high notes in unison with the music, which ended with a loud dismissive fart from Doli.

Everyone in the studio was grinning tearfully, even though they'd spent hours putting it all together. And afterwards the mail came flooding in and the phone went overtime. One of the callers was Fiona.

'I knew something like this would happen,' she cried. 'I'm on my way!'

Doli still stands the way Fiona drew her, her big behind in the foreground, feathered feet planted firmly and her beautiful head turned seductively over her shoulder. She does it on purpose.

'Posing,' said Mrs P, 'like a lily on a dirt-box!'

Chapter 9

If her public had been enchanted with the happy ending to Doli's story, Doli herself was not. She missed Sedley, she missed the other horses and she soon missed me, as I raced back and forth to London to complete the little TV job which would pay for her. There was nothing for it but to go dead lame again and panic me into providing her with some much-needed entertainment.

'Oh no,' sighed Bertie Ellis when I rang, 'not again! Are you sure she's not up to her old tricks?'

'Quite sure,' I said firmly. 'She's actually holding her foot up when I bring her in. It's obviously something deep-rooted because I can't feel or see a thing.'

'Oh, all right,' said Bertie, in a voice that boded no good for me or Doli if it was a false alarm. 'Leave her out in the field, will you? I'll watch her as she comes up to us.'

When he arrived, he left his car at the gate and motioned me silently to stay out of sight behind the barn while he went over to the gate and watched Doli as she pottered about. He called her and Doli swung round, neighed, and joyfully trotted up towards him. I emerged from behind the barn, Doli stopped, faltered, resumed her limp, drooped her ears and came slowly and painfully towards the gate.

'Ah,' said Bertie, 'I thought you said it was her near fore. That is her off fore. One of you has got mixed up. Lead her in, will you?'

Once in the stable, Doli looked depressed and eased the weight off her near fore.

'Thought so,' crowed Bertie. 'She can't remember which foot is lame. I'll have a good look, but I'm pretty sure there's nothing wrong with Doli except a low boredom threshold.'

Fifteen minutes later, after a thorough examination of her feet and much trotting up and down the yard, during which Doli didn't dare to limp, Bertie looked at me sternly.

'The only lameness in that horse is in her brain – or yours! I'll leave you some powders in case it's the odd twinge of arthritis, but I'd shove her in foal if I were you. Give her something to think about.'

I closed my eyes wearily. Getting Doli in foal was not easy. There was all of the autumn and winter to get through anyway before even trying would be possible, and the thought of Doli limping and feeling sorry for herself all that time was not something to look forward to. I wondered briefly if there was another Sedley out there who might take her on.

'Doli,' I now told Bertie, 'is getting on for eighteen, you know.'

'No problem,' said Bertie as he got into his car. 'She's in very good nick. Just keep her well and fit over the winter, try to ignore her little dramatic performances and keep an eye out for a patient and willing stallion.'

I spent the next few months looking out for him, making calls and writing letters, while Doli, relinquishing her lame phase, developed some warts that had to come off at vast expense, had the odd dash of colic to keep me on my toes, and bloomed with health. And all the time the love of Doli's life was living just a few miles away and one day their mating would produce the horse I'd always dreamt of. But that was all to come and meanwhile autumn brought gales and rain, and then smiled with brilliant sun on frosty mornings, before raging once more with temper at the rich gold and crimson which lay over the woods, till the trees were left in sepia silhouettes on hill and horizon.

The garden was suddenly full of blackbirds, robins fought pitched battles for their territories and at night the owls haunted the ash tree by the house and woke me with their long, lonely cries. The swallows had long gone and a family of noisy sparrows took over the goat-shed and roosted high in the rafters, unseen at night except for the shadows their tiny bodies threw on the walls when I switched on the lights. They made an awful mess, actually, so that I had to protect the goats' water buckets from their droppings, but Mrs P reserved her enmity for the owls.

'I don't know why they can't just stick to tu-whit-tu-whoo, like they're supposed to,' she said crossly one morning. 'That awful screeching they do! Sounds like a woman in labour. – And don't' – she held up her hand – 'give me a lecture about the habits of owls. Whatever they are doing, I think they should keep quiet about it. And when, might I ask, can I use the airing cupboard?'

'Not till that trap's gone off,' I said.

The airing cupboard is in Mrs P's bedroom. It is not a great example of the carpenter's craft. In fact, its construction was the final piece of work that particular builder did for me. When I came up the stairs one day and saw six-inch nails sticking through the wall, as the airing cupboard was being made on the other side of it, I gave him his marching orders. I doubt if he ever intended to fill in the gaping holes in the wall, where he threaded the pipes from the Rayburn through, but there they remained and, in spite of being stuffed with old tights and jumpers, afforded an entry into the airing cupboard for the odd mouse or, more lately, rat. Mrs P had stoically borne with the occasional mouse, even the one that sat up and polished its whiskers as she threw her slippers at it, but she was not putting up with the rat.

The rat, of course, could not actually get out of the airing cupboard, although, due to the generous gaps left round its doors, the mouse could. The rat, however, caused the most disturbance by skittering its paws on the copper tank, testing the doors for strength, gnawing them thoughtfully and totally ignoring Mrs P's strangled cries on the other side. Already she had fearfully heard it land in the loft with a bump and track its heavy-footed way down into the cupboard.

'How do you know it's a rat if you've never seen it?' I asked my mother, reasonably enough.

'Well, if it's a mouse it's wearing blucher boots,' she replied witheringly, 'and either it goes or I do.'

As a matter of fact, the rats were out in force all over the farm. After years of peace, they were staging a return match.

When we first came here, the rats were in total control. Mighty gangs roistered by day and night in the loft; they had wild, drunken parties on the lawn, thumbed their noses at us from the rafters in the barn, took baby chicks from under the hens, slaughtered goslings, attacked every bag of feed, flung the rubbish all over the yard and even sat, enjoying the moon, on the branches of the old plum tree. They reigned unchecked, until a small, three-legged cat called Kate repaid us for saving her life by getting rid of the rats. How she achieved what all our guile and force had failed to do is a mystery, but for years, in company with the two ginger kittens we'd bought for her to train up, she kept the farm more or less free from rats. But earlier that year dear old Kate (who was already a grandmother many times over when she came to us) had mewed silently at my feet, she who never liked to be in the house, till I picked her up and brought her in to the warmth by the Rayburn. And there, twenty-four hours later, she died.

Max and Muffin, now big strong hunters in their own right, went on with the work Kate had begun, but somehow the rats, sensing the lack of the tiny fierce personality, had gradually crept back. Fortunately, so far, they hadn't infested the loft as they had done before, jeering at us through the knot-holes in the wooden ceilings, gnawing at the plaster under the slates and making sleep impossible, but one had obviously found the holes in the airing cupboard and was currently driving Mrs P mad.

For a while, however, I didn't believe her. Mrs P's vivid descriptions of the various noises that afflicted her at night had dulled the edge of my sympathy. There was the rogue slate that went KERPLONK every time there was a slight breeze; there was the tree that whined and creaked; there were the bats thundering home in the wee small hours; there was the mouse which rustled around in her waste-paper basket; and now there was the rat banging about in the airing cupboard. I had actually sat up with her to catch these various noise freaks at their games, but her room had remained quite still and silent.

'You can have mine,' I said irritably, 'and then you can put up with the ash tree shrieking and the wind hitting that end of the house like an explosion. And it's cold, too, without any nice warm airing cupboard.'

'With a rat in it,' said Mrs P stubbornly.

She was right, as it turned out, but it took the outside rats to convince me that things had gone too far.

I do not share my mother's hatred of rats. They are, after all, just another animal trying to make a living the best way it knows how. They're intelligent enough to take advantage of the wasteful human ways and scavenge what they can. Why live out in the uncertain wild when there are people about to provide warm buildings and lots of food for free? And, although city rats are pretty disgusting and carry diseases from the drains and the sewers, somehow I've never felt the same about country rats. The ones the cats bring in are beautifully clean and healthy-looking and if they were less destructive and didn't have those creepy tails, we'd oooh and aaah over them and think how sweet they were.

But rats, like people, always go too far. Where one rat leads, thousands will follow and, by turning a blind eye to the odd one or two, I extended an open invitation to all their friends and relations.

I knew things were getting out of hand as feed bags were gutted, holes began to appear at the base of the walls and nearly every bale of hay and straw had had its twine bitten through. For a while Max and Muffin lined up enough corpses for me to hope that they were coping naturally with the problem, and there would be no need for poison or traps. And then the rats went too far. Replete on oats and corn and baler twine, they began the slaughter of the innocents. They chose the very creatures which had been, till I found their mangled bodies still on their perches, one of my greatest delights, not just for themselves, lovely though they were, but for the almost enchanted way I'd found them.

It had been the previous year and I was in a village in South Devon feeling extremely fed up. I'd had a few interviews to do in the surrounding countryside and all of them had gone reasonably well, but I had left one whole afternoon to see a gentleman who, I'd been told, was a great character and bred prize-winning Old English Game.

Now getting people to talk knowledgeably about Old English Game is not easy. They were the breed used for cock fighting in the bad old days, and, although it's illegal now, breeders have to guard their stock carefully from thieves who still practise it. I had promised this particular breeder that I would not give his location away and he'd seemed happy enough to talk to me about his birds and lots of other things, like the old cider orchards on the farms when he was younger. In order to give him plenty of time to cover these and a few other subjects, I'd arranged to stay in the village overnight, so that I wouldn't have to hurry off to meet the usual B & B deadline somewhere far away.

I was less than pleased, therefore, when I arrived at his small-holding to be told that he'd had second thoughts and was not going to be interviewed, no matter how I pleaded and reassured. Finally, seeing my look of desperation, he said grudgingly, 'You might like to try John Lear Hoskins at White Mill. He might talk to you,' and he shut the door firmly in my face.

For someone who's been interviewing as long as I have, it's amazing how bashful I still feel about pouncing on people unannounced. Only the thought of the long, wasted afternoon and evening, when I could have been miles away doing lots of other interviews, made me seek out the Hoskins' farm. When I found it, it looked very deserted. I creaked open the gate, went to the house and knocked feebly on the door. Nothing happened and I turned to go, when a voice behind shouted a greeting and there he was, tall, beaming and welcoming. The interviewee in a million.

I hardly had to explain the situation. Of course he'd talk to me about anything I liked. So we talked about cider making in his own orchard; we pumped up water from his own well; we discussed the art of putting a thin wash of cement on slate roofs to give them an extra lease of life (parging, they call it), as he'd done on that roof and look at it now twenty years later; we talked about his farm cats and how to tell a good ratter, as we investigated a litter of kittens in his barn; we talked about his Old English Pheasant Fowl and their rather schizophrenic habits (fowl or pheasant?); and, last of all, we talked about his delicate little Silver Sebright hens. The tiny birds looked as if they'd been made of lace, with each minute white feather sharply outlined in black.

John Hoskins smiled at me as I squatted down to get on a level with his Sebrights, as they scratched about in their pens, with their spunky little cockerels, wings held down like Western gun-fighters, guarding them.

'Would you like a setting of their eggs?' he asked. 'They're prize-winning birds, these, so you might be lucky and get something good. I can only let you have a few because there's quite a demand for them and my wife sold a couple of settings just this morning. But I see there are six eggs in the pens and you can have those.'

At that moment Mrs Hoskins herself appeared, returning from the Royal Cornwall Show, where her husband should have been, too, except for some reason I was never quite sure about.

'So it was lucky you found me in at all,' he said.

And the luck held because, in spite of bumping and rattling in the car home to Wales, all the little Sebright eggs hatched out and, even more remarkably, they were five hens and one cockerel, an unheard of ratio. Mostly I'm lucky to get five cockerels and one hen.

John Lear Hoskins' interviews had been the stars of that year's series. I spun them out over the weeks and each one was so full of colour and life, and his rich Devon accent so evocative, that everyone kept demanding more and more.

As for the little Sebrights, I found them so precious that they were kept apart, in a shed which is attached to the main barn, is warmly lined with wood and has its own electric light. At night they perched high up on their roosts and always they were a constant reminder that sometimes even disappointments turn out for the best. Until the morning I found two of them slaughtered on their perches and the rest hysterical with shock. The rats had finally tunnelled through the thick walls of the barn and repaid my tolerance by shattering my dreams.

Tears of horror. Tears of rage; rage not only at the rats but at the way Sod's Law wins every time. The big chicken house at that time, with its rotting wooden floor and sides, was far more likely to be an easy rat target. The tin shed, with concrete floors and high perches and three feet of barn wall behind it, had seemed so safe for my little Sebrights. And it was there that they'd been murdered.

It was a Saturday when I found the carnage and, oddly enough, I was hoping to find another special interview that day. There used

94

to be a Christmas edition of *A Small Country Living* then and, with November well on its way, I had to get on the road again. It wasn't quite the same as the main series in that I tended to do a lot of interviews in Wales itself and only sometimes made a quick dash to some other part of the country. This time it was the promise of a thistle stick which had tempted me as far as the Costswolds.

Back in the summer, Fred Archer, our resident rural historian and teller of unmentionable tales of village life, had told me about the walking stick that had a tiny shovel on the bottom of it, so that farmers could turf out any stray thistles as they wandered about their fields. As the owner of the best crop of thistles in the valley, I'd wondered longingly if there was still such a thistle stick to be had. There were, according to the letters that poured in, but most of them were in antique shops or prized family possessions, except for one which was mine for the asking. It belonged to Hugh McCallum, a Scotsman who had worked on a farm near Bourton-on-the-Water for many years. Now that he was retiring, he wanted the thistle stick, which he'd inherited from his grandfather, to find a good home. It just so happened that he lived quite near to another of our resident experts, the waterfowl breeder, Tom Bartlett.

Not that Tom's ducks and geese were the sort you'd normally eat for dinner, for all that most of them were domestic varieties. These were show birds and represented, in many cases, remnants of breeds which were almost forgotten. To give you an example, at that time, even if he'd sell you a pair, it would cost you £600 to buy a couple of Tom's Toulouse geese. Which was why I wanted to include Tom's birds in the Christmas programme. With everyone else on the media endlessly discussing how to cook poultry, I thought it was high time someone talked about the kind that survived the annual gluttony and gave a different kind of pleasure. Tom's farm was open to the public and, as it's in the winter that the ducks and geese come into their full plumage, that's the best time to see them.

Late autumn is also about the only time my neighbour Myrddin Parry can get away from his farm and, as he dearly loves an excuse to see a different part of the country, it had become something of an annual tradition that he would drive me to do the interviews for the Christmas programme if I was going somewhere he fancied seeing. Luckily for me, he wanted to see Tom's farm and he also wanted to go to some motor museum not too far away. So on that Saturday, when the murder of my beloved Sebrights happened, he was due to take me to the Cotswolds.

He arrived to find me tight-lipped and furious, giving final instructions to Brian Hancock, who was doing a bit of much-needed repair work to the barn doors.

'I want,' I was telling him, 'to come back and find this place like Fort Knox. I don't care how you do it, or what you use, but I want every last hole blocked up in this shed. On Monday I'm getting the Council in.'

Brian stared at me, shocked. 'You!' he cried. 'Use poison!'

'This,' I said, 'is total war!' And I scurried off to join Myrddin as he revved the engine impatiently. Fortunately, he had his friend Les Marshall, who looks after the lake, with him and they amused themselves in their usual way, talking about old cars and making dreadful jokes (the subtlety of which always escapes me), so I was left alone in the back of the car to try and clear my mind of rage and misery before I met Tom Bartlett and Hugh McCallum and plan my next move in the anti-rat campaign.

Tom, of course, was deeply sympathetic when I arrived at Folly Farm. He had his own rat war at all times and had found only one person able to cope with them. His name was Bill, he lived in Mousetrap Lane in Bourton-on-the-Water and he earned his living entirely by ridding local farms of rats and rabbits.

'He's really a warrener,' said Tom. 'He gets the rabbits in the old-fashioned way with ferrets and his terriers, but he deals with the rats for us in the winter. Bill understands them, you see. He knows their habits and how they make their runs. It's no good just putting stuff down; it's got to be in exactly the right place. Before Bill helped me, I lost a fortune in young birds to the damn things. It's a shame you live so far away. Bill's your man, all right.'

Tom himself is tall and bluff and he has a laugh like Father Christmas. His voice has the faint burr of a Cotswold accent and he moves like the farmer he was, until he turned the beef and arable side of the farm over to his son and made his old hobby of breeding waterfowl into a business.

When you turn into the drive of Folly Farm it looks like any other traditional Cotswold steading, with great beech trees sheltering the old stone house and barns. In summer, it is true, you'll probably notice a lot of brilliantly coloured poultry wandering about, anxious broody hens trying to restrain clutches of adventurous ducklings and, from somewhere behind the garden wall, strange and strident sounds. In summer you will have to run the gauntlet of Tom's wife, Diana, quietly taking your money so that you can penetrate behind that garden wall, but in winter she'll be more likely to be tucked up in her warm kitchen, spinning, or making bread, or keeping a hot meal on the go.

Now, as Tom and I sat brooding darkly about the hideous problem of the rats, Diana removed our coffee cups and spoke firmly.

'Meanwhile, if you want to see Hugh McCallum's sticks before it gets dark, you'd better shift yourselves and go to see those ducks.' And she shooed us into our coats and out of the door.

She was right to get us moving. Once Tom and I start wandering amongst his birds and arguing about how to do the interview, we get lost to time. The ducks and geese and a small collection of rare breeds of chickens and turkeys are all kept in large, natural-looking pens on sloping fields, in which a series of ponds have been made, until, right at the bottom, are two huge flight ponds.

It always takes us forever to get as far as the flight ponds, because each of the breeding groups stops me in my tracks (no matter how often I've seen them) and Tom finds himself doing an update on nearly every variety we pass, from the delicate little Trout Indian Runners or the true, deep-breasted Aylesburys, to the massive Toulouse or frizzled Sebastopol geese. But once at the flight ponds and the sight of dozens of varieties of waterfowl swimming for dear life and honking and quacking in one great explosion of sound as Tom calls them, it's almost impossible to drag me away. Time becomes quite irrelevant.

Diana sighed and pointed to the table when we got back to her kitchen a good hour and a half later, frozen stiff, Tom bemused and speechless and me hunting around urgently for a point to charge Gert on.

'Soup,' she said sternly as she filled up our bowls and pushed brown bread and butter at us. 'I've told Mr McCallum you'll be late and don't forget your friends will be back to pick you up at three.'

I started guiltily, remembering that Myrddin and Les wanted to see the ducks when they'd finished with their motor museum. Diana smiled.

'Don't worry,' she said. 'I'll show them round if you're not back by then. I don't suppose you will be either.' And she glanced at the clock which was remorselessly pointing at two o'clock. 'Get that hot soup down you now or you won't be able to do any more interviews. You're blue with cold.'

It was a good half-hour before we thawed out and Tom and I scrambled into his old car and rattled away down the little side lanes, the dried beech leaves in the hedges shifting slightly as we passed, and deep autumn shadows lying across the frosty fields. As we drove, the sound of horn and hounds followed us.

'I forgot,' said Tom impatiently, 'that the Hunt is around today. I hope we don't get held up by followers blocking the way.'

But the lanes were clear and of the Hunt we saw nothing as we dipped into a small hollow, ringed by wooded hills. A stream chattered under an open-sided bridge, a large stone barn stood on one side of the road and, on the other, a pair of cottages. In the garden of one cottage stood a short wiry man who grinned with relief as he saw us. He opened the door of his cottage, beckoned us inside, and waved his hand at the collection of walking sticks with carved handles. He had obviously spent some considerable time arranging them for maximum artistic effect. In their midst was my thistle stick.

'I've made a new shaft for it,' he said in a thick Scots accent. It sounded odd in that classic Cotswold setting. He began to tell me about his stick making but I held up a hand to stop him.

Tom let out a great laugh. 'She'll want to do the interview outside, you know. Likes to get all the country sounds in the background. And you'll probably have to demonstrate the thistle stick, too.'

Hugh McCallum was deeply disappointed. He looked regretfully at his stick display.

'We'll take most of them with us,' I reassured him. 'Tom here can hold them for us. And then you can tell me all about them.'

And so we stood outside in his garden. Around us the air was still and cold and silent, except for the trickling of the stream. Tom stood solemnly holding aloft the choicest examples of Mr McCallum's sticks, looking a bit like a scarecrow with a badly suppressed fit of the giggles. Well trained as he's been over the years of being browbeaten into doing the perfect recording, he stood quite still as we plucked each stick from him to illustrate some point their owner wished to make about one or the other. Tom understood, too, that to suggest we lay them out on the damp earth would not have gone down well, and so he stood, bravely acting as a hall stand.

The first member of the Hunt to come trotting down the road had actually clattered onto the bridge before he did a double take at Tom, and nearly sent his horse into the river. He went slowly up the hill, head over his shoulder as he gazed back at the tableau in the garden.

'I *know* him,' muttered Tom, going a deep red.

'Don't move!' I commanded, and held up a hand to restrain Hugh McCallum, who was launched on a saga of how one particular ash branch had been discovered in the woods and honed into the stick he was holding.

'I want,' I whispered fiercely, 'to get the sounds of this Hunt. It's a perfect echo chamber here – clopping hooves, hounds in the distance and, with luck, more horn. Now, Mr McCallum, tell me about the thistle stick itself and don't stop, no matter what happens. I'll mention that the Hunt is passing and try to get all the sounds under your voice. Right! Here comes another lot. Tom, don't you say anything, or I'll have to explain you too.'

Tom turned agonized eyes on me as a group of five riders came cantering down towards us, all of them checking as they saw Tom and hailing him gleefully. Then up the hill they went, staring back at his unresponsive figure festooned with walking sticks.

'Hey, Tom!' yelled a voice from the woods. 'Tell 'em there's a fox gone over to Cold Aston.'

'Don't you dare,' I hissed. 'I can hear hounds. I want those hounds uninterrupted.' And I got them, faint, then loud, then fading, and the horn calling and echoing and the horses' hooves and the shouts of the followers, frost-clear on the still air, echoing around the little hollow and up through the woods. And all of it behind the story of Hugh McCallum's grandfather and his thistle stick. A Christmas card of sound.

Tom was a nervous wreck by the time I delivered him to Diana, who was busy entertaining Myrddin and Les.

'I'll never live it down,' Tom moaned. 'Standing there with armfuls of walking sticks in a vegetable garden while the whole Hunt went by and never saying a word.'

'Now that,' said Diana wryly, 'they will find surprising.'

'One day I'll lend you my thistle stick,' I said soothingly. 'You were brilliant, Tom. Didn't move a muscle and I got a perfect recording. The trouble with that kind of coming and going background is that you can't edit it properly. Well, you can, but far better if you don't have to.'

Myrddin and Les, who have both been made to stand out in all kinds of weather while they've done interviews for me, nodded sympathetically at Tom and removed me from his sight.

When I got back to the farm, Brian had gone. He left a message with Mrs P to say that if anything got into the tin shed now they'd be rats with high-speed drills for teeth. Every conceivable nook and cranny had been firmly plugged with wire.

'I asked him to do the same for the airing cupboard,' said my mother bitterly,' but he thought you wouldn't be too happy about that.'

'I'll call the Council first thing on Monday,' I promised. 'And if that doesn't work, I'll import Tom's friend, Bill, from the Cotswolds.'

The man from the Council didn't say a lot. He clicked his tongue and shook his head and silently pointed out the runs where the rats had come from. There were runs everywhere and it appeared that my rat population could be very large indeed.

He frowned impatiently when I kept asking if there wasn't some more humane alternative to the poison he was about to dispense from a very long-handled spoon. He explained that he didn't use the really nasty stuff, but had a mixture he'd made up himself which, if finally lethal, was more gradual and not painful. He went to work, carefully making sure that no other animals could get at his brew, and a few days later came back to collect a sackful of bodies.

As I saw the fat, healthy bodies, with their clean, shining fur, laid out pathetically, I had to keep the memory of my slaughtered Sebrights firmly in the front of my mind, and remember all the diseases which rats can carry to contaminate the feed they raid, to stop myself feeling dreadfully guilty. I still felt awful, even though I had tried for ages to capture the rats in humane traps – tunnel-like things which don't harm the animal, so that you can either dispatch it quickly or take it somewhere else. The rats had simply stuffed soil in them.

'That's right,' said the man from the Council. 'They know, all right. And if they have a tunnel that one of their own kind has died in they'll block that up too. Look, there's one, so there must be dead rats down there.'

Once again, this evidence of their cleverness caused a surge of sympathy for the rats.

'Rubbish!' said Mrs P when I tried to explain this. 'What I want to know is when you're going to get rid of *my* rat.'

'You don't want poison in the airing cupboard. And,' I added sarcastically, 'if I remember correctly, it was you who once said that if you speak to them severely enough they'll go away. Have you tried that?'

'Of course I have,' she snorted. 'Damn thing's deaf.'

So my friend from the Council set a large trap in the airing cupboard. And I, in turn, trapped him in the stable as he was doing his undertaker duties, and made him do an interview. It had become very clear that he was like Tom's friend, Bill, and knew a great deal about rats.

I didn't hold out much hope of him speaking too much, though, because he was that very rare being, an almost silent Welshman. But, after his initial horror at the sight of the microphone and a few faltering minutes, he suddenly revealed a wonderful flow of words. Rats were his prey and his passion. He told me stories that would make you weep: of rats helping other rats, of their ability to 'think' through a problem (like how to get an egg down a flight of steps intact) and of their horrifying breeding rate. And when it was all over he smiled for the first time since I'd met him. At last he could admit in public his secret admiration for the animals he'd spent his working life destroying.

This time, one of the rats did get away, however.

'But I don't think it'll be back in a hurry,' crowed Mrs P. 'I heard it come THUMP into the cupboard and then it sort of whiffled around. The next thing there was this terrific BANG and I heard it do a sort of EEK and then it went mad, dashing up and down the copper tank. SLAM! BANG! BOOM! And it went flying up into the loft and I heard it eeking and squeaking and then fling itself out onto the roof with a KERPLONK and slide all the way down.'

I looked at her wonderingly. Sometimes I think my mother does a better line in sound effects than Gert and I could ever hope to get.

'Are you sure you didn't dream all that?' I asked slowly.

'Well, just look in the airing cupboard and see,' she shrugged.

The trap had gone off, all right. All it contained now was the tip of a tail. Its owner never came back for it and thereafter Mrs P had nothing but the owls and the kerplonking slate to disturb her rest. And I began to hunt for peacocks.

Chapter 10

'**U**nlucky things, peacocks,' said Mrs P.
'Not the peacocks themselves. Just their feathers, they say. All rubbish, of course. You're far too superstitious, you know.'

'Oh yes?' smiled my mother sweetly. 'I must have imagined it then, that time when you were hopping all over the place because someone brought you a few as a present. They were hardly out of the gate before you were burning those feathers on the fire.'

'Oh, well, that was different,' I mumbled. 'I didn't have anywhere to put them and they looked a bit tattered anyway.'

'This cottage,' said Mrs P, 'is full of tattered things people have given you. No. If they'd been tattered old hen's feathers you'd have found somewhere for them. But peacock's feathers, straight on the fire!'

'Well, it's all your fault,' I growled, 'always warning me about what happened to so and so and their peacock feathers.'

Mrs P shrugged. 'It never hurts to take precautions. Anyway, what do you want with peacocks?'

'*I* don't want any peacocks. I just feel there should be some in the Christmas programme. Could be something to do with those glass baubles for the tree in the shape of peacocks, or it might be because they used to serve them up, feathers and all, at feasts. I don't know, I just keep wanting to talk to someone about peacocks.'

My mother nodded. She's used to these odd hunches of mine. And, when it came to the programme, I never quite knew why I wanted a particular story. It was a bit like making up a tapestry, wanting a certain colour or texture to create the whole effect. Sometimes I think that I had nothing to do with the whole business, except to do the leg work, and that something or someone else actually decided what or who I needed to see. It was hopeless to explain this to producers, or other people who wanted to know in advance what I was up to, but there it was, and if I tried to do as they asked and planned everything carefully, it was a disaster. Anyway, for the moment, my subconscious (or whatever) was drumming out the sight and sound of peacocks.

Much good it was, though, because for some reason there was not a peacock owner to be found who was handy enough for me to see in the short time I had left. Those who had had peacocks had sold them or they had been taken by a fox or just died of old age.

'So I think I'll go and see Ruth Ruck's llamas instead,' I told Mrs P as I hunted up a phone number.

Mrs P peered at me over her glasses as she lounged, deep in some tale of blood and thunder, by the fireplace. Winston sat up on her lap and peered with her.

'The connection,' she announced at last, 'is not obvious. Not straight away, it isn't. But I'm sure you'll find one.'

'There isn't a connection, except that I was getting really frustrated about not finding any peacocks when I just had this clear thought, 'llamas and North Wales' – and that means Ruth Ruck. I know she's got a new young llama and that might put people in mind of cuddly toys round Christmas.'

'Oh, very subtle,' said Mrs P and she raised her eyebrows at Winston. He disappeared under the rug on her lap and she returned to the mean streets in her book and left me to try and charm Ruth Ruck into seeing me at very short notice.

My stubborn determination to find some peacocks had delayed me far too long and, llamas apart, I knew that if it was Ruth Ruck I was going to see, I would probably be able to persuade Myrddin to make another of his lightning dashes to get me there and back in one day. My old green Beetle would take far too long and probably get lost in the mists of Snowdonia.

Myrddin is a great fan of Ruth Ruck's and, many years before, he'd lent me her book *Place of Stones*. I didn't read it for ages. It lay, in its dull red cover, a constant irritation whenever Myrddin asked me how I'd liked it. As is so often the way with books I come to love, I read it finally so that I could give it back with a clear conscience.

Basically, it's the story of how the young Ruth and her parents bought their farm, Carneddi (Place of Stones), in North Wales, and of how Ruth set out to try and make it pay. But it's much more than that. It has a great sense of the grandeur of the mountains, of the determination of Ruth to try everything from turkey rearing to growing strawberries, and of her own further studies with the author of yet another classic on self-sufficiency, *The Farming Ladder*. It even has a chapter on how Ruth made a few extra pounds driving supplies around for the crew and cast of the film *The Inn of the Sixth Happiness* when they turned the Welsh mountains into a little piece of China.

As soon as I'd read Myrddin's copy, I ordered my own, along with its sequel, *Hill Farm Story*, and, much later, *Along Came a Llama*. For Ruth Ruck never gives up and, although now married, the mother of two children and a sufferer from multiple sclerosis, she had added a llama to the stock at Carneddi. By the time her book about Ñusta had been published, *A Small Country Living* was in the pipeline and one of the first people to appear on it was Ruth Ruck. Sadly, that first much-loved llama had died in the meantime, but by now Ruth's interest in llamas and the possibility of using them as productive working animals on the high, rocky hills of North Wales, had caused her to continue to breed them and by now she had quite a few, including the new one.

When I got through to her, Ruth was only too happy to do an update on her llama breeding and Myrddin just as happy to drive me to see her. Before we could go, however, there was another little matter to attend to. One by one, the goats came roaring into season.

This year, for the first time, their manic yells and wild leaping about did not send me into a panic of organization. I simply rang up and ordered the billy. There was now a travelling stud service for goats. And not just any old stud goats either. Margaret Shackles usually had a couple of males, with excellent pedigrees, of her own to offer and at least one on loan from another part of the country. This swopping around is fairly common. Once a male has been standing at stud in his own district, different blood is soon needed, so he's sent to another part of the country and his place is taken by one from somewhere else. Wenlock Heron was spending his second season in Mid-Wales and I'd already booked him in advance.

He made several visits that year. None of the goats had the consideration to come into season at the same time, of course, which would have saved me a bit on Heron's travelling expenses, but the relief of not having to mastermind the transport of a rampant, hysterical goat to him was wonderful. Already Gorgeous and Sophie had spent a blissful time with Heron in the loose-box and now there was just Minnie to go. And go she did, one dark evening when an early, rogue fall of snow made the roads treacherous and all my plans for a stress-free goat mating began to fall apart.

It was not as if the Shackles' had a Land-Rover, or indeed any four-wheel drive vehicle to transport Heron in. They didn't even have a car with four wheels. Their travelling Billy Service relied completely on a small, yellow three-wheeler. Margaret Shackles is not a small woman and her daughter Adeline, though slim, is not short. Heron was a large male goat in his prime. Somehow they all fitted into the yellow three-wheeler and emerged, if scarcely fragrant, at least fairly unruffled and eager to get down to business.

Twice already that year I had watched this cavalcade in wonder. For this last time I'd decided to record it. But down slithered the snow and would the little car make it?

'We'll have a damn good try,' said Margaret Shackles gruffly and I went back to stop Minnie smashing the door down and assure her that help was on the way. I hoped.

And so we waited, Minnie and I, I with one ear cocked for the phone in case the mission had been aborted or come to grief. Personally, nothing would have made me go out on a night like that and I marvelled, as so often before, at the incredible hardiness (and optimism) of country people like Myrddin and Ruth Ruck and the Shackles' and so many others, to whom the weather is simply a boring inconvenience to be bested if need be, and not, as it is to the likes of me, a terrifying message of doom to make me stay exactly where I am and dig as deep a burrow as possible. I strained my ears and peered out through the drifting snowflakes for the first sign of lights and envied Minnie, lost to everything but her raging lust.

Far from benighted travellers falling, exhausted, through my gate, there was an air of gaiety emanating from the little car as it wiggled its uncertain way around my yard. Margaret and Adeline burst forth, clad in their billy-proof overalls, and from behind the seats Heron snorted and bubbled his impatience.

When they met in the loose-box, Minnie flung herself on Heron and began biting his ears. Heron, taken aback, grumbled in his beard. Even the Shackles' were shocked.

'It's supposed to be him that bites her ears,' said Margaret loudly. 'Here, stop that, you,'

'Stop it everyone!' I cried. 'I can't do a recording with everyone waltzing around like this.' Adeline reached over and stopped Heron biting the microphone lead in two. She then frogmarched him to the end of the stable as if he were a kid, while Margaret gave Minnie a wallop and made her stand still.

All of them looked extremely bored as I fiddled with the equipment and adjusted the levels on Gert. Heron kept up a running commentary of groans and snorts. When Adeline released him, he ambled over, climbed on Minnie's back, still muttering to himself and proceeded to have a rest.

'He always does that,' giggled Adeline. 'Never in a hurry is Heron.'

'Well, while he's having a think, perhaps you could tell me about the travelling service and about the exchanges of stud goats,' I said.

Adeline, who was only sixteen at the time and still wearing her hair in long pigtails down her back, also threw in a lot about pedigrees and blood lines, while Margaret explained the economics of keeping a male goat at stud and Heron chimed in with his deep voice from time to time. Meanwhile poor Minnie wiggled and squirmed, until at last Heron lost interest in our conversation and served her, with a snort of satisfaction, and had another little rest on her back.

'I think that was OK,' said Margaret, releasing Minnie and cuffing Heron down. 'They can stay together for a bit while we go inside and write up all the particulars for your service certificate. Then we'd better go before the roads get worse. Was that recording all right?'

'Mmmm, fine, especially Heron's remarks,' I said.

'Oh, he can do more of that for you,' said Adeline, and she held a long and loving dialogue with Heron to which he responded as if he understood every word.

He was still in fine voice as they packed him back into the three-wheeler, eased themselves into the front, and said goodbye. As they went through the gate, with me still recording every last moment, Heron stuck his head over Adeline's shoulder and let out one almighty crashing snort, straight into the mike. Dear old boy. He was a perfect gent, a great broadcaster and a hell of a good sire. Just how good I didn't know then, but amongst the crop of kids which arrived next spring, was a very special one. Naturally, it was Adeline who spotted her and foretold her future.

There was no snow, but the cold smelled of old dried apricots and there was a haze over everything that threatened freezing fog that night, when Myrddin and I set out for North Wales a few days later. As soon as we were far enough north, Myrddin turned off the main road and drove up into the hills along a tiny road which had endless gates to open and shut. At last I persuaded him to stop, out came the Dilly Bag and we sat gazing down at the estuary and away to the sea, while around us the small, pure Welsh Mountain sheep grazed on the little hummocky hills.

With time to spare we went on to see the village where Robert Owen, a well-known speaker and poet whom Myrddin had much admired, had lived, and then on through deep, dark avenues where we found a strange deserted well, and on again past a stately home with a garden full of sculpted trees and not a sign of anyone all the while. So still it was and strange that at any moment I expected the Green Knight to come riding up and challenge us – or at least the White Knight to fall off his horse in front of us. We crept the car on tip-wheel on and beyond till we passed through an archway and out onto a main road again.

'That,' I said at last, 'was one of your more inspired diversions. Are you sure this is the way to Nantmor now?'

'Pretty sure,' said Myrddin, 'but we've still got a bit of time and I was hoping we'd see some kind of gift shop. I haven't got my mother's Christmas present.'

'What were you thinking of, then?' I asked.

'Oh, something like a shawl,' he said.

'So you need a crafts place. Look! It says "Crafts" on that little sign. There's an arrow, pointing up that road.'

Myrddin's eyes lit up. It was a small road and promised another interesting diversion. He did a quick U-turn, frightened the life out of a motorist coming the other way, and followed the arrow.

We followed it for an awfully long way. It was like those bush tracks which peter out and then suddenly, just when you've given up hope, appear once more to lure you on before they vanish altogether. Every so often, as we slid along the little road, another tantalizing arrow would sparkle from the hedge, only to leave us in serious doubt for more and more miles.

I looked at my watch and began to regret seeing the original signpost. Give Myrddin a road to follow and follow it he will to the bitter end. But at last even he began to doubt the existence of this craft shop and he groped for a map to see how we could cut across to Nantmor. And then the arrow appeared again, this time pointing firmly left. A sign beside it promised, once again, "Crafts".

Myrddin stopped the car.

'Up to you,' he said. 'Do we go left or do you want to go straight on to Nantmor?'

'Let's just see,' I said. 'If it's another road, we'll come back straight away and forget it. It *is* getting a bit late.'

Myrddin swung the car round and drove almost at once into an open forecourt, where two other cars were parked. There were stone walls behind it and, on one side, a tall house loomed out of the hazy air. A large sign announced "Crafts. Wood Turning".

'Damn it,' I said crossly. 'You won't find your mother's shawl here. But it does say something about wooden bowls and spoons.'

'It also says "Closed",' Myrddin pointed out.

It came from the dark trees around us, that long, high shriek that splinters time and echoes a noble past that should have been, but probably never was.

'Peacocks,' I breathed. 'I wonder who owns this place?'

'You'll soon find out,' said Myrddin and he gestured towards the chain-link fence beside the house. Just beyond it a man was hurrying towards us impatiently.

'I'm sorry,' he called as we walked towards him, 'we're closed at this time of the year.'

'Do you own those peacocks?' I demanded, ignoring his frown as we kept coming. He looked at me warily and the frown went deeper.

'Er . . . yes,' he said.

'How many have you got?' I asked.

'I'm not sure,' he faltered. 'My wife deals with the animals.'

'Does she know anything about peacocks?' I pressed on.

The man's expression turned rather nasty.

'Enough,' he said tersely. 'Why do you want to know?'

'I want to record an interview about peacocks for a radio programme,' I explained impatiently. 'Do you think she could do that?'

'A radio interview? About peacocks?' He began to relax a little and then turned and called over his shoulder. 'Tina, there's someone here wants to do an interview about peacocks.'

A small woman, bundled up against the cold, appeared from around the side of the house.

'Come in,' she smiled, and opened the gate.

'I'll get your stuff from the car,' said Myrddin and, moments later, we all stood under the trees around their yard while above us, on the stone wall, a line of peacocks peered down.

'They're not looking their best right now,' said Tina. 'You should come back in the summer. That's when they make more noise too.'

'I thought you were coming to complain about that,' said her husband, Frank, sheepishly. 'Why do you want to do an interview about peacocks?'

'Oh, it's just that I'm doing this Christmas programme and I wanted to give it a slight medieval touch, but at the same time do a practical thing about how to keep peacocks. The medieval Welsh nobility seem to have had a particular thing about peacocks.'

Tina and Frank glanced at each other.

110

'Do you know where you are?' asked Tina.

'Haven't got a clue. We just followed your signs,' I said.

'This is Cae Dafydd,' said Tina. She looked across at Myrddin. 'The home of the medieval poet, Dafydd.'

Myrddin gazed at her enchanted. Finding the homes of famous Welshmen is one of his passions, and here he had stumbled on one without even trying.

Tina smiled and went on. 'There have been peacocks here for centuries, we believe. Dafydd the poet wrote a poem about one. Anyway, when we bought Cae Dafydd we thought we'd better keep peacocks. They roost out in the trees. Won't come into a pen at night.'

'Yes, and when there's a frost you can hear their wings creaking,' chimed in Frank. 'In summer, they wake the whole district up, very early in the morning.'

'Dafydd,' continued Tina, dismissing the present, 'wrote a love poem to a girl called Gwen. In it he sends his peacock as a messenger. And another poet wrote a poem telling a fox to kill Dafydd's peacock.'

'Popular girl was Gwen,' said Frank.

As we talked, I got a funny tingling up my spine. I'm used to the way coincidence seems to play a large part in whatever I do, but this time it had surpassed itself. Llamas, North Wales, an arrow in the hedge, and somehow I'd pitched right up to the place where peacocks had the real medieval significance I'd been looking for. I found something else at Cae Dafydd too, but on that visit I didn't recognize it, and put off another of my animal love affairs for a whole year. Now I was too eager to pursue the story of Cae Dafydd and its peacocks.

Tina and Frank shaped up to the microphone beautifully, in spite of the cold and the complete indifference of the peacocks to come down off their wall and take part.

When it was all over, Frank coughed and asked hesitantly, 'Which programme is this for, by the way?'

'Oh, it's called *A Small Country Living*,' I said absently, busy packing things away. When I turned back to them Tina and Frank were looking shocked.

'Are you,' asked Tina slowly, 'Jeanine McMullen? Because, if you are, you're one of the reasons we're here at all.'

If I'd had a tingling feeling before, now I went ice-cold. One of the things that terrifies me is the thought that if I make country life sound attractive (I try very hard not to) someone will leave their nice cosy city living and go out to try an anything-but-cosy rural one. If anyone writes and asks my advice about this, I tell them not to unless they know exactly what they're doing. Now my doom was upon me and I was face to face with a couple who'd gone and done it anyway. I gave them a hunted look, flashed a warning with my eyes at Myrddin, who was beaming all over his face, and wished we hadn't come so far from the gate.

But Tina and Frank were smiling delightedly. 'We used to listen to all those people you have on,' said Tina, 'and one day we said, "If they can, why can't we?" And here we are!'

'Successful?' I asked hopefully.

'Oh, we do all right,' said Frank.

'And we have a lot of fun,' said Tina firmly. As she spoke, there was a fluttering of wings and what looked like a flock of long-legged starlings flew towards her and began settling around her feet and up onto her hands.

'Modern Game bantams,' she cried, as they chortled happily at her. 'We call them Stilt-Walkers because of their long, long legs. You should have some. They're *so* tame, right from the day they hatch out. I could let you have a trio.'

'Perhaps,' I said, 'but we're already very late for our next interview. Did you say you have a craft shop with other things in it for the visitors? Could we have a quick look round in case you've got something for Myrddin's mother?'

We didn't find anything that looked like a shawl, but I did find a book which I thought would make Mrs P a very suitable Christmas present.

As we packed ourselves back into the car, Tina put her head in through the window.

'If you change your mind about the Stilt-Walkers,' she said, 'give me a ring and pick them up on your way home.'

'Perhaps I will,' I called back, as Myrddin started the car forward.

112

We got to Ruth Ruck's farm very quickly indeed and as we drove up the long, winding drive, through the strange rock formations embedded around it, we saw above us a llama silhouetted against the sun, which had finally pierced through the cold mist that engulfed everything below.

Half an hour later I was crouched in one of the innumerable hollows ringed by the great stone boulders which make up the strange moon landscape of Carneddi. Standing on the rim of it were five llamas of varying sizes, all of them gleefully aware that I was a perfect target for a spit.

'They're just excited,' said Ruth Ruck. 'They're usually very good, but perhaps it's your equipment they don't like.'

'I don't think they mind my equipment one bit,' I said as I dodged. 'It's just me they're after.'

Ruth held up her hand and fielded a spit. It made a lovely sound.

'Get 'em to do it again,' I said quickly, waving the microphone. And Ruth, who's used by now to the mad ways of the media, did. And put up with the smell. Llama spit is regurgitated cud. It's the only thing I've got against them. Apart from that, llamas and alpacas are the nearest thing to a mythical creature I'll ever behold.

When Ruth Ruck began her llama keeping, it was still considered a rather eccentric thing to do. Now they fetch fabulous prices and there's even a British Camelid Association which has a devoted membership of people with llamas, alpacas and guanacos. I've seen a lot of them and loved them all with their bell-like voices and their elegant, other-world bodies, but nowhere have I seen them look so splendid as they do at The Place of Stones, which has a faint air of the High Andes about it.

It was dark when we came back down the hill to the village of Nantmor itself. I had one last call to make, to a delightful lady who owned a lot of sheep. Most of them were castrated males she'd bought to save them from being slaughtered. Janet Rossell was warm and round and very very kind and her house was as neat as a pin in spite of all the dogs who lived with her. She worked hard at her little bed-and-breakfast business and if she didn't have a lot of money, she did have a great amount of heart. If Myrddin was a little shocked at all her useless sheep eating their heads off, he enjoyed the warmth of her leaping fire and the great plates of home-made biscuits and the cups of tea she pressed on us.

We went home swiftly along the dark roads, with the shape of great mountains dimly seen, and talked over the day on which so much had happened.

'All we didn't achieve,' I said, 'was your mother's shawl.'

'And you didn't get a copy of that poem of Dafydd's,' said Myrddin.

But I got that from a more modern, literary Dafydd; Dafydd Ifans of the Manuscripts Department at the National Library of Wales in Aberystwyth. He looked it up for me in *Medieval Welsh Lyrics*, translated by Joseph Clancy. Dafydd of Nanmor's poem, in which he sends his peacock as a messenger to Gwen o'r Ddôl, is quite a long one, but I think the last few lines are the best:

> Fair, peacock, above the glade,
> The same hue as a rainbow.
> A fair sight, like coils are you,
> Green dragon of church windows.
> Go to the the spot, passion's choice,
> And hurry, azure adder,
> And come there like fowler,
> Fetch Gwen from her husband's home!

And Dafydd Ifans also sent a bit more information about the peacock-loving poets of medieval Wales:

Another poem, a *cywydd*, urging a fox to kill Dafydd Nanmor's peacock is *not* to be attributed to Rhys Goch Eyri, according to Sir Ifor Williams ... Rhys Goch Eyri's poem is a satirical ode to a fox for killing his peacock. It was described by George Borrow as

'a piece so abounding with hard words, that it was termed the drunkard's choke pear, as no drunkard was ever able to recite it'. Indeed it would be difficult enough for a sober man to recite it, consequently it is not surprising that an English translation of it has not been found ...

By the way, Rhys Goch Eyri also kept goats! In one poem he attacks the way Siôn Cent had slandered him in a poem for keeping goats for his mother!'

And, while we're on the subject of mothers, Myrddin found a hand-woven shawl for his, in Swansea after all. As for mine, amongst the other presents she had for Christmas there was a book of Welsh recipes. It was called *First Catch Your Peacock*.

Chapter 11

The squirrel clung onto the swaying branch with one paw and shut its eyes. It was an extremely fat squirrel and it had misjudged both the distance across the swollen river and its ability to jump it. The branch was thin and whippy, and below it stood Lily, the lurcher, mouth open, waiting for the squirrel to fall.

Lily had been trying to catch that squirrel for months, but always he'd flicked his tail and flown to the top of a tree and taunted her.

The squirrels have a very good living in the woods and on the meadow. There are all kinds of berries, hazel nuts and acorns in autumn, and in summer, seeds from the tall grasses and the herbs which grow wild. Apart from the owls and buzzards, which also live there, the squirrels haven't got a lot to worry about. Well, they didn't until Lily made it her life's work to catch one. It was not a threat the squirrels took very seriously as she always made enough noise, as we went down into the woods, for them to get well aloft. And I rather welcomed her obsession, because while she was going from tree to tree, gazing up into the branches with her paws on the trunk, I could go on with my quiet contemplative stroll without worrying where she and the whippets had got to and if they were up at the top of the woods poking their noses into the badger setts.

I had taken this situation so much for granted, that it was a while before I noticed that one squirrel in particular was having a battle of wits with Lily. Instead of staying fairly close to the trees, it was straying further and further out onto the open grass of the meadow, and leaving it later and later to fly for safety. I once saw it look up at the oncoming cavalcade of dogs and goats, calmly get on with what it was doing and then, timing it perfectly, make a dash right under Lily's nose.

'One day,' I shouted after it, 'you'll do that once too often.' A derisory flirt of its tail and a moving branch and it was gone.

That had been back in the autumn. It was now January the 5th and I had gone to the woods to escape. All day Mrs P and I had been arguing about Twelfth Night and the vital importance of taking the Christmas tree down before midnight. It's something we never agreed on. She said January the 5th was Twelfth Night, and I stuck out for January the 6th.

'Twelve days after Christmas,' I had said as my mother began the argument when I brought in her early-morning cup of tea. 'That means you start counting on 26 December.'

Mrs P set her jaw and intoned, 'You count Christmas Day. That's 25, 26, 27 . . ., and on she went, holding up one finger after the other till she reached 5 January. 'That's twelve days.'

'No, no,' I said impatiently, 'it's on the sixth, the Feast of the Epiphany, that you take the decorations down.'

'You know what will happen if you don't get the tree down and all the holly berries out before midnight,' Mrs P went on, ignoring me. 'All the bad luck will come back into the house.'

'Oh, Mother!' I groaned. 'As if a few Christmas decorations and holly berries could really matter!' But I was faltering. What was it Katharine Briggs, the folklorist, had once quoted to me? Something about, for every holly berry left in the house 'so many goblins shall you see'. If I rant and rave at my mother for her superstition, I'm enough of her daughter to share her misgivings. But I did have a good reason for wanting to delay the dreary task of dismantling the tree, and unplucking all the bright cards from the bookshelves and suffering agonies of indecision as to where I should put the holly. Katharine Briggs had also told me that it was not advisable to burn it.

Every year, just as the Christmas fever is hotting up, I go cold on the whole idea. Finding the time to buy, write and post dozens of cards appals me; buying presents is fun, wrapping them a desperate and personal battle between me and rolls of recalcitrant paper and ribbon. The very thought of organizing a tree, somehow getting it to stand upright in its accustomed corner and then braving its

117

needles (to which I'm allergic) as I painstakingly decorate it with the old blue, green and rose silvered balls, makes me feel very tired indeed.

Every year I moan and complain and swear I won't do any of it and why not forget the whole thing?

'Yes, why don't you?' asked Mrs P. 'So I gather you won't be wanting a Christmas cake or pudding or mince pies.'

'Oh well, we could just have *those*.' I always replied hastily. And so, gradually, Christmas catches up with me. The cards come and mine go out. Somehow the presents get bought and wrapped and extra food is organized. But still I stick out against the tree until, in spite of my intransigence, somehow one always arrives.

For the last few years, my neighbour-beyond-price, Gwynneth, had taken that responsibility upon herself. I had once given her a spare tree of two which had appeared, miraculously, from another friend. Until then, Gwynneth and her family had never bothered with a tree. In fact, when I first came to the valley, few of the Welsh families did bother. New Year was their big day then. For Gwynneth, that first tree had looked so splendid in the hall of her regal old farmhouse, and her children had enjoyed it so much, that from then on she always got one. The very next year, it had been Gwynneth who had taken me on a long, cold jaunt to a remote farm that advertised trees for sale and, after that, it became a tradition for her to give us one. Not that anything was ever said about this officially. There would simply be a knock at the door and Gwynneth beaming at me through the branches of a Christmas tree. Once, it was a close-run thing and, with the remains of a blizzard which had closed the road for ages still cooping us up, a tree had seemed out of the question. But on Christmas Eve there it was, tied to the gate with a bottle of whisky and a message saying 'Love from Gwynneth'.

The holly usually arrives with Myrddin, who has a wonderful tree that seldom fails to bear a brilliant crop of berries. Sometimes he leaves it a bit late, but somehow, whether I will or no, by the time I light the candle at midnight on Christmas Eve, to welcome the Christ child, the room is complete with glittering tree and scarlet holly.

And then I fall in love with it all. Gone is my irritable complaining and, unlike so many families to whom the tree and the holly become nuisances as the Christmas spirit tarnishes, for me they grow in beauty as they become more familiar. By the time Mrs P reminds me of Twelfth Night I will do almost anything (even argue about the calendar) to have another day and night of them.

On this particular fifth day of January, I was resisting Mrs P's nagging more stubbornly than usual. It had been a particularly lovely tree that year, the holly berries were of a rich fatness and depth of colour seldom seen, and the cards had been especially vivid and jolly. Once they all came down the room would look drab and dreary in the grey winter light. There would be nothing to look forward to except bleak January and spiteful February before the March gales came raging in, and with them the back-breaking, sleep-shattering job of lambing. In all my gloomy forecasting I ignored the fact that somewhere ahead was spring.

Finally I grabbed the new thistle stick, collected the dogs and announced that I was off to look for the sheep. Most of them were up on the home field but I'd noticed, earlier in the morning, that three of them were missing. For the past few days they'd been ranging around on the meadow and up through the woods to clear up any last shreds of grass and the odd bramble leaf. There was a lot more down there to pick at than on the field, but nevertheless, as usual, they'd streamed back through the gate and were now below the house. Except for three young ones, who, I suspected, had reached too enthusiastically into the bramble patch and were now stuck fast.

I'd often thought of having the brambles cleared out from the bottom of the wood, but a succession of naturalists had begged me not to, because they provide wonderful cover for all kinds of wildlife. Surrounded as I am by farmers who've opened out the fields into bigger ones, where the grass is of bowling-green consistency, I've left the meadow and the wood as natural as possible. When the wild flowers are growing, I keep the sheep off it, but in autumn and winter they do a good job of cleaning up. Well, at least they're supposed to. Mostly they prefer to be within sight and sound of me coming out with a bucket of nuts or an armful of hay. The older, wiser ones, that is. The yearlings find the drooping sprays of ivy and the few fluttering bramble leaves irresistible.

The dogs raced ahead of me towards the wood, Winston bouncing and barking through the mud, as we crossed the fields. The sheep looked up hopefully and Doli gave an inquiring whicker, but seeing nothing except a long stick in my hand, they went back to dozing in the sun, which had appeared miraculously over the hills that morning. It was that rare thing in winter, a mild, sunny day. Mild usually means wet in this valley, and sun means frost. But occasionally a day like this comes as a gift and the earth yawns in her sleep and the animals stretch themselves out and soak up the luxury of it.

As we reached the little gate leading into the wood, a bleat hailed me and Dolores and the rest of the goats came galloping from the platform outside their shed, where they'd been lying, backs to the wall, long legs out, eyes closed, jaws working over their cuds, looking like a mob of gum-chewing gangsters on holiday on a Sicilian beach.

I took a firmer hold of the thistle stick as they came roaring to a halt behind me and began a search of my pockets. Rescuing the gloves and the clasp knife I'd shoved in to deal with the brambles, I retrieved the toggle Dolores was detaching from my coat, shoved a boot out to ward them off and started down the track through the woods. The goats fell into single file and followed me closely.

The thistle stick was wonderful. Being winter, there wasn't much thistle destruction to do, but the sharp little shovel on the end was wonderful for steadying me across the muddy fields, or down the steep paths of the wood, slimy with decaying leaves and the water that trickled off the hill on its way to the river. It needed something more than an ordinary stick to stay upright on those paths, especially when there was a gang of pushy goats queueing up behind. Now the little shovel dug into the soft ground and supported my weight when I zigzagged downhill, and even allowed me to stay still as I paused to gaze up in wonder as a joyful flock of long-tailed tits came calling and darting through the bare branches overhead, like tiny winged bells.

The dogs gazed back at me impatiently, the goats began to shove

and clown about, and on we moved till we reached the path beside
the river and the open meadow beyond.

It must have been the false promise of spring which had tempted
Lily's squirrel so far from base. She spotted it at once, sitting
without a care in the world, right by the river bank. It would
have known nothing about the silently surging lurcher and the
two whippets, if Winston hadn't yapped as he tried to keep up with
them on his fat little legs. Even then it wasn't overly concerned,
and leapt almost casually for the trunk of an alder with its coral
roots trailing in the river. But its leap was not as agile as usual.
It made a bad miscalculation, fell back, leapt again and only just
managed to cling onto the trunk in front of Lily's snapping jaws.
Badly frightened for the first time, the squirrel scrabbled frantically
out onto one of the overhanging branches, lost its grip, made a
desperate grab with one paw and dangled over the river.

Gazing up at the soft underbelly, I realized what a very portly
squirrel it was. I suspected that it had been returning from a
sortie across the river, where I own a small half-moon of land
which is thick with rowans, hazels and brambles. Nothing ever
grazes there; in spring it's a stunning mass of bluebells, and in
winter, with the river raging between its banks instead of ambling
peacefully over the boulders, which provide stepping stones for
the odd fox or rabbit, the squirrels have it to themselves. It was
obvious that this one had meant to leap from the alder back onto
the opposite bank again. But aerial acrobatics like that require a
certain quiet calculation, even for a squirrel, and this overweight
squirrel had got it wrong. In its panic it had grabbed for a thin
little branch that bent and stretched under its weight, and below
there was either the rampant river or Lily's gaping jaws.

'You are one very lucky squirrel,' I called up to it as I grabbed
Lily's collar. 'I suggest a bit of hibernation and a good diet.'

By now it had managed to clutch the branch with its paws
and was edging its way carefully back to a fork in the trunk. I
left it to figure out its next move in peace and, keeping a firm
hold on Lily, roaring at Merlyn and Gloucester to leave it alone
and laughing at Winston as he came panting up in time to miss all
the action, I set off to the main part of the woods to look for the
missing sheep. The goats had been waylaid by the gorse bushes

121

in the middle of the meadow and were delicately nibbling at the prickles as if they were made of spun sugar, or biting off shoots and rolling them carefully round in their mouths till they could crunch them safely.

As the dogs and I reached the foot of the steep slope on which the main part of the wood spreads upwards to the fields, two black sheep broke cover and dashed past, trailing long swathes of bramble. A desperate, abandoned cry came from somewhere further up. I sighed, dug the thistle stick firmly into the soil and began heaving myself up towards the sound. When I reached the great bramble patch there was no sign of another sheep. I began to climb higher when a frantic movement from deep within the patch attracted the dogs, who dashed forward to investigate.

'Back!' I yelled, and then I swore. I could see the sheep now, just visible within the brambles, which were wound so tightly around it that it would need a large billhook to free it.

To see better, I pushed a bramble, at the edge of the patch, to one side with the thistle stick and stumbled so that it dug into it and cut it clean through.

'Brilliant,' I said to the dogs as they followed every move. 'The Lord and Hugh McCallum's grandfather be praised!' Within another couple of minutes, by stabbing down at the brambles, I had a patch cleared through to the sheep, which then did everything to prevent me cutting it free. Struggling and leaping as its bonds came clear, it managed to wind them around me as well. It scrambled away at last and left me scratched and bleeding, hating sheep and realizing too late that, with me safely occupied, Lily had taken the whippets up to the badgers' sett. Just disappearing above me was Winston's fat little rump bobbing through the dead bracken. Painfully, I followed it.

One of the things I never move without, is a piece of baler twine in my pocket. It came in handy now to haul Lily back down the slope and make her sit still while I caught my breath by sitting on the trunk of the holly tree at the bottom.

Once, long ago, the wood was separated from the meadow by a thick hedge. Probably then, the hazel and oak were a coppice crop and the hedge stopped the sheep from breaking through to nibble at the stands. Whatever the reason, it had been a good hedge and well laid, because even now, so long after, there are big trees striking upwards from thick horizontal trunks. Such a one was the holly. As a bearer of berries it is not prolific and what there are tend to be a paler shade than those from Myrddin's tree. Also, his tree needs cutting back from the track down to his farm, so he waits till Christmas time and gives me the berry-laden trimmings. My own tree, therefore, usually remains unmolested, except, that is, by the birds.

There were two of them, hanging upside down from its top branches, as I sat on the trunk and watched – a couple of blue tits, seeming oddly out of place there, so far from suburban bird-tables. Further below, a robin sat eyeing their revels thoughtfully before finding his own bunch of berries. Watching them, I knew exactly what to do with the holly branches in the house.

I got up slowly and towed Lily across the meadow. Merlyn and Gloucester trotted behind and Winston followed us, peeing on every molehill he passed. Trees are a bit daunting to a dog his size. Molehills are perfect.

The goats had disappeared, of the squirrel there was no sign and, still determined to enjoy what remained of my walk in the sun before going back to make decisions about the Christmas tree, I wandered over to the river. Two mallards, a duck and a drake, rose into the air from the wide bend where the river pauses for breath before hurtling over the rocks in a frenzy once more.

I smiled happily and raised an arm in greeting. Once I'd had a little mallard duck, called Mitzi, which flew around the farm like the pigeons. She had disappeared one day and for a while I thought the fox had taken her. But not long after, for the first time, I saw a pair of mallards on the river and hoped that Mitzi had fallen victim to love instead. The next summer I'd surprised a group of half-grown ducklings being hurried to safety by their mother. Since then, rightly or wrongly, I always greeted the mallards as if they were either Mitzi herself and mate, or at least their descendants.

Now, as this pair rose up from the river, bright showers of water trailing from their legs as they climbed to tree height, banked and flew off downstream, I wondered how long they'd been quietly sitting there as all the drama of Lily and the squirrel had been going on.

'Must have been Mitzi,' I told the dogs. 'Mitzi was used to you and your noise and never took any notice. Anyway, that's why we haven't seen any brown trout today, what with you and your racket and two ducks about. Poor things.'

I have a great affection for the little brown trout which congregate amongst the rocks at the bend of the river, or under the high bridge further back by the road. Usually I make the dogs go very quietly as we approach, so that I can see the trout, little more than shadows, darting for cover. And fishermen who excuse their trespass on my side of the riverbank by declaring that they're 'only after the little old brown trout and I'll bring you a few up for your supper', are likely to get a furious lecture on the increasing rarity of the brown trout as the dogs and I rumble them on their way. As for the sea trout which labour up the river to spawn by the lake, I leave their protection in the hands of the water bailiffs and, although when I see them battling against the current, I am moved by pity and wonder and try, by moving the boulders which have come down in the floods, to make their passage easier, it is the permanent inhabitants, the little brown trout, that I love best.

A martyred sigh from Lily, a tentative whine from the whippets and a sharp bark from Winston reminded me that it had been a long time since we'd left the cottage where, they hoped, Mrs P would have their dinner ready. And, I suspected, a whole new line of argument about the urgent necessity to get the tree down.

In spite of the dogs' agonized glances, I didn't hurry back. I seldom do when I'm by the river. Down there one is completely hidden – no buildings, no people and usually no animals except the wild ones and those I take with me. Until I get to the top of the path through the woods, my responsibilities seem ridiculously unimportant. If I waver in this view, I have but to look across the river at the few remaining stones of the old mill. Once people worked hard there, even diverting the river; once they hedged and hoed and worried. Now only the grass and the river whisper and the trees live their secret lives, as they will whisper and live when I and mine are long gone. So, no matter how agitated in spirit I am when I arrive on the meadow, by the time I leave it everything is in perspective again – until I reach the top of that path and the problems come rushing back. So I do everything I

124

can to delay setting foot on it. One way of doing that is to look, very slowly, for fir cones on the way back.

The tall fir trees grow just by the road and below the bridge which takes it over the river. Once the bridge was lower down, to connect, presumably, with the mill on the opposite bank. Nothing remains of it now but a buttressing of stone on my side of the river. Between this and the new bridge are the fir trees standing on their sterile bed of needles and, sometimes, after the gales, fir cones. The slope they stand on is almost vertical and one slip lands you in the river. Hunting for fir cones, therefore, requires considerable concentration, balance and foresight. Towing a reluctant lurcher on a length of baler twine is distracting; and worrying about the fate of a small, fat, but infinitely courageous chihuahua as he flings himself up and down the slope is very wearing on the nerves. If you also have two impatient whippets whining at you from above, it is wise to abandon the search, wedge your back against the trunk of the largest tree and gaze heavenwards, before you do anything rash, like scrambling to the top of the awkward hill and belting the lot of them.

So I wedged and gazed and became, as always when I stare straight up into the high branches of a tree, rather hypnotized. Above me the branches stayed quite still and I noticed a large piece of bark caught in a strange way on one of them. It was not in a fork, but suspended, upright, in the middle of the branch, quite motionless. How had it come there and, more important, how was it staying there?

The dogs by now had sat down resignedly and hoped to catch my attention and pity by shivering. I looked away from the mysterious piece of bark to frown at them and, when I glanced back, surely it had moved its position slightly. Craning upwards to see better, I moved my back away from the tree and the bark moved too. A pair of eyes opened slowly and stared down at me.

'Shh,' I whispered to the dogs, which, seeing my movement, had got to their feet hopefully.

But it was too late. The eyes closed and opened again, two blunt wings were extended and the owl left the branch and glided across the road and into the woods on the other side.

'I don't suppose it will ever come back to that roost now,' I said mournfully to the dogs. But it did, and for weeks afterwards, every walk on the meadow finished with the dogs and me going silently to gaze up at our owl sitting on the same branch of the same tree. After that first time it never moved, even bearing with out hunt for fir cones patiently, unless we stayed until the wood was almost dark, when it would lumber away to its evening hunting.

When we got back to the cottage, Mrs P was not in any mood to be beguiled by stories of owls, mallards or fat squirrels. Even my announcement that Hugh McCallum's thistle stick was a marvellous bramble cutter left her unmoved as she dumped the dogs' food down in front of them. She gestured towards the tray of scones by the Rayburn.

'Almost cold by now, of course,' she said. 'You've been gone for hours. Now, about this business of the tree.'

'The stock!' I cried, stuffed a scone into my mouth, grabbed the cats' food and fled.

By the time the animals were fed, the brambled sheep caught and divested of their trailing glory, and everything counted in, locked up and double-checked again, a frost was beginning to sparkle in the lights from barn and cottage and stars sharpened their sparks and bobbed and winked through the trees. Away over the hill a fox barked, and still I waited on the yard until I heard that shrieking cry from the woods. Somewhere down there our owl was hunting. I went back to the cottage where the little Christmas tree shimmered and danced a welcome and the holly berries glowed in the firelight.

'Now what are you doing?' asked Mrs P sternly as she emerged from the kitchen.

'Looking for a book,' I muttered and continued my search along the shelves which form one side of the room and are stuffed to danger point. Move one book and the lot are likely to collapse on your head, along with the shelves.

'Well, you'll have to remove those cards before you can do that,' said my mother. 'Of course, if you'd done that earlier, you'd have no trouble now. Anyway, I don't know if you want any dinner tonight, but if so it's ready.'

'Got it!' I cried and I pulled forth a small book with a bright pink cover.

'*Hogmanay* and *what?*' asked Mrs P as she tried to read the title upside down.

'*Hogmanay and Tiffany*. Tiffany as in Epiphany. And I think it might settle our little differences about Twelfth Night once and for all.'

'Oh, will it? Well, what does it say?'

'It says . . .' and I riffled through the pages till I found what I was looking for, began to read and then smiled triumphantly. 'It says we're both right. Listen to this: *In England only the learned spoke of Epiphany. Commonly the season was called Twelvetide or Twelftide, and the feast itself, January 6th, Twelfth Day.*'

I held up my hand as Mrs P began to sputter indignantly and continued: '*This dates back to the time of King Alfred, who is said to have promulgated a Law . . . with relation to holidays, by virtue of which the twelve days after* [and here I paused and repeated the word *after*] *the Nativity of our Saviour were made festivals – the twelve days of Christmas as they were later known. Nor did the people need urging to be gay; in medieval courts and great houses feasting and celebrations continued undiminished till the final revel of Twelfth Night. Nowadays the superstitious amongst us mark Twelfth Day merely by taking down our Christmas decorations, if we haven't already burned them because they harboured the dust.*'

I paused and gave Mrs P a very meaningful look. 'So you see, mother,' I said, 'you take down the decorations on Twelfth Day which is the *sixth* of January, Feast of the Epiphany. *However,*' I went on as she began to tighten her lips, 'Gillian Edwards, the author, also goes on:

'*Twelfth night, of course precedes Twelfth Day. There is increasing confusion* [and here there came a loud snort from Mrs P] *over this because we have forgotten the ancient custom of starting the day not at midnight but at six the previous evening. . . . So the last great festival of Christmas . . . eating, drinking, dancing, mumming, foolery and plays . . . was actually held on what to us would be the night of January 5th to 6th.*'

I closed the book with a bang and grinned at my mother.

'So you see! Twelfth Night is when you have the party. Twelfth Day is when you have to make sure the decorations are down.'

127

Mrs P began to protest but I assumed an air of sweet reason and said, 'It makes sense doesn't it? You have this thing about Twelfth Night because you want to have a party and wish on the tree. Now, you can't wish on the tree if it isn't there. So let's make it the house rule. Party and wishing on Twelfth Night. Tree down on Twelfth Day. By the way, Gillian Edwards goes on a bit later about the special cake they had for Twelfth Night. It had all sorts of things in it – including a bean. Whoever got the bean was King for the night. It was an iced and decorated cake,' I concluded wistfully.

Mrs P tossed her head and marched out into the kitchen. She came back bearing in front of her a wonderful cake. On it, in bright green icing, it said: 'HAPPY TWELFTH NIGHT. JAN *FIFTH*.'

'I was frightened you'd come back before I got it finished,' said Mrs P with a smirk. 'Just got it hidden in time before you and the dogs came in. There's no bean in it, though.'

'Never mind,' I said happily, 'we'll both be King.'

It was a very good party and the room was full of people. Not that anyone peering through the little windows would have seen them. But we could. Mrs P once read a story about a lady who was on her own on Twelfth Night with nothing but her Christmas tree for company. Her family was scattered all around the world, and the only thing she could wish for on the tree was that she would see them somehow. As she sat there, the woman fell asleep and in her dream all her children and all her friends gathered around her and, when she woke, it was as if they were still there.

So that is what Mrs P and I do for our Twelfth Night party. We imagine that all the people we have loved (and all the animals) past and present are with us, and we wish for them all on the tree.

The next day, without any fuss, I took the tree down and put the silvered balls on their cushion of tinsel and into their box under the stairs. The cards were packed up to remind me of next year's list. Only the holly remained. I gathered it up and took it down to the pond below the house. There I stuck every branch into the soft soil around its banks, so that the berries gleamed amongst the withered grass. As I walked back to the cottage, the blue tits and the robin were already gobbling them up.

Three days later, Lily finally caught the squirrel. Or to be more precise, the squirrel caught Lily.

You could hear her screams all over the valley. Rushing suicidally down the path through the woods, I could only imagine my beloved dog lying with at least a broken leg, or strung up on an ancient strand of barbed wire, cut to pieces. When she came to meet me, I could hardly bear to look for the damage. There was nothing except a minute jewel of blood on her black nose. But still she howled and shivered and cowered and nothing would comfort her.

Lily, it has to be said, is an appalling coward. Just giving her an injection is a nightmare. Curiously enough, this terror of pain makes her a very good guard dog. The fact that she's protecting herself, not me, doesn't really signify. For some reason she doesn't like men, and, although female visitors are likely to be greeted with a great big gurning grin, men had better watch out or else.

I peered closely at the bead of blood. A thorn? I touched the spot and set Lily off howling again. Suddenly the whippets, who'd been dancing around behind us, streaked past.

'Oh, God! The squirrel,' I cried and raced after them.

It was lying, not a mark on it, but obviously in a state of complete mental collapse, at the foot of an ash sapling. Once again it had left the leap for freedom too late, its fate had overtaken it in a blinding flash of black and gold and all it had time to do was bite hard. Its 'fate', being the coward she is, had saved its life, but when you're as fat as that squirrel being winded is no joke. Any naturalist would have left it, out for the count with shock, to its inevitable end in the claws of the buzzard wheeling hopefully overhead. Grey squirrels, despoilers of trees, eaters of birds' eggs, would not have won their sympathy vote. But this squirrel was different. It had become part of our daily ritual. I couldn't abandon it now.

It was not easy to get one hysterical lurcher, two furious whippets, a shrieking chihuahua and a comatose squirrel back up through the woods, across the fields and into the full blast of Mrs P's disapproval. Neither did I get any thanks from the squirrel, which came to in the middle of the night, got out of its warm, hay-lined box and roared round my office creating total havoc. It was still trying to bite me when I released it in the wood. I wished the buzzard joy of it.

We never saw it again, but Lily, in spite of her wound and the course of injections which followed it, still lives in hope.

Chapter 12

'It all looks very dull,' sighed Mrs P, gazing around the room emptied of its finery.

I paused in the doorway, my arms full of bare twigs.

'Sorry,' I said. 'There's not a sign of anything in the garden. You'll just have to wait till Tolly's magic works.'

'I can never believe it will,' said my mother, as I began arranging the twigs as artistically as possible in the old brown game-jug on the table. 'Of course, if you'd remembered to plant your hyacinth bulbs in the pots earlier, we'd have those out by now.'

I shrugged. Every autumn I buy hyacinth bulbs to bloom after Christmas, invariably forget where I've put them and only rescue them far too late for them to be able to cheer us up when we most need it. The current ones were still showing nothing more than coy green tips above the earth in their pots. Our only hope was this tasteful display of twigs which would, sooner or later, burst into flower.

Tolly's magic.

I call it that because, every January, when I go out into the dead winter garden to cut the shoots of flowering currant, forsythia and hazel, I think of Tolly arriving at Green Knowe for the first time and gazing in wonder at the thick, twelfth-century walls with their great mirrors and carvings of cherubs and '*vases everywhere filled with queer flowers . . . branches of dry winter twigs out of which little tassels and rosettes of flower petals were bursting, some yellow, some white, some purple. They had an exciting smell, almost like something to eat, and they looked as if they had been produced by magic, as if someone had said "Abracadabra! Let those sticks burst into flower."*'

If you have not already met Tolly and his great-grandmother

Mrs Oldknow, I strongly recommend you to do so at once. In fact, when I went to look up that passage again to get it precisely right, I found my hands collecting all five of the Greenknowe books and once again losing myself in that enchanted house, which is a border of time for all those children who lived there and loved it. To leave it and come out again into the real world of a January howling and screaming with storms, with nothing but the demanding cries of animals waiting to be fed, watered and mucked out, and with no faint bleat or neigh of thanks, is hard indeed. Greenknowe, where the animals are as delightful as the people (and haunt it just as much), and where even the most frightening adventures are soothed and calmed by the most understanding of grandmothers, is one of my indulgences which make winter possible to bear.

Where Greenknowe's stout walls keep out the storms, mine let in the damp and draughts; where Greenknowe's furniture and myriad old and precious objects are polished and gleaming, mine are scratched and dull and dusty; where Greenknowe has the taciturn but most obliging Mr Boggis to row through the floods or bring in armfuls of apple-scented logs, here there is only me to struggle through the mud or heave the endless buckets of coal and the heavy logs up the steep steps. And, if there are ghosts of past residents here, I fear that they are united in appalled disapproval. All I can do, to bring part of Greenknowe here, is to fill the vases with those branches of dry winter twigs and watch them shoot into life. The ribes (or flowering currant) appears first, with tassels of white bells (although in the garden they are bright pink), which soon mingle with the catkins on the hazel, and the bright yellow of the forsythia, as if indeed someone had said *'Abracadabra! Let those sticks burst into flower.'*

Now I said to my mother, 'It will happen. You'll see.'

'Meanwhile, I've got a nasty feeling something else is about to happen,' she replied tersely. 'That woman was on the phone again about those whippets.'

'Oh, no! Poor little souls. I haven't made up my mind about them yet.'

'Well, I wish you wouldn't. It has been nice and peaceful around here with only four dogs.'

I looked at my mother guiltily. 'I know, I know. But I can't bear to think of Merlin's relations being sold off cheap to the first comer. Her husband has given her a deadline to get rid of them. They could end up anywhere.'

'Nice and peaceful with only four dogs,' repeated Mrs P firmly.

It was now some years since my first, much-loved whippet, Merlin, had died. At first, I had looked at the other whippets, tiny Bea and her daughters Misty and Gloucester, and almost blamed them for not dying instead of him. The three little bitches, however, had their own ways of coping with my grief. Bea and Misty followed me everywhere and took his place on my bed, but Gloucester took my attitude to heart and ignored me completely. By the time Mrs P's chihuahua, Winston, had arrived, and soon after a black whippet related to Merlin (which I also named Merlyn in the hopes of replacing the first, but learnt, too late, that he was quite irreplaceable), and finally Lily the brindled lurcher, Bea and Misty had become so much my shadows that I took then for granted. Until, one awful December, with blizzards raging, Bea suffered a stroke and gentle Misty developed a clot on her spine which killed her. A few short weeks later, dear, clownish old Blossom the pig died. None of those deaths can I bear to talk about even now, but they had a long-term effect.

'I've had enough horror and heartbreak with animals,' I stormed at the great moon which shone relentlessly over the white valley, helplessly buried in huge drifts, endorsing with its bitter light the sharpness of the wind which screamed insanely as it flicked the castles of snow into even more bizarre shapes. 'You will have no more new hostages, you old hag!'

It was a full moon and, when the wind is in the east, there is nothing more cruel. It is not at all the same moon which floats, large and golden and languid, from behind the hills in late summer and autumn. Neither has it any of the spark and joy of a spring moon. It is hard and cold and dead and I hate it. This one was so bright that it washed out the stars themselves. In my rage and grief I blamed it for everything and, true to my promise, no new animals came to the farm for a long while, except the lambs and kids that were born there.

I even found it possible then to sell those animals which were less than 'viable' (horrible word), and during that period, I regret to say, several goats, sheep and poultry went to very uncertain futures – futures I heard about eventually and which have haunted me ever since. At the time I was too busy gloating over my new-found thick skin, which protected me from my own emotions and deluded me into thinking that at last I was as hard-nosed as any of my farming neighbours and from now on need not apologize for my inadequacies as a sentimental fool. And, if sometimes I heard a faint cry of despair from that child I once was long ago, who had never had a real home of her own and had promised herself that one day she would have a place where any animal who needed a refuge would be welcome, I ignored it.

Fortunately, this bleak, unloving time was beginning to thaw by the return of Doli, but there was still enough of it left for me to remain fairly unmoved when I heard of the plight of the two whippet pups. In order to be helpful, I did make quite a few phone calls on their behalf, but didn't offer to have them myself, even though they were related both to the original Merlin and his replacement. The latter had been bred specially for me by a lady who owned Merlin's sister and her daughter. There had been five pups in the litter and one of them, a bitch, had been bought by an acquaintance of mine. Some years afterwards, she bred from her, simply because she'd seen a dog she fancied at some dinner party at a friend's house. There'd been no trouble selling the bitches in the litter, but the two dog pups were now five months old and her husband was determined not to keep them any more. There was to be no more nonsense about them going to 'good homes'. They were to be advertised and sold at once to the first comer. His wife had rung me to see if I could suggest a good home before the deadline came up.

'Cheek,' said Mrs P. 'She's got more space and more time than you and a husband to give her a hand. Why does she have to dump the problem on you?'

'Probably because she knows I can do as I please. Which she obviously can't. I don't know why she had to breed from her bitch.'

'True. But you won't have them yourself, will you? You swore when Bea and Misty died there'd be no more new dogs.'

'Not a chance.' I said and I tried to forget all about it.

My conscious mind succeeded very well, but at night I began to have dreams. I kept seeing the original Merlin's face gazing at me in anguish, and beside him stood Prince.

Prince was a little whippet which we'd rescued, years before, from an appalling fate, and who had found a wonderful home with my friend Terence, in London. He'd been bought cheaply by a farmer's son for rabbiting, been tired of, replaced by a couple of terriers, and left to starve to death in an old pigsty, still full of muck. They couldn't be bothered to waste a bullet on him. An old lady on a pension had got him away from there, but couldn't afford to keep him and advertised for a home. The Artist (who used to look after the farm for me then) saw the ad, collected Prince and nursed him, still covered with fleas and dreadfully emaciated, back to health. He would have stayed with us, for he had a lovely, happy nature in spite of everything, but when Terence saw him it was instant love between them. So Prince went to a life of utter luxury, with his own duvet, central heating and as many walks and as much food as he wanted. Terence's other whippet had cost a fortune and was of impeccable looks and pedigree, but Prince, who had every design fault possible, was very greatly loved. When he died, two short years later (the awful neglect of his first year did finally kill him), Terence was broken-hearted.

At last, after a week of these dreams and memories, and with Mrs P snorting disapproval in the background, I rang and offered to have one of the pups, the black one.

'But what about the other one?' cried their breeder. 'They've never been separated. I'll let you have them very cheaply if you'll take the two.'

I sighed. 'Have they been vaccinated?'

'No, I was going to let the new owners do that.'

'So,' raged Mrs P when I explained what I'd done, 'You've agreed to pay her £60 for the pair and about another twenty-odd to have them vaccinated. You must be out of your mind.'

I agreed with her but, haunted by the memory of Prince, I stuck to my bargain, if bargain you could call it.

Ike and Ginger Meggs were sick and shivering when they

arrived. The visit to the vet's en route, for their first jab, and the car journey, left them a pack of nerves for the next few days. Eventually it was possible to see that Ike, the black one, was the boss and a coward to boot. Ginger, the smaller, brindled pup, was more retiring, but very brave and very lovable. He had a look about him I'd seen somewhere before. Carefully I checked their pedigree certificates. And then I rang their breeder.

'Did you know much about the dog you mated your bitch to?' I inquired innocently.

'Not really,' she said. 'I just thought he was a good-looking dog.'

'Well, if you had bothered to do some research, you could have sold all the pups in that litter for anything you liked.'

There was a deep silence as I continued.

'You see they have, between them, some of the best racing, coursing and show blood in the country. Of course, on their mother's side there's the great Koh-I-Noor, who's won on the track and in the show ring. On their father's side there is none other than Madishan Moonlake. And goodness only knows what else.'

I've told the story of Luke (Madishan Moonlake) elsewhere. He was another rescue job when he was a puppy, and lived to become a legend in his own lifetime. He also resided in the flat upstairs when I was in London and Bea's litter of pups had been sired by him. Although those pups had either stayed with me or been given to very special friends, Luke's progeny was much prized normally and did not usually go begging a home.

After I had delivered this bombshell with some satisfaction to the breeder of Ike and Ginger, I rang Gay Robertson, Luke's owner, and told her what had happened.

'How strange!' she said. 'Koh-I-Noor's owner and I were only saying the other day that it's a pity nobody had ever combined our two lines. And now it seems someone has.'

'Without knowing what she was doing,' I said crossly.

'You'll have to race them,' said Gay.

'I'd love to,' I said, 'but they're nervy little things and Ike is only interested in fighting when he's running. Funnily enough, he's very like the original Merlin to look at and Ginger Meggs is very like Luke. It's all a bit *déjà vu* – reminds me of the two of them playing in the park.' For Luke and Merlin had been great friends and had met every day in Kensington Gardens when they were pups, tunnelling through the leaves, or haring round the great trees together. 'It's all very odd, really.'

'Too odd by half,' chimed in Mrs P from across the room as she eavesdropped on our conversation. 'You and your hunches and your dreams!'

I never did race Ike and Ginger, but it was good to see the pack flying across the fields with Lily. Two black, two brindled and one white dog, with fat Winston yipping along behind, and Doli galloping beyond the fence with her tail up. Everything looked normal again and the great frost was over.

'And I must admit,' said Mrs P, 'I was beginning to worry about you. It might be a nuisance having a daughter whose heart rules her head, but the other way round was a bit boring.'

I shook my head at her lovingly. One of the best things about having her for a mother is that no matter what idiocies I commit she's behind me every inch of the way.

'Look,' I said, 'the twigs have burst into flower and a while ago I saw the first snowdrop in the garden.'

A week later there were drifts of them all over the garden and if the real snow returned once or twice it was only half-hearted about it. We could stand and admire it as it floated gently enough for us to see the loveliness of the soft flakes, and it left every gate and every tree an individual beauty. Soon March was barging its way in, lambs were popping out all over the valley and Cliff Griffiths came knocking at my door to borrow a spade. One of his sheep had given birth right over a badger's exit hole and her lamb had fallen straight down. Cliff got it out all right, covered in dirt, a trifle bewildered but alive and full of go.

My own lambs, of course, were being born in the hay-shed on deep beds of straw. In the goat-shed, Gorgeous and Sophie decided to resume their feud.

One of the reasons I frequently feel like the headmistress of a boarding school here (as well as an overworked waitress, lavatory attendant and the madam of a certain house) is that part of my job involves keeping the peace between a lot of females, shut up together. For a long time all will be quiet, and then suddenly two of the sheep will start fighting, for no apparent reason. All day they carry on banging heads, butting each other up the behind and even ignoring their food in the struggle to score points. I've known them carry this on for a good week or more, till both of them are worn out and even I've given up trying to stop the battle. If I separate them, as soon as they are released (no matter how long that separation) they'll pick up the matter where they left off, until it seems to cease as suddenly as it began. Once I thought it had to do with a pecking order being challenged, but it's too persistent for that. Pecking-order affairs tend to be settled quickly and brutally and seem to have a chain reaction, with the whole flock joining in. But these one-to-one feuds (although sometimes a daughter might give her mother some help) seem to be purely obsessional and nobody ever wins.

The goats fight too, but not in the same silent, determined way as the sheep and it *is* usually a matter of deciding who comes where in the hierarchy. Except that none of them have ever actually liked Gorgeous very much. Even her mother, Dolores, had little time for her. It takes a lot to annoy Sophie, that most amiable of goats, but, some time back in the autumn, Gorgeous had managed to do it so thoroughly that Sophie was moved to thrash her mercilessly. I found the rest of the goats looking on with deep satisfaction as she did so, until I broke up the party and gave Sophie and Gorgeous a good boot to be going on with. And now, months later, when any untoward violent activity could cause them to abort their kids, the fight was resumed.

In those days, there were no pens in the goat-shed. It was a big open space where the goats could potter about at will, but each had her own favourite place between the old cattle barriers, which were still in place. On the whole, these places were respected, but Gorgeous, now that she was coming up to her time, became full of her own importance and began to trespass. Her mother, Dolores, had but to fix her with a beady eye as she approached her spot to make her back off, but Gorgeous is a big goat and the rest gave up their beds reluctantly, only to have them spurned and another one prodded and poked. Until she came to Sophie, who rose to the attack.

When the sheep fight, they charge each other, head down, and keep it up till either one gives way, or they stay with heads locked, disputing inches of ground with single-minded determination. The goats, on the other hand, gain height first by rearing up on their hind legs and then crashing heads as they descend. When it's merely a greeting or a ritual reminder of who is who, they can come down and touch brows as delicately as a feather and that is beautiful to watch. When they're in earnest, the force of their impact is terrifying and often very bloody.

Now Sophie and Gorgeous stood back and prepared to rise in the air. Neither of them managed more than a few inches, hampered as they were by their enormous bulk. I was still travelling fast from the other side of the shed to stop them, as they settled into a kind of rumbling trot, like a pair of heavily armoured knights clumsily on foot, charging and missing, turning and charging and missing. The other goats settled into their hollows of straw and watched as Sophie scored a direct hit on Gorgeous's flank, just as I leapt the barrier of the feeding channel, too late.

Which is probably why Gorgeous kidded four days earlier than she should have (although, being her, it was more likely a desire to be as inconvenient as possible), choosing the very day that Mary Price was due to come and have a conference about the next radio series.

'Don't you think you could put it off till after lambing and kidding,' I'd pleaded when she rang.

'Oh, don't worry about that,' she'd cried. 'I'll help you. I don't mind being elbow-deep in placenta.'

I doubted that, but there was a bit of a lull in hostilities and no one was really due to lamb or kid again for a couple of days. I got out the broom and began to tidy up.

Having visitors at any time, even when I'm looking forward to them, is a pain in the neck because I have to clean the house up. I've learnt to ignore their assurances that I needn't bother for *them*. If they saw the mess I normally live in, the house always being the last to get mucked out in the usual run of things, all their illusions would be shattered. If they insist on coming, I do like to let them enjoy themselves, with warm fires, fairly well swept rooms and dusted furniture, the awful tide of mess hastily cleared away into my 'office' and myself fairly confident that, should they penetrate into the kitchen or the bathroom, both will be tolerably decent. Tall visitors are rather more of a problem, which is why I ask people their height if I haven't met them before. If they are over five foot six (my own height) it means more work dusting up higher, for usually what goes on above my own eye level I would rather not know about. It is for this reason that I do not appreciate people who 'just drop in'. Anyway, getting everything in some sort of order means frantic rushing about with broom and duster in the middle of the night (any earlier and the dogs will mess it up), a very early rising to get the stock done, fires blazing, loos checked, myself tidy, dogs walked and subdued, and a general air of sweet smells, peace and harmony pervading everything. I usually reckon a visit of three hours means three days' hard work. One to get ready, one to entertain and one to get over it.

Sometimes it has occurred to me to keep the place tidy all the time. But then I'd never get anything else done and, as Mrs P is fond of remarking, 'If you don't want any visitors, clean the place up, have plenty of food in the cupboards and nothing much on hand to do. You won't see a soul.'

It's a theory we have often tested and it never fails.

On the morning Mary arrived from Bristol, I was already bleary-eyed from the midnight housework, but everything outside seemed fine: all the lambs were thriving; those sheep still waiting their time looked good for a long while yet; the goats were reassuringly firm as to pelvic ligaments, and lacked their proper bagged-up udders. That is, except for Gorgeous, whose bag was balloon-shaped and stiff, as she fussed and dug into the straw, and her ligaments had gone soft and squishy.

I looked at her with loathing, marched her away into the freshly disinfected loose-box and left her there rearranging the bedding.

Mary arrived in a bright, clean BBC car and, with shining eyes, looked around at the waves of daffodils rippling across the lawn, the chubby lambs tottering around the hay field, the distant cliffs of the Fans etched in snow, and the evocative plume of woodsmoke coming from the cottage chimney.

'Oh, how lovely it is to get out of town!' she said happily and began unloading boxes of tapes, dozens of bulging files and a couple of Sainsbury's bags full of 'specials' I'd asked her to bring. No one travelling direct from Bristol would dream of coming without getting a list of groceries to collect from Sainsbury's. If they've come for no other reason than to see me, they call it 'doing a Sainsbury's run for you'.

Before I gave Mary a hand to carry everything inside, I glanced at Gorgeous. She was fast asleep.

We got a lot of work done, in between me dashing out to the loose-box to check on my goat. Lunch came and went, and I thought we might be safe to go for the walk on the meadow which Mary was pleading for.

'A quiet stroll by your river and I'll feel set up properly,' she said.

As we came outside, a sharp north-easterly breeze had blown up and a few casual flakes of snow drifted down. The sheep and lambs had retreated to their shed, the daffodils drooped and Gorgeous was yelling desperately. My hostess smile disappeared. I ran, tearing my coat off and rolling my sleeves up, and left Mary to follow me.

'Shall I call the vet?' she called, peering over the top of the loose-box door, as I frantically poured warm water from a thermos I had waiting, soaped my arms up to the elbows and began gently to probe inside Gorgeous.

'No. Come in, sit down and shut up,' I said grimly. 'I think it's a breech birth.'

'I'll get the vet, then.'

'No. I might need you. Just sit still.' I said and turned back to my task impatiently. It *was* a breech birth and, although I was fairly sure I could deliver the kid safely, it's got to be fast because if the kid's head is still inside when the cord is broken it could drown if you delay. This one didn't even have its back feet coming out first. All I could feel was the round hardness of its little behind. For once Gorgeous let me get on with the job in peace, find the legs, flip them out and then pull the kid as quickly as possible.

'Oh!' said a small voice behind me. 'How *wonderful!*'

'Get one of those towels,' I commanded over my shoulder as I tipped the kid upside down, and swung it to clear the mucus out of its nose and lungs. It gave a small strangled cry and I handed it to Mary.

'Keep that warm. I don't want this goat to move. I think the next one's got its head back.'

'The vet?' said Mary as she took the kid.

I glared at her and Gorgeous stood up.

'Leave that kid,' I said to Mary. 'Hold Gorgeous steady.' And, while the goat struggled to get her first-born, I wrestled with the second, a big kid with its head firmly pointing the wrong way.

'Bugger it,' I said as I tried to turn the head.

'Don't you think the vet?' whispered Mary.

I paused in my task. 'For someone who doesn't mind being elbow-deep in placenta, you panic easily,' I said nastily.

By the time the second kid was safely out and Gorgeous was deliriously washing both of them and whickering ecstatically, Mary had gone quite limp. She sat on a bale of straw and stared.

'One more to go,' I announced. 'With any luck this one might be coming the right way.'

It didn't. It was a breech birth again, but a small kid and not so difficult to pull quickly. I sat back on my heels and grinned at my poor producer.

'I think that's the lot. Hand me another towel, will you?' and I waved an imperious and bloody arm at her.

Mary didn't move for a moment, just sat on her bale of straw and stared at me.

'Do you know what?' she said at last. 'I *wish* I'd had a *tape-recorder*. That was magical.'

'As if someone had said "Abracadabra. Let that goat burst into kids",' I said.

'What?'

'Forget it!' I said and began to wash my arms in the bucket.

What I didn't tell Mary then, or ever afterwards, was that if she hadn't been there I *would* have panicked and called the vet.

'Which just goes to prove,' said Mrs P tartly, 'that you can do anything you want, provided you've got an audience.'

Three days later, while Gorgeous was once again screaming and yelling and indulging herself in a massive display of post-natal depression, Sophie, quietly, and without any fuss, produced her kids. One of them was a silvery fawn female and, as time was to prove, she really *was* magical.

Chapter 13

'I wish,' I wrote in my diary for the 2nd of April that year, 'that I could capture that feeling of birth and spring which is part of the very smell of a day like this, and store it somewhere for ever. This morning the sun beat up across the valley, lighting one side of the trees and barns, as it haloed out of the mist on the mountain. Douglas and Daisy ate their egg, the kids were out in the sun going wild, the birds were singing in echoes and Monkey Bum's lamb was chasing the Light Sussex hen. Over in the oak tree by the gate a demented blue tit was beeping its heart out. I feel tired to extinction, dirty, scruffy and very, very old.'

After Mary's visit (had she been from another planet?), March had gone on spitting with cold, the house had sunk once more under its pall of dust and bits of hay and straw, and I made infrequent contact with my bed as the sheep stepped up their lambing, usually in the middle of the night or at the first twitch of dawn. Mostly that year they had twins or triplets. If it was a single, it was so big that both of us sweated and cried to get it delivered. And every time Gorgeous heard me pottering forth she began her awful banshee wailing and woke everyone else up too, including Doli, who neighed imperiously for me to come and top up her hay net. It was not a peaceful time, but I forgot it all when April came in smiling calmly, the new moon loitered in the ash tree and the perfume from the scented violets under my window reminded me that there was life after lambs.

Not entirely, actually. Lambs and kids have a miraculous way of getting themselves into completely unforeseen trouble; sheep and goats alike can either turn homicidal, or decide it's all been too much for them and need persuading back from the grave. When my other bosses airily assume that once the actual birth

144

process is over, I'll be free to attack the work they've been waiting for, it's difficult to explain that the few weeks afterwards are even more fraught sometimes, and this time without the immediate lift of the heart that a newly born animal, which you have struggled for, can bring.

Ungratefully, then, as I scan the fields for marauding crows, rescue lambs from impossible places, hold recalcitrant goats while their kids feed, make sure the geese have laid their eggs in a safe place, hunt down broody hens in the bushes and worry about the patches of nettles, docks and thistles springing up everywhere, I forget that not long before, I was pleading for spring to come. For a moment I think back regretfully to the cold, still days: the quiet, plodding sheep, too heavy to be a nuisance; the long, deep slumbers of the goats; the huddling together peacefully of the hens; and Doli with her mind on food and nothing else. What she had it on now was a strong, virile stallion. Well, even a little weak one would have done her at a pinch.

'Sorry, old girl,' I told her as she pranced up to the gate, tail in air and snorting hopefully, 'they don't like their stallions to run out with mares like you any more. And you won't have it the other way. Go and stand in the duck pond and cool off.'

Doli tossed her mane and galloped back to the end of the field, followed by the kids having a great lark.

'You don't really want to put her in foal, do you?' asked Mrs P, as I sat down wearily after another session of phoning up people with possible stallions.

'Not really,' I sighed, 'but neither do I want Doli roaring and raging about and trying to hop over the fence for the next few months. Bertie reckons having a foal might sort her problem out.'

Doli, it has to be said, managed to come into season at any time of the year, except in the very worst of the cold weather. She had something called, most appropriately, nymphomania. I can never get the real hang of it, but it had something to do with the malfunctioning of her ovaries. It not only made her a nuisance on a day-to-day basis, it also meant that it was very difficult to get her in foal. The only way to make sure of catching the right moment was to let her run out with the stallion, but not a lot of owners like them to do that, and insist on them serving only 'in hand' – in other words, with both of them firmly on the end of a halter.

'Oh, well,' I said now, 'I'll have to leave it till I get this London trip out of the way. You'll be OK for a couple of days, will you?'

'Of course! When haven't I been all right? Gwynneth will be over twice a day to do the stock and carry anything in for me.'

'Thank God for Gwynneth,' I said, and tottered upstairs to try and find something respectable to wear. Being fashionable or even vaguely smart was not something I aspired to. Just clean, and clad in something with no holes and big enough to cover the multitude of sins Mrs P's cooking had laid upon my shape, was all I could hope for.

'Give me lambing any day,' I stormed that night as I slammed down the iron, rescued a blouse from the pups, flicked wet hair out of my eyes and remembered I didn't have a respectable pair of tights to my name. 'And I'll never get this purple stuff out from under my nails.'

It was the usual thing. If I have to go away, everything on the place starts limping, coughing, getting bloat or just generally curling up to die. The remedies for all these ailments are mostly smelly, sticky or brightly coloured, like the foot-rot spray.

'Does it matter?' asked Mrs P.

'Of course it matters. The first thing that's going to happen is a photo session with one of the Dailies and as the pictures are black and white it'll look as if I've got dirty nails.'

'All part of the country image! Country author comes to town. Take a few bits of straw with you.'

'I don't want to be a country author,' I grumbled. 'I want to be urbane and literary.'

'So?' said Mrs P, cocking an eyebrow at me. 'Why didn't you write that kind of book?'

'I couldn't,' I mumbled. 'I could hardly write anything.'

'I think,' said Mrs P slowly, 'that I will take my little dog and go to bed.' And, wise woman, she left me to pull myself out of the spiral of misery rapidly overtaking me. She'd heard it all before, endlessly, over the years it had taken me to write that first book.

146

If it hadn't been for the persistence of my editor, John Newth, it would never have got past the thinking stage.

Like half the world, I'd always said that if only I had the time I'd write a book. Not just any old book. A book to set the world on fire. A book of pure literary genius. Or at least an absolutely gripping one. And then, given the chance, I'd behaved abominably. Poor Mrs P had winced at the cries of rage and despair, the endless sound of tearing paper, and had listened patiently to me moaning and complaining and finding any excuse rather than go back into that office and write. It didn't help that the post brought so many other 'country' books for me to look at for the series. Some were very good indeed, some were funny and some were plain awful. And now I'd finally added to the pile, some other poor reviewer would have to read it, and I had no happy illusions about my literary ability left at all. They were about the last illusions I'd had left, so their loss was deeply felt.

'Well,' soothed Mrs P, 'if the publishers didn't think it was all right they wouldn't print it.' It was not the right thing to say.

'Ah,' I pounced, 'they only want it because of the radio series. That's all. It doesn't matter what you write these days as long as someone's heard of you.'

I suppose it's a little unfair of me, therefore, to feel quite murderous if anyone else says the same thing. As they do, very often.

But getting back to the matter of illusions. I had, over the years, greatly envied the authors I'd interviewed, especially the brand new ones who had lived in obscurity till then and were now, if only temporarily, the darlings of their publishers' PR teams. The look of amazed joy and excitement in their eyes (for – who knew? – their book might be a bestseller and meanwhile all the lunches and the concentrated attention of reporters like me made up a new kind of wonderland) was almost all I ever remembered about most of them. If their books and names have faded from my mind, their faces never have.

As I whizzed some curlers into my hair that night I peered into the mirror. Was it there, that same bemused look of euphoria?

Not a trace. Just sheer terror.

The next day, sitting on the train to London, a coffee sploshing on the table in front of me, the murmur of voices in the background and the soft Cotswold countryside flying past the window, sanity returned and I decided to enjoy the trip and pretend that it was the author in me they wanted, not the radio presenter. I wouldn't have to get up at five (as I had that morning), I could stay in clean clothes from morning till night, soak in deep baths without dogs banging against the door and whining at me and, with any luck, the hotel would have room service (breakfast in bed) and possibly a civilized restaurant. I could even see a few old friends.

It wasn't quite like that. To begin with, John Newth had left and I had to face up to a new editor, but in those days the publishers had their London offices in a wonderful old rickety building near the British Museum. Everyone who came in and out had to be vetted by Louise, she of the deep voice and an air of having seen it all before, and weren't they like a lot of children who needed reminding of their own names half the time! Getting Louise's approval seemed far more important than my new editor's at the time. It was Louise who said 'How nice, dear' when I showed her the unicorn tiles I'd bought in a little shop on the other side of the narrow street. I bought quite a lot of them and they were all different. There were big unicorns and baby unicorns, funny unicorns and deeply romantic ones, but there was no signature on the tiles. When, a long time after, I found the man who'd made them, he was just as diverse and surprising as his tiles.

Meanwhile, in the blur of taxis, studios and phone calls and newspaper interviews and more taxis, studios, and so on, the unicorn tiles gave me courage and, more important, stopped me losing my temper. I understood at last why all those other authors had gazed at me in astonishment and said breathlessly, 'Oh, but you've actually *read* the book.' It's obviously a rare phenomenon. Only one interviewer, at the dear old World Service in Bush House (where I got my own first training), had bothered to do more than glance at the blurb, and he knew the book better than I did. For the rest . . .

'Good heavens,' giggled Philippa from the publicity department, 'I've never been round with an author before who made the interviewer stop and ask proper questions.'

'Well,' I growled, 'they all seem to think that everywhere past Hammersmith is without benefit of electricity, running water and telephone. And the next one who asks me if I don't miss the dear animals in one breath, and then wouldn't I love to be back in London in the next – well, I'll do something a bit nasty, I think.'

But all I did was the worst crime of all. At the end of a long day, faced with yet another interviewer asking the same boring old questions which had very little to do with me or my book, I simply answered 'No' and left them to scrabble out of it unaided.

Of course the pro in me understood their dilemma. You can't read everything (especially these days, when the authors are lining up three deep outside the studios) but you can 'dip' read. You can do your victim the courtesy of at least appearing to be interested in what they have to say and let them feel, for that brief time, that they are the most important person in your life. Illusions again, but that's what it's all about. And if the interviewers had this deadening effect on me, who knew the score and felt at home in a studio, God knows what my poor first-time authors of long ago were like by the time they finished doing the rounds. Had it all gone, that look of heaven in their eyes?

My own eyes were just a bit depressed as I stood on the platform at Paddington Station. At least there'd be time for a good long doze on the train. All around me people shuffled their trolleys and suitcases into the charging position as the indicator above began whizzing and spinning and printing up the latest train news. A groan went up. The Swansea train would be delayed.

I didn't mind too much. I like Paddington Station. It's full of memories of exhilarating departures and romantic arrivals. There was, for instance, that incredible year when Mrs P and I still lived in London for most of the time, and the Artist kept watch at the farm, where we were to join him for Christmas.

It was the day before Christmas Eve and all of London was sheer misery, with a miner's strike, a rail go-slow and an IRA bombing campaign. We couldn't wait to get away.

We arrived at Paddington with suitcases heavy with food and presents, Mrs P's budgerigar Oscar, and my two Burmese cats, Pip and Suyin. Not wanting to join the usual charge for the Welsh train, I got us there nice and early and safely tucked up in window seats. No sooner had we settled ourselves, and our livestock and luggage than it was announced that this was to be the only train leaving for Wales that day, and indeed it would replace the boat train going on to Pembroke. People hoping to travel on that had better join this one.

They were mostly Irish, of course, travelling to catch the ferry, and they came roaring into the carriages with jokes and songs and crates of beer. They filled the seats, the gangways and the exits. Mrs P loved every minute of it. She likes an impromptu party.

'Though how we'll ever get out of here I don't know,' she laughed as we fended off the waving arms.

Grinning, I turned to look out of the window at the people still hurrying along the platform, desperately looking for a space to board the train. And then I saw it. A carrier bag, with two sinister wires sticking out of the top, placed squarely on the platform directly under our windows.

As I felt the blood descending rapidly to my feet, two tall, jackbooted motor-cycle policemen strode through the barrier. Frantically I tried to catch their attention, but in that hermetically sealed, sound-proofed train it was hopeless. They marched along, heads up, within feet of the carrier bag. What was it they'd been saying on the tannoy, before we'd boarded the train, about reporting any unattended parcels at once?

'Mother,' I whispered. 'Don't panic. Just get yourself and Oscar under the table if you can.'

'Why?'

'Just do it. *Please!*' And I pointed silently to the carrier bag outside. 'Don't say anything or there'll be a stampede. I'll just pass the message along quietly and see if they'll clear the doorways so people can get off.'

Mrs P looked at the bag, cast an eye over the press of people above us, tried the table for size, decided that getting under it was hopeless and took action.

'Hey! You lot in the doorway get out and let us off. There's a bomb on the platform.'

There was a deep, cold silence.

'What did she say? A bomb?' called someone from the middle of the gangway. I closed my eyes and began to say the Lord's Prayer very quickly. Above me I could feel bodies craning towards the window.

'Ah sure! That's no bomb! That's Liam's new radio! Someone get out and pass it in, will you?' And, as I opened my eyes, 'the bomb' was being handed overhead to someone far down the carriage. As everyone shouted with laughter at Liam and his forgetful ways, the train began to move.

It should have been a nightmare journey, but it was one of the best I've ever made. We had to change at Reading and somehow, in all that incredible mob, I got Mrs P, three very heavy suitcases, Oscar and the cats once again installed in window seats. As we lurched out of Reading, I began to wish I hadn't. The train was actually leaning to one side with the weight. And from then on there wasn't a dull moment. The large Irish contingent kept us all laughing with their jokes, sent up orders to the buffet (there was one, surprisingly) and handed coffees and sandwiches back down through the carriages. When that supply ran out, they cracked open the beer they'd been saving for the ferry. Other passengers shared out fruit and cakes and biscuits, and a charming Indian lady, looking like a flower in her sari, fed sesame seeds to Oscar.

At one point an alarming rumour shot through the train. It was not going to stop till Pembroke. Not even at Cardiff. Everyone (including the Irish who were going to Pembroke anyway, so it wasn't their problem) was appalled. But we put our heads together, paper and cardboard were produced miraculously and we got busy printing huge notices, 'MEET US AT PEMBROKE', to press against the windows at our waiting relatives and friends as we flashed past. We had just finished when the train slowed down and stopped at Cardiff. It took them a long time to unpack the passengers wishing to alight and no one was allowed on.

'Not that it's made much difference,' said Mrs P as we started moving again. 'How are *we* going to get out?'

'Don't you worry about that,' cried one of our Irish friends. 'We're big strong boys and we'll carry you out.' Which is more or less what they did.

The Artist told me later that when the train came lurching into view of Neath station he thought that nothing would ever be able to get out of it. Faces and hands were pressed against windows and bodies obscured everything. When it stopped, the doors exploded open and people came hurtling out. Meanwhile, inside, our Irish friends handed Oscar (loud bird noises accompanying him all along the carriage), then the cats (much crying of 'Pussies coming up'), those terrible, heavy suitcases ('This is where the bomb was all the time'), Mrs P, and finally myself, hand over hand, till they hoisted us all out onto the platform and wished us Merry Christmas. The whole carriage waved, as best they could, when the train lurched off again. As it dwindled away down the track, I suddenly felt very lonely.

I was still smiling at the memory when, back on Paddington Station such a long while after, a voice expressed British Rail's regret at a further delay for the Swansea train. All around me lips tightened and frowns deepened. This was no party crowd. We perched on our luggage and endured . . . .

And just as I wrote that last sentence the dogs began whining at the door of the little room I call the 'office' and I had to leave myself sitting on a suitcase on Paddington Station and go and feed them. There was no chance for quite some time, as I hurried about attending to horses and goats and poultry, to come back and move that other me forward in time and it seemed, when I gave it thought, as if I was looking down a telescope at myself waiting . . . . When I finally returned to my desk, ready to move that doll-like figure forward, it came to life and said, 'But don't you remember? Have you forgotten Archie Ogden and Tom Percy and "Sam" Weller and George Thomas?' And suddenly I did.

It's early morning and Paddington is a-bustle with commuters, as well as the long-distance travellers. There are no big high-speed trains with their sleek open carriages and their smell of aerosols and air-conditioning. There are no monstrous, wobbly luggage trolleys, but there are lots of porters hurrying around and, as I run breathlessly onto the platform where the Cardiff train is waiting, a figure in a gold-braided hat moves forward to greet me. He is a full inspector and he's all mine; Inspector Tom Percy has nothing to do for the rest of the day but look after me.

'I've got you a good first-class seat,' he tells me, 'and as soon as we're on the way I've organized a cup of coffee. Unless, of course, you'd rather have breakfast.'

'No, just coffee will be fine,' and I follow him up the steps and into the compartment where a Reserved notice hangs above one of the plush seats. I look around nervously at the other passengers, all of them men and already deep in their newspapers. Inspector Tom Percy whispers in my ear.

'I think, if I were you, I'd start with the ones at the other end of the train and work back. I'll go and warn them you'll be along and smooth the way a bit.'

'Thank you, Mr Percy,' I say and, as he leaves, my companions glance up, cast a quick look at my legs, nod affably and return to their reading. I rummage in my briefcase and try to look busy. The train give a lurch and begins to move.

It was a curious assignment. I was being employed to find out about the travelling habits of the better-heeled British Public. I'd already been wandering around East Anglia for weeks, with a Golden Pass, doing long unstructured interviews with amused businessmen, or academics returning to Cambridge. The market research firm which had sent me to Ireland had been so pleased with the results that they'd put me forward to British Rail as one of their best people and sent me straight off to East Anglia. I got to know every bump on that line, all the little stations, all the guards and even a lot of the drivers. And, as the firm was pretty generous with their expenses (if not the actual fees), I got to know some of the best hotels too. But I had no sooner finished with that job than the Western Region decided to carry out a similar survey. Which was how I first fell in love with Paddington Station. For three hilarious days, everything tingled with romance.

Not that I felt particularly romantic when the train began its journey to Cardiff. Apart from the fact that a real inspector had been appointed to make sure none of the passengers got trouble-some, trying to keep my concentration and jotting down answers as the train bent itself around the track, and then spending a couple of hours in Cardiff with nothing to do, was not a very pleasing prospect. This was far more organized than the East Anglian job, where I'd pottered about as the fancy took me. Now I had a definite train to catch each day and Tom Percy to make sure I kept busy. There was another interviewer travelling on an earlier train and it was vital we didn't get mixed up.

Tom Percy slid open the door of the compartment and beckoned me outside.

'Right! They're expecting you along there. No one objects to answering questions. Your coffee's waiting, too, and I've just had a message for you to meet up with your friend in Cardiff.'

'What friend?'

'The other interviewer. Thought you might like to have lunch together and a chat.'

'Oh dear!' I groaned, imagining some properly qualified psychologist (for these so-called 'depth interviews' they usually employed the real thing) all eager to compare notes. I followed my inspector, switched on my most winning smile and claimed my first victim.

When the train got to Cardiff I gave everyone the slip, found a park where the sun was shining on a brilliant display of daffodils and the birds were singing wildly, and buried myself in a book. Leaving just enough time to catch my train back, I skirted round the ticket barrier and was hailed by Tom Percy and a tall, gangling and wildly enthusiastic young man.

'Hi! I'm Archie Ogden. Tom and I have been looking everywhere for you. Guess what! My inspector's called Weller! I call him Sam.' The American accent halted the hurrying passengers and I looked up at the twinkling eyes and waving arms in astonishment. 'What a shame!' said Archie Ogden. 'You're train's just leaving. See you tomorrow. Tom here'll make sure you don't run away again.'

He stood waving happily and chatting and joking with 'Sam' Weller as Tom Percy and I gazed back at the distant station.

'Nice young chap,' remarked my inspector. 'Weller said he's a real character. Had all the passengers laughing. You should have waited for him.' He nodded sternly like a father.

If I'd any ideas to the contrary the next day, Tom Percy and the entire staff of both Paddington and Cardiff stations saw that I didn't get a chance to put them into operation. That both Archie Ogden and I might have been romantically otherwise engaged at the time didn't seem to enter their calculations. We were both young and not bad-looking and they decided to matchmake. Even the porters nodded and winked at me when I arrived for my train, Tom Percy settled me into my seat like a mother hen and, when we arrived in Cardiff, made sure I stayed around to meet up with Archie.

'Let's give 'em a run for their money,' said Archie, who was a bright lad, a postgraduate student and Dickens fanatic (hence his delight in 'Sam' Weller) who was earning a bit of experience and money in his spare time. 'It'll give 'em a kick to think they've fostered the big romance. Let's go off somewhere and come back all glowing.'

We went to see Llandaff Cathedral. As we stood beneath the altar I said, 'The last time I was here, I was a marauding Saxon. I had to leap over that bit there, pull up a cardboard cross furiously, make a terrible din, and exit left. I even had a helmet with horns.'

'Gee!' breathed Archie. 'What the hell were you doing that for?'

'It was when I was studying dance. They got our studio to stage a pageant about St Teilo, who brought Christianity to this part of Wales, and I was one of the baddies. The choirboys outside gave us a terrible time.'

'What were you up to with the choirboys?' asked Archie.

'Well, when we stopped being marauding Saxons, we had to skip round the back and put on long purple robes and take a lighted candle and process up the centre aisle behind all these sweetly carolling choirboys for the finale. We were a great deal older than them, but you'd never have believed it out in that dressing room. I threatened to set one alight with my candle if he didn't behave.'

'And did they?'

'Butter, as they say, would not have melted in their mouths when they came out into the Cathedral. But it's odd to see it now, all silent and empty. It was completely covered with scenery and people and sound then. Afterwards we were ushered straight back to the people we were billeted on, and went home to Surrey the next day. I've always meant to come back and see the Cathedral as it normally looks.'

'Speaking of which,' said Archie, 'I think your train awaits, madam.'

The following day, the whole of the staff on the line was in on the secret. When Archie and I met up in Cardiff they treated us as if we were a honeymoon couple. We fled onto a bus and went to the beach at Penarth, where we sat eating cheese and drinking wine, and suddenly I was sorry that the job was nearly ended.

'No interviews tonight?' said Tom Percy when he greeted me beside the train.

I yawned. 'No, thank heaven. I've done the full quota now. But do you think it would be possible for me to see the engine on the way back this time?'

'Of course,' he replied, and gave me a sympathetic glance as I cast melting eyes at the lone figure of Archie gazing up from the platform. 'I'll have a word with the driver and I'll come and collect you. The train's crowded tonight. I've got your seat safe' – he lowered his voice -- 'but I've had to put you in with the politicians. George Thomas the MP is in there with a few others.'

'Well, I hope they don't talk politics.' I stifled another yawn. The sun and wind and wine were working fast.

Apologizing, I stepped over the legs in the compartment, nodded at the man opposite, who smiled and offered to put my briefcase up on the rack for me, and settled back into my corner seat.

When I woke, the dark countryside had given way to brilliant lights and we were obviously approaching Paddington. Tom Percy appeared at the door.

'Mr Percy,' I cried scrambling up, 'I thought you were coming to get me to see the engine.'

'I tried to,' he said reproachfully, 'several times! But Mr Thomas there,' – and he pointed to the man opposite me – 'he wouldn't let me wake you. Every time I came in, he "sshhed" me.'

'Quite right!' said George Thomas, as he handed down my briefcase. 'You looked so peaceful. I made everyone stay quiet. It seemed a pity to wake you.'

I've often wondered since, whether that desire to let those who will slumber in peace, stood him in good stead when they made him Speaker of the House of Commons.

So I never did see the engine. Neither did I see Archie Ogden or Tom Percy ever again. But one day that journey from Paddington to Wales was to become the most familiar of them all . . . .

156

And now, will that figure slumping on her suitcase move nearer the present, and get back onto the train for Swansea?

'No! Because, if you remember, I nearly didn't catch it. I almost caught the one to Penzance instead.'

'A bit of an exaggeration. You *wanted* to catch it. Once, you might have, but not by then. So you sat there and pretended you were going to catch it. As once you caught it, hot, thirsty, tired and clutching a bundle of paperbacks you didn't really want to read. But you had to, to catch up on your homework. By then, of course, you thought you'd made it. A real broadcaster at last . . . .'

'It will only take you twenty-four hours. If you catch the late afternoon train, Jeannie and Derek will put you up for the night. I'm having all the books sent round by special messenger.' Rosalie Swedlin was another persuasive American and she'd been badgering me for days to do this publishers' tape with the Tangyes. I quite liked the idea of a trip to Cornwall, all expenses paid, but I was flat out with work at the time, including a daily live programme that week. Finally, I'd given in.

'How many books has he written?' I sighed.

'I'll send them all, shall I?' Rosalie had said.

'Yes. I'll read them on the train. I won't have a minute till then. I read the first one years ago.'

'*Gull on the Roof*? You know the story then. She was the PR at the Savoy and he was in MI5 and they threw it all up to go and grow potatoes and daffodils in Cornwall. The books are tremendously popular. This last one is *Cottage on a Cliff* and that's really what the interview is to be about mainly. Derek can't leave Cornwall, so if you do the interview we'll have it copied and send it round to all the radio stations. I'll get your tickets and send them round with the books. You'll be able to eat on the train.'

And that was the sole thought sustaining me as I leapt out of the taxi and caught the late afternoon train to Penzance, by a whisker. I'd been tied up in studios all day and hadn't had a thing to eat except a piece of toast early that morning. All the talking and rushing on that hot summer's day had left me with a raging thirst that only a gallon of tea would slake.

But even a thirst like that won't make me queue if I can help it. I decided to wait till things calmed down a bit and the multitude waiting to go in to the dining car had thinned out a little. I left it a bit too late.

'No, I'm sorry, madam. Afternoon tea is over now. There is no buffet on this train. I can't let you into the dining car now as it's being prepared for dinner. That is fully booked for both sittings. It's the height of the season, you see, and it's Friday afternoon.'

'I'll die if I don't have something to drink,' I declared.

The guard looked at my wild eyes and red face.

'I'll see what I can do,' he said at last, and returned some time later with a cup of coffee. It was the only thing that passed my lips all that long journey. I passed most of it trying to keep my eyes open and concentrate on the pile of books Rosalie had sent me. I'd managed to read *Cottage on a Cliff* in between one thing and another, but to do the job properly I felt I should look carefully at the others too. It was pretty hopeless. Hunger, thirst and weariness made me irritable. I began to resent these people with their flower farm and their donkeys and their gulls up on the roof. They'd probably be pretty spartan people too, all joyful skipping through the meadows and homespun philosophy. Not the sort of people who would understand the immediate necessity to feed and water me when I arrived. I couldn't bear to think what the beds would be like.

By the time the train began to stop at the odd station, I was in a foul mood. What I was reading went straight in one eye and out the other. People started to leave the compartment and at last I noticed the scenery – the deep rich haze of the setting sun, the little tucked-in villages, the distant glimpses of the sea.

'Lovely, isn't it?' said a voice. There was one passenger left. She looked as if she'd trotted straight out of an Agatha Christie village, sensible tweeds (summer and all), gardening hands and a round busybody face, which was beaming at me happily.

'I see you've got Derek Tangye's books there. One of my favourite authors!'

'Oh? Do you know him?'

'I feel as if I do. If you read his books you can't help it. Well, this is my stop.' She began collecting her various magazines and bags and departed.

It was growing dark now and the train began to run along the

158

sea. What was that large mound out in the bay? St Michael's Mount at last? The train was slowing and at last it stopped. Penzance and not a great deal of life visible either. Certainly no sign of anyone to meet me. And it was just on eleven.

'Is it Jeanine?' The man hurrying along the platform was waving and, as he panted up to me, he relieved me of my bag and looked around to see if there was anything else he could do to help. As usual, I refused to let Gert out of my own hands, but he insisted and took the brown holdall firmly away from me.

'I am dying,' I told him, 'of hunger and thirst.'

'Ah! Dinner booked out? I should have warned Rosalie. Right! Say no more. Car's over here.' He led the way to an estate car, ushered me into it, swung rapidly out of the car park and onto the road and said not another word until finally we turned left onto a small track, bumped down it and across a little stream and up towards the cottage glowing with light. He jumped from the car as the door opened and a woman appeared.

'Jeannie,' he cried, waving her back. 'She is dying of hunger and thirst. Dinner all booked out on the train.'

'Ah! Give me two minutes.' And she disappeared again.

Crunching gravel, the soft sea sounds and the warm scent of escallonia; dark into light, thick white on stone walls, bright colours in pictures and books and flowers, gay chintz on the chairs; the chink of cups, a kettle boiling and the frizzle of a frying pan.

'Whisky?' asked Derek, waving a bottle at me.

'I'd rather have tea for the moment.'

'Have both,' called Jeannie as she peered, smiling, through the hatch from the little galley where she was working at the stove.

It was very late by then, but not by a hint or a glance did the Tangyes seem inconvenienced. They fed me and they listened to me as if they had all the time in the world. They made me feel clever and brave and very very welcome, till the bored, cynical reporter was shed like a skin and back was the sense of adventure and surprise – the beginning of the holidays.

A gull crying on the roof, feet above my head, woke me early next morning and I knelt up in bed and opened the window. The light was brilliant and more gulls were wheeling in from the sea.

I wanted urgently to rush outside and see everything, but the rest of the cottage was silent. Remembering how late I'd kept my hosts out of their own beds the night before, I sat down and tried to see where the chickens had once perched. For my room had once been a chicken shed, bought by the Tangyes for some extra space. In those days they'd bunched violets in here, Jeannie had written her book *Meet Me at the Savoy* and friends had camped out in it. Now it was covered with bright, sophisticated wallpaper on ceiling and walls and there was a flounced dressing table with matching material, a built-in wardrobe and the lingering touch of an expensive perfume. At one end a sliding door covered the deep, cavern-like hole which had been made through the thick wall of the cottage and which led into the room I'd been in the night before. At the other was a bathroom with big taps, a roaring heater and a view of the meadows behind.

If you can imagine a chicken shed overlaid with a combined atmosphere of the Savoy Hotel, one of the old-style, grandiose P & O liners and a holiday beach house, you've got it. I wanted to stay there for ever. But Derek now appeared with a steaming cup of tea, there was the smell of fresh coffee and toast coming from the cottage, and somewhere, a donkey was braying.

We sat in the little sun porch and ate breakfast and watched the beat of wings through the glass roof above; we scrambled down the cliff path and saw the sea curling lazily against the rocks and a fishing boat out on the still, blue water; we fed the donkeys, Fred and Penny; and we listened to the breathless exclamations of a couple of fans who'd managed to find their way to Minack. We sat up on the 'bridge' above the cottage and we did a long interview in the sun and I wanted to hold up a hand and stop time. But at last they packed me onto the sleeper back to London and, as the train slipped past St Michael's Mount once more, I was utterly besotted with Minack and the Tangyes. I sat on my bunk and began to read all the books again, slowly and carefully, from top to bottom.

I went back again, eighteen months later, when November fog smeared the windows of the train, and this time I took careful note of every mile of the journey.

'Any adventures? Any adventures?' cried Derek as he met me

at Penzance. 'I am convinced your fate will be sealed on British Rail, Jeanine.' And, before they sent me to bed once more in the chicken shed that night, both of them listened and sympathized, because I was going through a very bad patch at the time.

The patch got worse, and for a long, long time I thought it would never end. What helped me to survive it, and to hang on regardless, was the image of Minack, superimposed over my own little farm, and the letters, full of understanding, from Jeannie and Derek. The Tangyes, too, had had their days of being broke and desperate and living in constant fear that they might have to abandon their dreams and return to the city, so when my own situation seemed to offer no hope I would suddenly hear the gulls and see the meadows and that bright cottage, and somehow get the courage to keep going.

By the time I went to Minack once more, my own clouds had more or less dissipated, but it was not an entirely successful visit. This time I arrived in the afternoon, direct from Bristol, and Jeannie was there with Derek at the station. And I shall always see her like that, in bright yellow, her face lighting up as she saw me. That was the time I finally saw her little studio where she painted her pictures, and Derek's hut in the wood, where he wrote his books. This time I grieved with them over the loss of Penny and spent a long time trying to get Fred's new companion, Merlin, to bray. He didn't manage it, his lack of voice being another Minack mystery, so Fred did the honours when I played him his own voice back on tape.

That afternoon I spoilt everything by being terribly sick (nothing to eat on the train again and gorging myself on crab salad when I arrived), but I did go back with some cuttings of the lovely perfumed violets which grew wild at Minack. Once Jeannie and Derek had popped a couple into their bunches of unscented commercial violets to give their unseen customers pleasure. Now I took some home and planted them under my bedroom window, so that I could lean out and smell the leaves when the rain fell on them. Until the year when they shrivelled and I grieved over them bitterly, not knowing that they were a mere whisper of a greater grief at Minack itself.

It was the hated east wind that killed the violet plants. It blew unabated for five whole weeks till the grass was as burnt and dry as it had been in the drought of 1976. The violets were like scraps of tissue paper and yet I couldn't bear to dig them out. I looked in vain for some sign of life, and watered them in hope, but at last had to admit that they were quite gone.

When the phone call came to tell me the news I had somehow missed, that that bright spirit Jeannie had died, I was so shocked and numb that I stumbled out of the door and went to the sad bed of brown leaves and roots and just stood there, unable to come to terms with what I had just heard. Now I would dig the violets out at last and admit that this much-loved link with Minack had gone. I bent down to pull the withered plants out and, as I did so, there, in all that devastation, was one solitary green leaf. And as I saw this tiny evidence of life I knew that nothing could ever snuff out the joy that Jeannie had spread all around her, and that the best of her was still there at Minack. A few weeks later the whole bed of violets was green and alive and buds began to show.

All that was in the future, however, and before that my own world would shudder and rock on its foundations, crumble at the edges and finally settle back into place with a decided list to one side. So, as I sat on the platform at Paddington, suffering from a massive dose of anticlimax and waiting for the Welsh train, I watched the one to Penzance slip away, and longed with all my heart to be on it.

The crowd around me stirred and began to move. I picked up my suitcase and followed.

'Everything OK at home?' I asked Gwynneth when she met me at Swansea three hours later.

'Oh, yes! Mrs P is tamping mad because the phone's never stopped ringing and old Doli's been running about a bit. Randy old thing. But I see there's a thoroughbred stallion not far away. They were advertising him at stud in the paper. Give them a ring. It's worth a try.'

So I did, and Doli went on the honeymoon of her life with an elegant flea-bitten grey called Tapanui.

Chapter 14

'**F**lea-bitten?' cried Mrs P. 'You haven't taken dear old Doli to a flea-bitten horse!'

'Mother,' I explained patiently, 'he's a flea-bitten grey.'

'I heard you the first time. And I don't think they can look after it very well if it gets flea-bitten. Doli might catch them too.'

Mrs P began to scratch in anticipation.

'Stop that!' I commanded. 'A flea-bitten grey is just another one of those weird terms horsy people use. I mean, all white horses are called grey, and so are grey ones for that matter. Tapanui is a white horse covered all over with tiny flecks of brown. Gives him a kind of speckled-hen look, actually.'

'So why don't they say he's a speckled white horse?'

'For the same reason that it's a crime to call a foxhound a dog and they don't wag their tails, they feather. But I quite like "flea-bitten grey".'

'Well, I don't suppose old Doli will mind what he looks like as long as he gets on with the job,' said Mrs P, practical to the last.

Doli was so far from minding that she was currently driving the Lloyds mad. Not on account of Tapanui, but because of her other great interest in life, food.

Gladys and Bill Lloyd had been very understanding when I told them about Doli's need to run with the stallion instead of being served in hand only.

'What we'll do,' said Gladys, 'is to let him out with her during the day, but I always bring him in at night. Then, just to make quite sure, we'll get him to serve her in hand as well. When is she due in season?'

'Any moment now,' I said, 'but the thing is that I've got to go away on and off for the next few weeks, so could she come to you now and then you'll be sure to catch her when she cycles?'

And so Doli had been marched up the fields by another neighbour, Cynog Davies, loaded onto his lorry and delivered to the Lloyds' farm, where for a few days Gladys kept her in an enclosed yard with mangers and a roof at one end. Doli could see the layout of the farm, call to the other horses, get used to the sight, smell and sound of Tapanui, just across the yard, and settle down.

'Not that she took any time about *that*,' Gladys told me. 'She might have lived here all her life the way she made herself at home. So we put her on the field with the others to get a nice bit of grass. Anyway, there I am standing in the kitchen, doing the washing up, and I look out of the window and there's Doli trotting down the drive. I thought someone must have left the gate into the field open, so I rushed out, caught Doli and led her back and there was the gate *closed*. I couldn't believe a great big horse like Doli had jumped over the hedge, so I just put her back with the others. I'm no sooner in the kitchen and I look out and there's Doli again! I thought I was going mad. She trotted straight back to her manger and when I went out she was nodding at it as if to say 'What's for tea, then?'

'Was Tapanui on the field too?' I asked.

'Oh yes, and all the other mares. None of them have ever got over that hedge.'

'Doli,' I said, having heard it all before, 'will always find a way if there's food at the end of it. Why don't you keep her in till she comes into season and then she'll be too busy charming Tapanui?'

She charmed him all right, so much so that he followed her (he who had been a model horse till then and never tried to jump out of his field) through the hedge and the reinforcing fence. This time, when Gladys Lloyd looked out of her kitchen window, both he and Doli were cantering gaily down the lane together, ignoring the various cuts and bruises they'd collected on the way. The vet had to be called out to patch them up. Gladys cut short my apologies for Doli's behaviour.

'Bill and I,' she said, 'haven't had so many laughs for years. I was worried about Tappy's leg, but the vet says he'll be all right.

But that Doli! How old did you say she is? She goes on like a yearling.'

'I'm not sure how old Doli is,' I said. 'But she has to be about eighteen by now. I'm really sorry about all this. Perhaps you'd better send her home.'

'Oh, no, she'll probably settle down a bit now that she's been served. And she's got another interest too. Doli is helping to look after a foal.'

'What?'

'Oh, yes, Doli is helping Beauty to look after her foal. And Beauty doesn't mind. If she wants to go off and graze, Doli guards the baby. She's a real mother is Doli. I hope she gets one herself. It'll be a really loved foal if she does.'

'Funnily enough, the last foal she had here used to be minded by one of the goats, Dolores. How's Tapanui bearing up under the strain, by the way?'

'Well, he's a bit puzzled by Doli. We got him to cover her in hand after all that nonsense and, do you know, when we bring him up behind Doli she waggles her left leg. Not kicks, mind (I've seen enough of them to do that), just waggles her leg. And not the right one, never the right one. Always the left one. Looks as if she's doing the Hokey-Cockey. Bill and I crease up every time. So what with Doli waggling and Bill and me laughing, Tappy's wondering what the heck's going on.'

'As long as she doesn't fart at him,' I said. 'That's what she usually does if you go round behind her. It's made strong men wilt before now.'

'Yes,' said Gladys, 'We've had a bit of that too. Talk about Doli's secret weapon! Anyway, I wonder what sort of foal she'll have to Tappy. He *did* serve her, a couple of times.'

What the foal (and I touched wood every time I thought about it) would be like was the big question. Tapanui is not a big stallion, but he had some very good breeding in him. At least it looked impressive on the card the Lloyds had given me. But I was more worried about temperament. Not wishing to admit to the Lloyds that none of the names on the card (except that of Colonist, Winston Churchill's horse) meant anything to me, I rang Fiona Silver in Cambridge to see if she could help.

'It says Tapanui's out of a Flying Curtis mare,' I told her. 'Who the hell was Flying Curtis?'

'Ah, now,' said Fiona, 'he used to stand at stud not too far from here. I've seen quite a few of his progeny and they are lovely animals. But as for character – well, not perfect. Bit wicked, I think. Got a way of their own.'

'Tapanui himself is a real gentleman,' I said. 'Gladys told me he does tend to carry his buckets around in his teeth, but apart from that he's very well behaved.'

'Hm, well let's hope the foal is too,' said Fiona. 'Flying Curtis was a grey, of course. Would you like a grey?'

'I'd love a grey,' I said, 'a well-behaved grey! But as Doli is bay with black points and her character is not perfect, I don't see much hope of either.' I went on to relate the dramas of the past few weeks.

'Dear Doli,' said Fiona fondly. 'I'll be most interested to see what she produces. When are you off on your trips for the programme? Anyone interesting to see?'

'Any day now,' I said, 'I'm off to see the Queen Mother's Buff Orpingtons.'

'I'd rather see her horses,' said Fiona.

'At the moment,' I said firmly, 'I've had enough of horses. The Royal Buff Orpingtons will be a pleasant change.'

I must admit, however, to being a trifle disappointed when I drew up outside the bungalow on the outskirts of the village near Sandringham Estate. I'd expected to be on the estate proper, being conducted around a confection of a poultry house like the one Queen Victoria had, by a gaitered poultryman standing stiffly to attention as the Royal birds appeared. Well, perhaps not quite that, but I certainly hadn't anticipated sitting knee to knee with this very elderly gentleman in a modern sitting room, albeit lavishly decorated with photographs of the Queen Mother.

It appeared that Mr Hammond-Brown and the Queen Mother and her Buff Orpingtons went back a long way. He had been in charge of the Sandringham Flower Show (where they also had classes for poultry and small animals) for many years. At one show, as he conducted his royal patron round the poultry section, she'd exclaimed over the pen of Buff Orpingtons.

166

'Do you know Buff Orpingtons, Your Majesty?' asked Mr Hammond-Brown reverentially.

'Oh, yes!' she declared and then told him how, as a little girl, she'd been a bit of a tomboy, tearing around the grounds of her home in Scotland on her bicycle. One day she'd careered right into her father's flock of prize Buff Orpingtons. Instead of being picked up by her nanny and consoled for her grazed knees and bruised pride, she'd been given a good shaking and everyone was far more concerned about the precious chickens.

In spite of this childhood trauma, when the Buff Orpington Breed Society asked the Queen Mother if she would accept a trio, she agreed, on condition that Mr Hammond-Brown looked after them for her. This he had done with great pride and dedication, right here in his own back garden. Part of the job, of course, was to enter them in shows, but these particular Royal personages did not enjoy the usual security arrangements when in public.

'People come and put their hands in the cages and pull their feathers out' whispered Mr Hammond-Brown. 'As souvenirs, you know. Poor things, they come home all bleeding sometimes.'

'Do they win very often?' I asked.

'Oh yes! And Her Majesty is very proud of them when they do. She tells all the family.'

I put the next question a little delicately.

'Does she ever eat them?'

'Of course. When she's at Sandringham, I send over eggs and the odd bird too.'

Obviously, whichever way it went, being a Royal bird had its drawbacks. But where were they? I was taken, feeling as if I was being granted an audience, out to the small poultry runs at the back of the bungalow.

A Buff Orpington, no matter what its connections, is a magnificent bird. They look for all the world like gigantic animated golden chrysanthemums.

These were prime show specimens and, as far as I could see, still had their full complement of feathers and were happily clucking and singing to themselves as we peered at them in awe.

'Where's yer mate, then?' inquired Mr Hammond-Brown of one particularly chatty hen. 'Don't tell me she's layin' an egg!' And it occurred to me that these must be the only members of the Royal entourage actually to be encouraged to lay an egg in public. I recorded the happy event and much of the clucking and singing and general sound of deep content. When it was all finally broadcast, I played the programme out with a slow and dignified performance of 'Pomp and Circumstance,' accompanied by the Royal Buff Orpingtons. As one of the Studio Managers exclaimed ecstatically, 'Elgar and chickens! It's so beautifully simple!' And, it must be said, those Buff Orpingtons did have a very regal and dignified cluck.

Only Mrs P was deeply disgusted.

'I thought you were going to see the Queen Mother herself, feeding her chooks,' she said. Mrs P is an ardent fan of the Queen Mother's, and it all goes back to when, as the Duchess of York, she was on tour in Australia.

Poor Mrs P was a very junior nursing trainee and had been told that, whilst the other nurses were out on the balconies waving and cheering at the Duke and Duchess, she was to stay at her post and get a great mountain of bedpans properly scoured out. But no Cinderella was she, and she climbed out through a window and got onto a little ledge high above the street, where she waved and waved and waved and nearly fell off. All this passionate activity so far above caught the Duchess's eye and she looked up, saw the skinny teenager balancing on for dear life, and smiled and waved encouragement. Mrs P has been her slave ever since and I would have done anything to get her within waving distance of her idol, but the best I'd been able to do was to go and see the Buff Orpingtons. Which was actually going a long way for me, because my own royal sympathies cancel out with the Plantagenets. It was to indulge my own medieval preferences that, with the Sandringham hens safely tucked up on tape, I went to see the willow man.

Once, willow growing and basket making of all kinds was a most important part of the Suffolk economy, but when Crawford Balch tried to revive some small part of it he was hard put to find even the old varieties of willow which had been grown. And when someone told me about him I was not much interested, to tell the truth.

'I've done basket makers in Somerset,' I sighed.

'Ah! But this is not just a basket maker. He makes whole fences out of woven willow. Not hurdles put together. A complete, unbroken fence.'

Woven willow fences, curving in one continuous line? Where had I seen those before? Sitting on my own wall, in my own house. Snow, the brilliant blue of the woman's dress as she warms her feet at the fire and, outside, sheep huddled behind a woven fence, 'December' from the *Très Riches Heures du Duc de Berry*, one of a set of six beautiful reproductions from that glowing book. This was my favourite and I'd often wondered what the fence was made of that held the sheep in their open-sided barn. Indeed, I'd often pointed to them when people scoffed at me for bringing my own sheep into the hay-shed in winter.

Now, of course, those very scoffers have got their own sheep inside big custom-built sheds, as indoor lambing has become the thing to do.

Not that the fences Crawford Balch made would be used for sheep – unless their owners were very rich indeed. What was once done as a matter of course by the medieval shepherds was now a rare craft, and these fences were woven for gardens, and in them Crawford Balch would make you arches, or willow pigeon lofts or summer houses. As we sat in his own willow hut, looking across a garden surrounded by this amazing piece of continual sculpture, the evening sun blushed scarlet, bells rang distantly from the village church, a lone bird sang its final notes and, for a moment, the fourteenth century swirled around us and was gone.

There were other, more recent, time warps on that journey – the old wooden-rake factory, where pulleys and chutes and miniature guillotines whirred and banged and shimmied on the pull of a rope; the farm where huge, muscular Suffolk Punches were getting the hay in; the couple with the herd of Red Poll cattle, still working their farm as others had done in the fifties and making, if not as grand a living as their prosperous corn-growing neighbours, one that kept them, their cattle and their land content; Denis Watkins Pritchard (the author 'BB') in his perfect round toll-house, his exquisite garden and the 'ghost pig' who used to haunt it, vocally, if not in person. I got home at last, picked up the phone and began all over again. Ten days later I was in Lancashire.

Curlews sang their song of high, wild places, a cool breeze drifted up from the green, stone-walled fields, and the horrors of the drive up the M6 eased out of mind and muscle. To have arrived at all seemed remarkable, for if the motorway had been crowded, hot, endless and dreary, the Forest of Bowland had seemed determined to keep me out of it. No wonder that in the past it's been a hideout even for the likes of Henry VI. Not that there's too much of a forest about it any more, but it is a secret sort of place.

One of the few spots in the Forest which attract tourists is the Village of Chipping and, about a mile away at Gibbon Bridge, is a hotel which is a mixture of opulence and stark provincial 'take it or leave it'. It had once been a small farm and, if the large room I was ushered into had been part of the hayloft, it was now a frenzy of flounces and gold taps, deep-pile carpet and a terrifying newness. The yard below had been laid out in ornamental walks, rustic bridges, massed flower-beds and lampposts. Since that first visit, the original barn has almost totally lost its character under soaring buttresses and neo-gothic archways and stonework and glass. The story of the hotel is a bit like a certain type of novel: tenant farmer's daughter, by sheer guts and hard work, creates luxury hotel out of old home and – well, I don't know the end of the story, just the beginning, and I didn't even know that as I stood breathing in the sweet evening air and listening to the curlew's song. Eventually, I was restored enough to totter downstairs, have dinner, and later meet up with Shelagh Holmes and her husband, who did know the story and had advised me to stay at the Gibbon Bridge because it was also very reasonable then. Now, with typical Lancashire kindliness, they'd driven several miles to make quite sure I was all right and keep me company, although I'd never met them before.

'We'll see you tomorrow, then,' said Shelagh as they left me at last, 'about mid-afternoon?'

'Now, you've got the directions,' said her husband. 'Anyway, just look out for black and brown sheep once you get near.'

'Fine,' I said, and waved them off. Tomorrow was going to be a long day. If I'd known just how long, perhaps I wouldn't have been in such wonderful spirits the next morning.

170

The curlews were bubbling their song again, it was a fine clear morning and a bustling elderly lady was serving me piping hot coffee, fresh rolls and delicious home-made lemon curd (which, as you may have gathered already, I am extremely partial to), and asking me a lot of questions. Who I was, where I'd come from and what I was doing here? I gave her the answers (which she remembered perfectly a good two years later when I returned to the Gibbon Bridge) rather absently, keeping my eyes on the view soaring away in front of me. It was a high, bare fell with a solitary cottage clinging to the top. How on earth, I wondered, did anyone ever get up there?

'Well, you'll pass it this morning,' said my friend, who was actually the owner's mother and responsible for much of the excellent cooking. 'If you look, you'll see the road goes all the way up there and beyond.'

My old Beetle snorted a bit as we climbed, but sure enough we passed the cottage and, in passing, it lost some of the mystery it had had when seen from below. And still the road climbed on, entering now into mist, which the sun was piercing in great shafts as, eventually, the farm I was seeking came into view. And there, on the top of Lancashire, a Welsh voice hailed me.

Now I understood why Phillip Morris had been recommended as a 'good speaker'. I have never interviewed a Welsh man or woman who wasn't. Even when they're translating from Welsh into English as they speak, what usually comes out is sheer poetry and often very witty as well. And poetry and wit about the Lonk were not what I'd expected. Well, not after I'd spoken to the secretary of the breed society, who was obliging but sparing of words. Some of the breeders she'd put me in touch with were even more sparing, until someone had suggested Phillip Morris, who was perfectly happy to put off his trip to market till a bit later that morning.

The Lonk, according to the book *British Sheep*, 'from time immemorial . . . have existed on the hill ranges of Lancashire and Yorkshire.'

'So what,' I demanded, 'is a Welshman doing keeping Lancashire sheep?'

'Well, it's a long story, but they're the best sheep in the world.'

cried Phillip Morris. 'Come on and I'll show you.' And he set off at a rapid pace away into the mist and left me to stumble after him in such a way as to arouse the collective interest of a group of young cattle, who romped merrily behind, bellowing to any stragglers not to miss the fun. They sounded so gleeful, I simply had to stop and record them. Mr Morris and his dogs came back to find me happily conducting his cattle in an impromptu concert, which all of us were enjoying enormously. I was led firmly away to where the mists were lifting and there, on a long, curving field sheltered by trees, were his Lonks, grazing calmly as the sun lit their backs.

The face is pure black and white, legs speckled black and white .... The fleece is trim and even from head to skirting, white, free from kemp .... In the ram the horns should sweep well round with a good bump ... and in the ewes they should be strong and flat ....

Brought up in a country where the vast majority of sheep are of one breed, the variations of the native British sheep fascinate me. Short, chubby sheep that look more like bears; tall sheep with flowing Rastafarian locks sweeping the ground and long blue faces; solid sheep with great big ears; downland sheep and upland sheep; white and speckled and grey and black and brown; even some with no wool at all. Each of these breeds has a nucleus of dedicated breeders who've stuck to them loyally when fashion and fellow farmers scorned them, and each and everyone has its special reason for being what or where it is, on which terrain or near which port. Each breed history is sprinkled with monks or kings and queens and royal preferences and, except in those breeds termed 'primitive', somewhere along the line there'll be a whisper of Bakewell and his Dishley rams.

Given their name, I had expected something a little more spectacular of the Lonks. But stand in a golden mist on the top of the world and watch them being collected by two dedicated collies reacting in perfect co-ordination to the shrill whistles piercing the air, listen to a man, who is passionate about the breed, tell you of their background, their wool that is fine enough for baby clothes, their hardiness, their mothering abilities, the quality of their lambs and his own fierce determination that the breed can be bettered by none, and they acquire a glamour all their own. By the time Phillip Morris had finished, I was convinced there was nothing like a Lonk.

But almost immediately I became a traitor. I had lunch with the secretary of the Derbyshire Gritstone Breeders Association. Now the Derbyshire Gritstone is not unlike a Lonk without horns, although members of both societies would probably kill me for saying so. Not that Eric Halsall was as furiously partisan as a real farmer would have been. The reason he met up with me, as Phillip Morris and his collies returned me to the farmyard and rushed off to market, was that Eric was longing to show off his beloved Forest of Bowland. And I wanted to have a word with him about his role as the commentator on the TV series *One Man and his Dog* and sheepdog trialling in general.

Eric's own dog was a little Shetland, a kind of mini-Lassie type once used for rounding up sheep in the Shetlands, but now more usually a fluffed up, pampered pet. Eric's dog, Gail (about whom he's written a book), did still do the odd bit of work, however, mainly when the snows came and she used her excellent nose to find buried sheep. Now she pottered along with us as we wandered deeper into the forest, where hidden glades and streams caught the spring sunshine and Eric, as he pointed out its beauties, wondered why this lovely place had never attracted the tourists. He told me many stories of the people who'd hidden there over the centuries, of its archers and its ghosts and its tough, weather-wracked farms.

All of this took a long time, and the lunch we found in a warm, matey pub took even longer. It was getting late, therefore, when I remembered my appointment with Shelagh Holmes over in Whalley. By then, however, we'd twisted and turned around the forest roads so much that I didn't have a clue how to get there.

'No trouble,' said Eric, 'just follow my car and I'll guide you.'

If I hadn't followed him, they'd have found my whitened bones somewhere in the forest a long time later and my ghost would still be wailing and weeping with the others.

To this day, if I think of Portfield Farm, I see the colours of gold and tan and fawn, and I hear thunder. The cats were tawny Abyssinians, the goats were Golden Guernseys, the geese were

Brecon Buffs and most of the sheep were the little caramel-coloured Manx Loghtans.

'But we have the black Hebrideans and the grey North Ronaldsays too,' said Shelagh, as she led me out of the house and up the lane to the sheep fields. Both of us were bundled up in wax-proofed coats and we had a stout umbrella each. Great rain clouds had been looming over the fells, with the odd flick of lightning giving them a sickly glow.

'Are you sure you wouldn't like to leave all this till another time?' asked Shelagh anxiously as the first heavy drops splashed down.

'It's now or never,' I said grimly. 'I won't be back this way for a long time.'

So it probably wasn't the best interview I've ever done. Certainly it didn't do justice to the Hebrideans with their four horns spiralling out like the top of a hat stand, the seaweed-eating North Ronaldsays or the Manx Loghtans from the Isle of Man. All of them are classed as 'primitive' sheep; all of them were on the way out until the Rare Breeds Survival Trust sounded the alarm; all of them have stubby, triangular tails; and all of them are hardy and milky and their fleeces have a colour and quality all their own. It was their fleeces that Shelagh Holmes was particularly interested in.

Some of the clothes I wear most frequently, when I'm not grubbing around the farm, originally came off the backs of Shelagh Holmes's sheep. I have kilts and jackets, cardigans and sweaters, hats and cloaks. They are warm and smart and comfortable and they don't crease much. Shelagh, who worked as a lab technician to support her sheep until she could find a way of making them pay for themselves, was fortunate enough to have a husband who worked in the textile industry. He arranged to have the fleeces professionally spun and woven; Shelagh designed the clothes and then had them made up by small local firms.

'But right now,' I said bitterly, as the rain pounded and pattered on our umbrellas, 'their fleeces are a lot more use to them than they are to us. I can't do this interview with all that noise on the umbrellas, so we'll just have to get wet.'

We got soaked right through our wax jackets and down to our

174

pelts. Even our wellingtons were full of water. When we got back to the house, it took us a long time to dry out, and still the thunder rattled and crashed around us as we raced into the goat-shed to talk about the Golden Guernseys. The goats were less than happy and yelled above the sounds of the storm.

'Don't stop them,' I shouted at Shelagh as she tried to bribe the goats into silence with some hay. 'I want that noise – goats and thunder!'

'Why?' cried Shelagh above the racket.

'You'll hear.' As usual, my mind was racing ahead to the finished results on the air and for a while I was exhilarated enough to egg the goats on to greater efforts and grinned happily as each crack of thunder shattered the air.

I was not grinning too much when I swung the Beetle out of the Holmes's yard about an hour later. The storm was gone, but it was after nine, I had to get across country to the other side of Thirsk, and I had barely a quarter of a tank of petrol. There was not a single garage open anywhere.

'And I'll tell you for nothing,' said the policeman, when I flagged his car down, 'you won't find any this side of the Yorkshire border. And I doubt you'll find much over there.'

He banged the nose of the Beetle and shook his head.

'All you can do is drive slowly. You might just make it if you drive slowly.' And he tipped his cap, got back into his car and drove off.

Thinking about it now, I should have rung the AA, but I was parked in a lay-by on a dual carriageway, there was not a phone to be seen and somehow, not knowing the road ahead, I was sure there'd be an open garage somewhere along the way. There wasn't, of course, and the road, which seemed fairly civilized for a while, narrowed and began to curve out into wild country, where it bent under brooding cliffs with a hideous drop on the other side. There was nothing to do but keep driving. By the time the road levelled out again, the motorbike was behind me.

The bike had popped out from some side turning and it made no attempt to overtake me, slowly as I was driving, but stayed close, blinding me with its brilliant light on full beam, reflected in the rear-view mirror.

175

Imagination, warped by exhaustion, took over. I was suddenly in that film of Cocteau's – *Orphée*, wasn't it? – where the messengers of death come clad in black on motorbikes. Or was it that other one, where the man looks into the rear-view mirror at the bike behind him and sees a skeleton riding it? Oh God, if only this one would overtake me and go away. Which it did, almost as I thought it.

'Silly fool,' I thought to myself. 'Stop fantasizing. It's just some poor soul trying to get home.'

He was waiting for me at the next lay-by with his lights off. I saw the shape of the bike dimly in my own headlights, saw it move towards me as I passed and soon it was behind me again, revving and growling and flashing. It moved out and sat directly in front of the Beetle; it shot ahead and repeated the lay-by trick. Now I was terrified, beyond reason, on that dark, lonely road, like an animal being hunted and chivvied, and when the friendly lights of a pub did finally appear I was in too much of a blind panic to stop. I'd forgotten to check the needle on the petrol gauge for miles, but when I did it had swung down well into reserve.

The mad motorbike left me somewhere just before Harrogate, where the garages on the outskirts showed a united blind front. Still trembling and bewildered, I swung the car on to the A61 and went on fatalistically towards Thirsk. If I had to stop by the side of the road, the dear old Dilly Bag was fully charged, the big quilted coat I always carry in the car would serve as blanket and pillow combined, and in the morning help would come.

On I went, driving slowly and automatically, and I hardly noticed that I was passing through Ripon. I didn't give the dead garages more than a glance in passing, knowing that it was well after ten anyway. I began to go down the hill and out on the other side of the town, when I saw it, bright and gleaming and, above all, open for business.

The man was a bit surprised when the crazed-looking woman told him he was Sir Lancelot, A Perfect Gentleman and Arthur, King of All Britain, rolled into one. And when she cried, dancing round his forecourt, 'Fill 'er up! Fill 'er up!' he hesitated and looked decidedly alarmed. As the petrol finally gushed wonderfully into the Beetle's tank, I told him of my nightmare journey.

'And then there you were! A bright light in a naughty world,' I concluded.

'Yes,' he said slowly. 'I only decided to stay open till ten-thirty at the beginning of this week.' He gestured towards the town where all the big garage chains had their outlets.

'That lot,' he said contemptuously, 'they want people's money, but they don't want to give them the service. There's not a lot of business at this time of night, but that's when people really need to keep going.' Which had been my feeling exactly.

Before I left, I got him to top up the oil, bought a spare can (which I didn't really need) and raided his store of chocolates and crisps. One way or the other, he'd make a few pennies profit out of me. He had flatly refused to take a tip.

As I finally crossed the A1, I saw a big garage open beside it, but whether I'd have made it that far without my saviour in Ripon I was never too sure. I've always had a great fondness for that town ever since.

At last Thirsk itself came up, empty and bleak under the street lighting and completely different from that day, so long ago, when I'd been trotting around the busy streets with the author James Herriott, and Gert, and having our photos taken in the market square. An eternity away.

The road to Scarborough was not hard to find and there I was on the last leg. It should be easy now. The directions had been quite clear, but I wasn't too sure about the part that said 'if the water is high in the ford, go round behind the old tree and come along the road.' I left the main road and made for Thirlby.

One of the villagers told me that they heard me lots of times that night. Arriving, departing, arriving, reversing, departing and arriving and stalling the Beetle in the ford.

'I was just coming to help you, when you got it right,' he said. 'I told my wife, that'll be Penny's visitor all right.'

Penny, meanwhile, was about to set out on a search party. It was nearly midnight when she hauled me, babbling incoherently, from the Beetle. A gallon of tea, a stiff whisky, endless sympathy, dogs settling on my feet, exclamations of envy at the outfit I'd bought from Shelagh Holmes, a warm comfortable bed in a room where the old polished furniture looked as if it had been loved forever, and the horrors of the road receded and I sank into a dreamless sleep.

Each night, as I came back from seeing cheese makers, wood carvers, carp breeders, purveyors of old farming prints and the man who'd actually bred the Royal Buff Orpingtons, Skipton Hill Farm enclosed me and fed me and ironed out the creases. But on the last day of all I nearly didn't get back, and this time the lonely moors, covered in fog, almost claimed their victim for good.

The day began well enough, in spite of a cold wind keening around the tall windows of the house. I left Penny feeding her stock in bright sun, and the Beetle made the perilous climb up Sutton Edge without too much trouble. As I spun through the villages, blossom lit the streets of old stone cottages and it wasn't until I was out on the moors themselves that the rain came smashing down against the windscreen and a fog swirled in from nowhere.

It was cold when I arrived at Goathland and, as I parked the car by the road and walked, loaded down with equipment, across a wet meadow, over a rushing beck, under huge dripping trees and through a roundabout sort of farmyard, I was already worrying about getting back.

Joyce Fussey was so terrified of me coming to interview her that she simply laughed nervously when I growled about my poor wet Gert. Which lack of understanding I took hard, so that I took longer than I should have done to get my professional self in order and do my job of calming her down. I almost missed the beauty of the house hidden amongst its old trees, with the beck rippling at the bottom of a garden already scented with the new Sweet Briar leaves. And I almost didn't get the essence of the extremely funny lady Joyce Fussey can be. As in my own life, 'Sod's Law' attends everything she does and the only way she can bear it is to write it all down on paper. Read her books, and you'll see what I mean.

'But if you're going to get over to Glaisdale, we'd best be getting up to see Max Graham quickly,' she said now, as I packed Gert and the microphone back in their bag. 'He'll be waiting for us. And, er, I know you want to talk to him about his Swaledale sheep, but if you could have a quick word about his walking sticks too – he's ever so proud of them.'

'Oh, not another stick maker,' I groaned.

178

'Well, if you could just have a look,' pleaded Joyce as we drove higher up onto the moors.

The farm kitchen was warm and steamy and I didn't want to leave it. Outside the wind whipped down over the stone walls and I shuddered to think what it must have been like in winter. And Max Graham had a pretty bleak way with idiot interviewers too, especially if they imagined they were in a hurry. But, if it took a long time, he did tell me a lot about his 'Swales', if not with the ebullience of Phillip Morris, at least with as much passion. And he uttered one phrase which, as the weather forecasts send me into a frenzy, I remember vividly, and which summed up that solid endurance of all upland farmers. I had mentioned, rather brightly, that they must get terrible snow up here.

Max Graham sniffed and flattened me with a look. Finally he said, 'Ay. When it snows, we gets it.'

As we walked back towards the blessed warmth of the kitchen, he stopped and, for the first time, smiled at me.

'Come in 'ere,' he said. 'I'd like you to see summat.' And he opened the door of a small lean-to. Hanging all around its walls were walking sticks with horn handles.

'I only ever uses me own sheep's horns,' he said proudly. 'All Swales', these are.'

The horn handles with their polished creaminess streaked with grey had a rough texture to them, unlike the fancy ones I'd seen so often, so fancy that they were purely ornamental. These were made by a shepherd from his own land and animals, and they were made to use.

People still say to me, 'I'll never forget that man who sold you a stick. The way he said "Ay, you look good for a bob or two. I reckon I could ask you a tenner." And you said "Done" and he laughed like anything.'

It was worth every penny of it, my Swale stick, if only to remind me of that dour man with a look of pure mischief in his eye as he got the better of the silly woman from the radio. And later when, as is the way with producers with a time limit, Mary was looking for something to cut in that week's programme and picked on Max Graham's interview, none of the studio managers would touch it. As one of them said, 'Even his pauses said everything.'

'Oh dear,' said Joyce Fussey as we rushed back to Goathland. 'You'll be ever so late, Jeanine. Are they expecting you for lunch? I don't think you'll make it.'

I didn't either, but in that extremely civilized house in Glaisdale they'd kept me something hot to gulp down before I followed Lady Simon's car endlessly over the moors. She'd written to me about an amazing woman who bred Cleveland Bay horses, had invited me to lunch and offered to lead the way to Fryup Gill – a name I still couldn't believe in. I wasn't entirely confident, either, about her claims that I'd always regret it if I didn't interview her friend, who was a complete 'one-off'.

She was absolutely right, though. An ex-barrister, very elderly, dressed like a stable boy but with the presence of a judge, Ruth Kitching was indeed a 'one-off'. Her rich, cultured voice boomed across the fields at the mares and foals grazing on the hillside; it roared at the massive stallion to 'get on over'; it spoke like a history book, a romantic novel, an encyclopedia of horse management and almost like the horses themselves. Miss Kitching seemed to know every Cleveland Bay who'd ever been in a stud book and she knew just as much about the past of the breed as she did of its present. There was even a touch of Royalty thrown in again.

'That stallion is the father of the horse the Queen has just bought for the Royal Mews. You've probably read about it in the paper. They always make a big fuss. Now that horse's mother (see her coming down the hill with her foal) is back here to be served again. I'll just see if she's in the mood yet.' And she led the stallion out as if he were a poodle, tied him up and charged off through the mud to catch the mare. She led her up and down in front of the stallion, which snorted politely but got a quick nip in return.

'Nope! Nothing doing,' declared Miss Kitching. 'Go on, you old baggage, out of it and feed your foal.' And she sent the mare packing, returned the stallion to his box, fended off a couple of pet lambs which had been following us everywhere, made sure the hay-racks were full, as the other mares came down from the hill, and led me back to the house. At no given point could I keep up with her.

She fed me with strong tea, thick beef sandwiches and a stream of witty anecdotes; she collected a dozen Buff Rock bantam eggs for me to set when I got home, she drew me a detailed map of how to get across the moors a shorter way, and she tucked me up into the Beetle with the following warning:

'Now, that damn fog's coming in badly. Follow those directions exactly. There'll be a part of the road when you'll think it's the end of the world. You'll see and hear nothing and nobody. Whatever you do, don't panic in the fog. Don't leave the road. And if you do get lost or in trouble, don't leave your car. Sit there. If I don't hear from you by nine o'clock, I'll send my nephew up to look for you in the Land-Rover. Remember, don't leave your car. Just sit there till help comes.' And, with those ominous words ringing in my ears, I set out for the fog-bound moors.

I peered, I prayed, I crept and I promised God anything he wanted, but I followed those directions to the letter, even when they seemed about to lead me into the mouth of hell itself. I got back to Skipton Hill Farm just before the deadline.

'I told you it was a good short cut,' said Ruth Kitching when I rang her. 'Come and see me again soon. We'll have a good chat.'

'I'd like that,' I said truthfully, 'very much indeed.' But I never got the chance. By the time I was in her part of Yorkshire again that legendary lady had left.

Penny celebrated my safe return with a perfect meal. It was washed up quietly and efficiently by a girl called Sue. Sue kept Penny's horses spotless in their big roomy stables across the yard. I hadn't seen much of her and couldn't know then that the next time we met it would be on my own farm and she'd be looking after a great deal more than horses.

As for the Shelagh Holmes interview about her Golden Guernsey goats, we played the programme out that week with 'Silence is Golden'. Every time the singer paused, we popped goat and thunder noises in. If it lacked the simplicity of the Elgar and chickens combination, it caused a riot in the studio.

Chapter 15

I went to Cornwall that year too, a blistering journey that ended up in a garden full of roses – roses that climbed everywhere, roses with tiny flower buds which were picked painstakingly by Penny Black and her husband, pressed carefully and used to decorate fine linen and lace sachets and pillows, which Penny also embroidered. Their old cottage was full of colour and perfume and the garden seemed to be part of it. I returned to that small, jewelled world every night after hunting down bee-keepers, a couple who made little felt mobiles which were a triumph of humour and imagination, a small commercial tannery which would cure your own sheepskins for you, traditional Cornish drystone wallers, an expert on old-fashioned clotted cream, the farmer editor of an alternative magazine which put the wind up the local councils, a couple who lived out on the Lizard and bred waterfowl, Shetland ponies and beautiful big, chestnut and brown Barnevelder hens, which laid chocolate coloured eggs, an artist who painted rare breeds and had a thriving postcard business, and finally a flower-farmer-cum-donkey breeder who had actually bred the Tangyes' new donkey Merlin. This lady also had whippets and I ended that day bowling along a Cornish cliff in a donkey cart, with two blue whippets galloping behind and gulls shrieking overhead.

I didn't go to see the Tangyes' themselves because I was trying to achieve all this in a couple of days (and had a lot more interviews to do on the way back) and, just for once, I wanted to go to Minack when I was relaxed and calm enough to take it all in properly. In view of what was to happen two short years later, I've regretted that decision ever since.

I left Cornwall with pots of herb-scented honey, a collection of mobiles to brighten up our lives and a Threepenny-Bit rose in a pot.

When she saw it, Mrs P touched the tiny leaves in wonder.

'Does it always stay this size?' she asked.

'The flowers and the leaves do, but the plant itself throws out long arms covered with tiny thorns. It's quite a tough customer.'

'Well, that's a relief,' said my mother. 'All those other miniature roses you've given me never seem to do very well here. And none of them have got such tiny buds and leaves as this.'

'It reminds me of the one Tolly gave Mrs Oldknow,' I said, 'which had *leaves no bigger than bird-seed, and flowers like tiny wild strawberries.*'

'You'll do yourself an injury one day if you don't stop quoting out of books,' said Mrs P impatiently. 'I'll just go and find a safe place for this little pet, away from those awful dogs.' And, although the Threepenny-Bit rose has indeed sent out long fierce arms, the thorns are more like little hairs and the leaves and roses are still the size of birdseed and tiny wild strawberries.

While Mrs P was planting out her rose, I set some eggs. One contented broody was already covering the bantam Buff Rocks I'd brought back from the north. Now I had to find a couple more to sit on some Barnevelder eggs, and on two duck eggs which had been laid right in the middle of my annual interview with Tom Bartlett, whom I'd gone to see on my way back from Cornwall.

'The Crested Duck,' Tom had been explaining, 'is really something of an abnormality. If you breed two that have big crests together, you end up with mad ducks, because the crest can be so big it damages the brain. So you breed a small crest to a big one. And then, of course, only a percentage of the ducks will have a crest – you know, Mendel's Law and all that. So that's why the Admiral there has a marvellous crest, but all the ducks with him have only little ones.'

He picked up the Admiral so that I could feel the great powder-puff of feathers on his head. I'd seen old prints of white Crested Ducks, but this one was a marvel of fawns and browns and cream, with green tips on his wings. As Tom put him back, one of the females came waddling out of the bushes in the big open pen, with a self-satisfied look on her face.

'I think,' I said slowly, 'that that duck has just laid an egg.'

Tom hopped over the low fence, rooted about in the bush and emerged with a warm egg which he presented to me with a flourish. He went back to find me another one and, when finally they both hatched out, I got a duck and a drake, both with magnificent crests which were a swirl of delicate colours. Any hairdresser would have wept with envy. I called them Tom and Diana and their theme music on the programme was, of course, 'Where Did You Get That Hat?' with duck accompaniment.

There was a lot more to do that year and by the time I finished running around the country the cottage was bursting with tapes. The editing machine ran hot, the dogs kept barking at all the sounds of livestock seeping out from under the door of the office, the phone never stopped ringing, the outside work was done on the trot and Mrs P made sure I remembered to eat.

The series began: wild dashes to Bristol in the middle of the night; slower journeys back the next night with the Beetle loaded down with files of letters, more books to read and boxes of food from Sainsbury's; little sleep and much agonizing. It was all very much as usual, a tightrope of time and work and the terror (firmly damped down) of any minute disruption which would cause it all to come tumbling down. It didn't need a lot – a sick animal, the editing machine breaking down, my car not starting, Gwynneth being unable to attend to the stock when I was in Bristol, a storm to stop me getting there or . . . The possibilities appalled me, as they did every year. That I might personally fall by the wayside (mostly likely through sustained lack of sleep) was not too much of a problem. I relied on that good old belt of adrenalin that the body of any broadcaster is used to pumping in when needed and, if the aftermath left you feeling like the dead, there was always the next programme to start it all up again.

And so the weeks went on, the halfway mark was reached and the home stretch was in view. We'd make it to the end. Or would we?

'Mother,' I said slowly one morning, 'why are you trying to put the electric lead into the spout of the kettle?'

Mrs P looked at me for a moment as if trying to remember who I was.

'Jush havin' a cupatea,' she announced and nodded her head up and down to herself.

'Are you all right?' I asked, peering at her closely.

'Eh?' She started violently, seemed to focus properly, looked down at the kettle and lead in her hands and said in her normal voice. 'Oh dear! Aren't I a silly old fool?' As she smiled at me and began to put the lead into the proper end of the kettle, a huge wave of relief swept over me.

'Thought you'd gone off your rocker,' I said gaily, although, in fact, the awful word 'stroke' had been beating in my mind.

'Oh, well,' she said now, 'that's always on the cards with me. But I *have* got an awful headache.'

'Why don't you go and lie down,' I said, 'and I'll bring you a cup of tea?'

I helped her up the stairs and left her sitting on the edge of her bed. When I came back with the tea, she was still sitting there, looking puzzled now.

'I can't remember whether I'm getting up or going to bed,' she said with a frown.

'You're going to have a nice lie down and I'm going to call the doctor,' I said gently. I removed her clothes and tucked her up in bed.

The doctor, when he came, was one I didn't know. By then, Mrs P was fast asleep and he raised his voice at her to wake her up. When she opened her eyes, smiled vaguely and said 'Urroo! 'Oo are 'oo?'.

I suppose he must have examined her, but I was too angry and too frightened to remember much about it. Finally he finished and as he was leaving, he told me he wasn't sure what was the matter. Yes, it could be a stroke but we'd have to wait and see and if, in the meantime, I was worried, to ring him again.

If I hadn't been so desperate with worry and an awful feeling of complete isolation, I might have thought the ensuing night was funny. Mrs P, instead of quietly lying still, was up and down the whole time, getting her words back to front, giggling and pointing at me, picking things up and putting them on her head and generally behaving like a very active, mischievous child. But, in between, she would have moments of complete lucidity and tell me of the awful pain in her head.

I rang the doctor again in the morning. He came back some time in the early afternoon, by which time Mrs P had ceased her merry activities and was lying, breathing heavily, groaning and failing to recognize me at all.

This time the doctor took one look and rang for an ambulance. I suppose I can understand his irritation with me when, like a child clinging to the familiar, I asked him if it was really serious and should I ring the BBC to tell them there'd be no programme that week. I was actually relieving the pain of one situation by worrying about another, but for this doctor, what I did or did not do was no concern of his.

I followed the ambulance to the little local hospital and they showed me into a room where the screens had been pulled round the bed in the corner. Mrs P opened her eyes as I came near and said very loudly, 'Am Tam!'

'Yes, love,' I said, 'you just lie nice and quiet till the doctor comes.'

She frowned, pointed her finger at me imperiously and repeated 'Am Tam, Am Tam!'

I did a quick translation.

'*A pan?*' I asked. '*Now?*'

She smiled happily and nodded. 'Am Tam!'

I found a nurse and she came quickly with another one.

It took two of them to heave my mother up and she sat like a queen enthroned, beaming delightedly at her subjects. There was a loud report from under the bedclothes, which caused her immense satisfaction. She bowed from side to side to each nurse in turn and did a kind of royal salute.

'Ank 'oo! O mutz,' she declared loftily. And in spite of every-thing we all got the giggles. No wonder they used to call her 'Duchess' when she was younger.

It was short-lived, that moment of hilarity. In fact it made me feel much worse. Was I to lose this wonderful parent who had always, no matter what the horrors of any situation, been able to make me laugh? Even now, with her conscious mind in retreat, she was busy entertaining the troops.

186

I rushed out to find one of the doctors I knew coming towards me.

'Go home,' he said. 'You can't do anything here. We've done some X-rays and the best thing we can do is to let her rest. You're so close that if you stay she'll sense your worry and try to stay awake. If there's the slightest change, we'll ring you at once. You look as if you could do with some rest yourself. You'll be more use to her after you're rested.'

'But what is it?' I cried.

'We don't know. It could be a stroke, but it doesn't seem like that somehow. I've asked Dr Williams to come over. He's on his way now.'

'Thank heaven!' I said. 'Dr Williams knows all her other ailments and she likes him.' He is also one of those doctors who isn't afraid to try something new if he has to, and he treats his patients as human beings instead of ailing morons.

'Do you think I should ring and cancel this week's programme?' I said now. 'They'll need quite a lot of notice to replace it.'

'No,' said Dr Richards. 'Don't do anything till we've had a better chance to look at her. At least wait till the morning. Just go and get some rest yourself now.'

I tiptoed back to the room where Mrs P lay, now asleep once more. As soon as I sat down by the bed, she opened her eyes and I could see she was trying to reassure me. We are both so close mentally that even in her fog she could sense my terror, in some deep core of her being. I realized that Dr Richards was right. While I was there she wouldn't rest and, after the night we'd had, waltzing round with her temporary madness, she needed it badly. I smoothed her hair back from her face and crept away.

The ward sister was waiting for me at the door.

'I can't bear it,' I said. 'She isn't really there.'

'I know, dear,' she said. 'It's the thing most people feel the worst. When someone they love isn't there in themselves. It's the loneliness, they say.'

And she was so right. My mother has always been something of a creaking gate. I was no stranger to her being ill and in hospital, but every other time she had been normal in mind and spirit. This time there was the merest flicker of the person I knew on that bed.

I must have driven home, I suppose. Gwynneth came over to help me with the stock and, when I told her I couldn't find a single respectable nightdress or towel fit for hospital use, she collected a vast bundle from the linen basket and took them off home to wash in her automatic machine, something I didn't have in those days.

I didn't sleep that night. I sat up editing tape. It was the one way to keep me from going mad. Instead I drove them crazy at the hospital, ringing up every hour. 'No change' was their only reply all that long night. And, all the while, Mrs P's dog Winston, who'd never been parted from her in all his life, sat on the back of her armchair and howled and howled and howled.

Next morning I rang Mary and told her to go on red alert. Mary is wonderful in a crisis.

'Don't worry,' she said, 'if the worst comes to the worst we can always bring a couple of sound recordists out and do the programme there. Don't worry. We'll cope somehow.

When Gwynneth and I arrived at hospital, Mrs P just about knew who I was, but was clearly puzzled by Gwynneth. She still looked like a bewildered child. The general feeling was that it was a stroke, but one that would get better. All her limbs were working normally and the only symptoms were the lack of sense and the headache.

I left her to rest, came home and attended to the stock and went on editing. Like people hunting through their ruined homes after a flood or fire for some sign of the normality of their lives before disaster overtook them, salvaging the programme was all I dared to think of. If I took my mind off it for one moment the horror of what was happening to my mother engulfed me completely. I felt that if I could just get this one thing done I could cope with the nightmare better.

Now, convention decrees that in cases such as my mother's desperate illness my place was at her bedside. The first doctor had been deeply shocked at any suggestion of me going off to do my work. I suppose most people would be. But I knew that Mrs P would understand. She had sacrificed as much time, years of being broke and emotional effort, as I had to get that programme on the air, and the fact that we'd succeeded at last had been a matter of immense pride to her. She, could she have said so, would have been adamant that I go on with it.

There was another aspect to it and one which very few people would comprehend. We have been so close knit, my mother and I, that always the actual physical presence of one or the other has been of little significance. My body may have been at home, looking after the animals or engrossed in editing, but the real part of me was with her in the hospital and I knew that she would be far more conscious of that than anything else. And, although the surface of my mind and its connecting nerves were jangling with fright, deep down inside I knew that she would be all right.

'I could get you to Bristol early tomorrow morning and, if you were needed, have you back in a very short time,' offered Myrddin.

'All you have to do is fling the edited tapes at me, record the script and I'll do the tidying up,' said Mary.

'My sister Becky will come and look after the animals and sit by the phone,' said Sara Ellis, Bertie's wife.

'Your mother has been able to sit up and eat a bit of supper tonight,' said the nurse when I rang the hospital very late.

So I sat up all night and edited and scripted. At some time there was a timid knock on the door and when I opened it a small person in khaki trousers, a pink overshirt, a long plait and dangling earrings announced that she was Sara's sister and what could she do to help. When I gestured at the incredible mess everywhere, she simply smiled and disappeared, to come back with strong coffee, which she kept me supplied with most of that long night.

I checked with the hospital before Myrddin collected me at seven the next morning. Mrs P was demanding room service and obviously getting it.

I tried to catch up on some sleep as we flashed along the morning roads to Bristol, but the Red Shoes danced in front of me all the way. I thought I'd got rid of them long ago, but there they were every time I closed my eyes. Mrs P had told me the story when I was a little girl, probably to stop me rushing off somewhere I shouldn't – the beautiful Red Shoes, bewitching the feet of the young girl so that she left her ailing mother and went off to dance in them. But when at last she tired of dancing the shoes wouldn't let her stop, but made her dance on and on and on, till the girl was worn out, and still the shoes made her dance until the only release was to have them cut off, feet and all. A dreadful story that had haunted me for years, till I thrust if out of my mind ruthlessly so that I could get on with my own life. But it was lingering all the time in the background, waiting to pounce. Like now, for wasn't this just the same sort of thing? Could I really trust that inner sense that all would be well?

Mary said I put the programme together like a zombie. Not all her smiles and wiles could get my voice up off the studio floor. And when we finally turned back home for Wales the full terror of what I might find at the hospital rushed over me, the lesser emergency no longer dulling its intensity.

'Of course, when I was a young nurse, we wouldn't have been allowed to do it like that.' The voice was strong and clear and very much in command.

Myrddin and I stood outside the ward and grinned at each other.

'Sounds familiar,' said Myrddin; 'more like someone we know.'

'Yes,' I sighed happily. 'If she's complaining, she's feeling a lot better.'

'Did you really think I'd gone mad?' my mother demanded when I filled her in on the forty-eight hours she'd missed. 'Did I say some very awful things?'

'You said some very funny things,' I said, 'and I shall blackmail you with them for ever.' And I told her about her Royal Personage performance on the 'Am Tam', to her great embarrassment but even greater amusement.

She wasn't completely out of the woods yet, they told me. But it hadn't been a stroke. They thought it was some extremely nasty virus which had affected her lungs and cut down the oxygen supply to her brain. Hence the confusion and the headache.

'But I did think she was a goner,' said Dr Williams. 'She's a tough fighter, your mother. A lot of other people wouldn't have made it.'

'You were fighting, too, weren't you?' said Mrs P. 'I could feel you here by the bed all the time.'

'I wasn't, you know. I was at home for some of the time.'

'But the real you was here. I know, I saw you clearly,' she said, and she settled back contentedly on her pillows. I left her at last, dozing peacefully.

I wished I could have just curled up in the chair beside her and slept too. The thought of the awful mess at home made my own prospect of sleep a long way off.

When Myrddin turned his car in at the gate, Becky was out by the gate to meet us. Inside, the house was spotless, Winston had stopped howling, the rest of the dogs were calm, and Becky had a piping-hot meal waiting for me.

'And I've made you another quiche and this tart for tomorrow,' she said in her quiet, unfussed way.

'But the house!' I exclaimed.

'Oh, Sara came over and we both had a go at it. The only place we didn't touch was your office.' And, while I was still marvelling and gulping my thanks, she collected her things and was gone.

Dr Williams kept Mrs P in hospital until the series was over. And, if ever I had occasion to be grateful to anywhere, it was that hospital, where the staff had time to care about more than the physical needs of their patients. I think if Mrs P had been sent off to the big county hospital she wouldn't have made it, in spite of the superior technology and equipment. What she needed, and got, was the encouragement to fight and the subsequent kindness to make her fight worthwhile. But I regret to say that my mother's impact on that little cottage hospital was profound. She told the staff endless stories of her own days as a nurse in the good old days; boasted about me till they could have screamed; reminded them forcibly at all times that being older didn't mean stupid; and caused a mini-riot when a geriatric escapee from the men's ward arrived at her bedside, stark naked, and tried to hop in with her.

I heard about it all as I dashed in every day to see her, and for a while the world of the little hospital became as important as the one at home, where each week Becky came back to let me get away to Bristol. Except for once, when our old friend Jane Crawford did a split shift with Adeline Shackles.

191

Adeline had been at the farm during the day, feasted her eyes on Mrs P's collection of Agatha Christies and dived in. When I got back, the dogs had eaten half a pound of butter and assorted other trifles lying about, had dragged all their bedding out into the garden and applauded Lily when she hopped up and did a rapid tango on the only decent table I've got – or had.

'Rotten dogs!' I yelled at them. 'Taking advantage of a stranger!'

'I thought they were allowed to do those things,' said Adeline, who had a low opinion of my animal discipline. 'By the way, you've got a hell of a good kid out there. I mean one that could win at national shows.'

'Which one's that?' I asked as I tried to clear the dog havoc.

'I think it's Sophie's kid,' said Adeline. When it comes to goats, her eyes are very sharp indeed. 'Anyway, she's really good. I'd show her if she was mine.'

'Oh, I never show my goats,' I said dismissively. 'No time. But you probably mean Rebecca. A little devil! She's the wildest of the lot. Not a bit like her mother. I was thinking of selling her.'

'Don't!' cried Adeline. 'She's really something, that kid. Show her!'

'Not a chance,' I said. But the conversation was to spring back at me one day and prove that Adeline knows a thing or two about goats.

Meanwhile, the series finally came galloping to an end, Mrs P, to the intense relief of the staff at the little hospital, came home, and Winston went into a state of suspended bliss and didn't bite or bark for days and days. But the tightrope had twitched and wobbled a bit and things were never to be quite the same again.

Chapter 16

'**O**h, look!' exclaimed Mrs P. 'Ray's got the chimney brush all the way to the top.'

'Sshhh, Mother,' I hissed, 'that's not a chimney brush . . .'

'Hello, Mrs P,' cried the face that now appeared beneath the 'chimney brush'.

'. . . it's Mandy's hair!' I continued lamely.

'Hullo, Mandy,' called Mrs P. 'I thought you were the chimney brush.'

'Mother, did you have to tell her that?' I said fiercely.

Shrieks of laughter came from on high.

'Oh, my Afro again? Yes, I suppose it must look like that from down there. It's a wonderful view from up here. Ray says there've been a couple of kites coming over to see what we're doing.'

I glared at Mrs P and went inside to get some coffee for the couple balancing on the chimney stack. My thoughts were bitter. If I'd told Mandy her hair looked like a chimney brush she'd have clouted me. But Mrs P could say things like that and everyone just laughed. Which was extremely unfair, because, whilst I have a fatal tendency to assume that everyone is lovely until proved otherwise, Mrs P is a firm believer in the saying 'It is always a sin to think the worst of people, but it is not always a mistake'. She has, as I'm fond of reminding her, a mind like the proverbial sink.

'Love many, trust few and always paddle your own canoe,' she would reply blithely. 'Your trouble is that you hold open house on your canoe and when it tips over you can't understand why.'

'Whereas you repel boarders very firmly and still stay the best of friends. If I do it, they hate me for life.'

'Well, I've been on the river a bit longer than you. But I'd hoped you'd have learnt a thing or two by now. I get a bit tired of watching you being ripped off.'

Being ripped off by builders, of course, isn't difficult to achieve, especially in those areas where the good ones are booked up for years ahead and the cowboys gallop the range of home repairs unchecked.

But this time I'd struck it lucky. I'd found Ray and Mandy.

Ray was big and blond and gentle. Mandy was his girl-friend and had a dark mop of an Afro hairdo which Mrs P, who'd never seen one before, was constantly mistaking for something else if Mandy wasn't immediately visible beneath it. As she had now, as Mandy helped Ray to repoint the chimney. It was the one just above Mrs P's room and had been leaking badly onto her ceiling and provided a noisy, twig-filled nursery for generations of jackdaws. The annual jackdaw problem was not yet upon us, but the damp ceiling was about to collapse. So Mrs P was out at the back of the house peering up to supervise progress.

It had been raining (oh, how it had been raining!) for weeks. Water from the road, out of sight at the top of the hill, had poured down the field at the back of the house in a great, white, frothing torrent, blocked the yard drain, rushed through the barns and even threatened the house itself. The bottom meadow had flooded and one wall of the house was glistening with damp. In the kitchen, black oily water poured down both the outside and the inside of the Rayburn flue and spread evilly over the floor. I'd rung in desperation for a builder to come and do something about the flue and one inspired soul had suggested Ray.

He was a bit pale when he came down from examining the rusty pipe that thrust up through the slates.

'Who the hell put *that* up?' he demanded. 'Whoever it was used a rubber seal, the kind you use for septic tanks, and it's a wonder you haven't been burnt to the ground before this. As for the flue, it's the wrong size, the wrong material and it's cracked from top to bottom. Come up the ladder and see for yourself.'

I did as I was told and felt a bit pale myself when I came down, as much because I'm terrified of going up ladders as for the dangerous state of the flue. Ray was right, we should at least have been smothered by fumes, if not burnt in our beds, long before this.

194

I began to wonder if Mrs P's unidentified illness might have been caused by seepage from the Rayburn flue getting into her room, through the dreaded airing cupboard.

Within a couple of days Ray had stripped everything out, replaced the old flue with a shining, insulated one, found exactly the right kind of flat 'Chinese hat' to go on the top, and charged me a very fair rate. So I let him loose on Mrs P's chimney and, when he and Mandy had finished admiring the view and chatting to the two kites wheeling overhead, they'd done an excellent job.

'But, do you know,' said Ray, 'that chimney is full of sticks. I hope you don't use it any more.'

'Not since the last time I cleared it of sticks,' I said. 'The jackdaws just stuff them down till they fall into the fireplace in my office.'

'We'll put some wire around the top when we've finished,' said Ray, 'and we'll clear the sticks out from the bottom.'

We took six sacks of dusty twigs from the chimney, most of them bearing thorns, but although the jackdaws can no longer nest in it they still sit there poking sticks hopefully through the wire and the chimney's solid with them again.

Ray and Mandy were due to attend to the big chimney next, but the rain came again and went on and on, till the mud was ankle-deep and slimy with it.

'I know just what they felt like on Flanders Field now.' I told Mrs P. 'The mud stinks, too. Even poor old Doli's having trouble wading through it, the sheep are limping again and the goats are going stir crazy.' I looked in disgust at the glutinous mess still clinging to my boots. One of these days I'm going to invest in a tap just outside the door. A boot scraper would be a waste of time.

'So?' asked Mrs P, as I hopped over to the fire in my socks. 'What did Bertie say?'

'Bertie? About Doli? Well, after she'd trodden on his foot and he'd found an egg in the manger (that hen *is* laying, by the way), and he'd done his usual groping and feeling inside her, he said,' – I paused dramatically – 'he said that she's *in foal*.'

'Oh, *good!*' exclaimed Mrs P, already getting her midwife look on her face. 'What do you hope it will be?'

'A filly. And I'll keep it, so that when Doli goes eventually, there'll always be something of hers here.'

'Which probably means you'll get a boy,' said Mrs P, knowing my luck only too well.

'A colt, Mother,' I corrected her primly.

'A male anyway,' she said tartly. 'Did Bertie do a good interview?'

'Oh yes, he was on form today. Gave me lots of bits and pieces about how a horse's coat is designed to withstand the weather. He also explained why they roll so much in the mud when it's cold. Getting a 'mud duvet', he calls it, and then people go and ruin all that effort by brushing it off. When it's dry it keeps the cold out. How do *you* feel, by the way?'

'Me? Oh, I'm fine. Why?'

'Well, I've got to go and get some stuff for the Christmas programme again, up in North Wales. Myrddin says he can do his usual "lightning dash", but I don't like leaving you.'

Mrs P sighed. 'Gwynneth will keep an eye out for me,' she said, 'and I'll ask Nurse Williams to come that day instead of her usual one.'

Nurse Williams had been making weekly visits ever since Mrs P had come out of hospital. The excuse was to give Mrs P a proper bath and to see she was all right in general, but in fact the two of them spent most of the time having a lovely old nurses' gossip about ailments, known and unknown. It was the highlight of my mother's week and Nurse Williams did a great deal more for her mental state than her physical one. I loved hearing them giggle away together and always had a cup of tea and a dozen fresh eggs for the neat round lady in her spotless navy uniform. In fact, what with the friends she'd made in hospital and now Nurse Williams, her illness had done Mrs P's social life the world of good.

'Maybe Becky or Mandy would come and spend the day,' I said now.

'Oh dear, you do make me tired sometimes,' said my mother. 'I'll be fine.'

And so, once again, Myrddin and I set out for North Wales, with a short diversion to see a litter of Kelpie pups, some of the first in the country. And just for a while I felt desperately homesick, remembering that the last time I'd seen Kelpies was where they looked best, in the Australian outback, rounding up great mobs of sheep in that quick, highly intelligent way of theirs. For a moment the smell of the dust, the blasting sun and the great sea of woollen backs with dogs darting and diving, or running across the top of them, was superimposed on the green, wind-swept fields of that small farm beside the sea in Wales. I almost bought a Kelpie, but the breeder was doubtful if I'd have enough work for it and, as this litter had to make the name of the breed in Britain, I was not considered a right and proper owner.

I consoled myself with the unicorns, dancing and rocking, far away in the north in a house with huge chimneys and big chunky stone walls and the MacPhersons.

The MacPhersons repaired old rocking horses and made sledges (they were hoping for a really hard, snow-bound winter) and their own new rocking horses modelled on native British ponies. They also made a rocking unicorn, big enough for an adult to ride.

We were late, very late, to the next place, because I kept going back to have another ride on the unicorn. My original interest in unicorns is far too complex (and part of the story belongs to someone else, too) to explain easily, but once you start looking into the legend it grows and grows on you. There was no way I could afford either the space or the money to add the MacPhersons' 'Orion' to my collection, but I found it hard to leave him behind. However, the MacPhersons had cheered me up a little by telling me that I had something rather unique in that collection already. I had an early, signed, Sam Smith unicorn. Sam Smith, who had died recently, was, according to them, a kind of toy-maker's Henry Moore.

Stuart and Pam had gone quite still when I first mentioned, laughing, that I had a strange little wooden unicorn, with a blue and white spiralled horn, a zany look on its face and a rather tattered tinselled saddle.

'It was found for me by a friend,' I told them. 'It was sitting in an antique shop on their 'bargain' table, priced one pound. It's a queer little thing. It's got a stamp on the bottom which says 'Sam Smith' and then next to that in real writing, it says 'Sam Smith' again. Must have been some amateur to stamp it *and* sign it.'

'Did you say "Sam Smith"?' asked Stuart.

'Yes! Isn't it a great name to find on a unicorn?'

So then they told me about Sam Smith and his wonderful toys and how, in his earlier days, he'd made hand-carved wooden ones, which were now, if you could find them, collectors' items. And, as they talked so enthusiastically, apart from being pleased that my humble but much-loved £1-on-the-bargain-table unicorn, with its dotty face, was suddenly a star, I marvelled yet again at all the little worlds with their histories, their great people, their ambitions, their knowledge and their passions, which most of us pass by and know nothing of. And now, for a brief moment, my little painted unicorn had led me into this one of toys and toy-makers.

There was another such world waiting for us down a dark lane, not many miles away. Nothing lit our way except a hurricane lantern hung on a gatepost.

Gripping our torches, we stumbled past a tall barn, down a steep path, and found below us what seemed to be a house from which no light escaped.

'Are they having a blackout?' wondered Myrddin.

'No, I don't think they've got electricity at all.'

'So how do they manage, then?' he exclaimed.

'With hurricane lamps, by the look of it,' I replied, as a thin light wavered at us unevenly through the total darkness.

Candles and oil lamps in the big, flagged kitchen with the scrubbed table where a tiny, shell-like new baby lay asleep, face down on a pillow; another smaller room with a rocking chair and a leaping fire; dark passages which ended in a beamed workshop where the christening stools were made; the creaking of the old mill and the chiming of clocks; an owl screaming outside, and, inside, music on flute and guitar. We stumbled back past the gaunt barn, past the flickering lantern on the gate, and wondered if we'd dreamt it all.

At last Myrddin spoke. 'Why are they called christening stools?'

'They were given as christening presents and they had the child's name carved on them and quite often lots of elaborate decoration too. Richard Fox said it was an old Welsh custom, particularly here in the north. I should think they were a lot more use than a spoon.

You could sit on them and later use them as a little table and they were handed down as heirlooms. Richard Fox is just reviving an old craft, but they were usually made by a relation of the baby's.' I paused. 'Funny he should be called Richard *Fox*.'

'Oh, what's so funny about being called Fox?' asked Myrddin.

'Nothing except that we'd just been talking about my Sam Smith unicorn and the friend who gave him to me was called Sally *Fox*.'

'Mmmm,' said Myrddin doubtfully, sensing that I was about to wax esoteric, and said not a great deal more as he flung the car around his network of short cuts to make up for the time we'd lost as I agonized over Kelpie pups, rocked on the unicorn and listened to the Foxes' music.

A few days later I was trekking a flock of reluctant guinea fowl, watching my solicitor David Green sounding off his shotgun before he explained the game laws to me and then gave me the recipe for a special home-made liqueur that would take your socks off, rushing across country to hear about elegant Llanwenog sheep with their smart black faces and legs and curly white top-knots, and hunting down the man who drove our garbage lorry to see his vast collection of miniature fairgrounds, all in perfect working order.

Out in the wide world, Mrs Gandhi was assassinated and Ronald Reagan won the presidential elections. In our world, the goats came into season, the Shackles' arrived with a large male called Mousie, the rain came back with a good dose of thunder and lightning, the Rayburn flue had to be extended as the water poured in again and, frantic for time, I began to edit the tapes for the Christmas programme.

That morning, my first thought as I screamed into consciousness was 'This time I really won't make it. If I edit all day and all night, I won't make it.'

Feeble cries of alarm from the next room – Mrs P, eyes aghast, unable to speak, and blood everywhere. Ice packs and pressure and prayers did nothing to stem her massive Metro-Goldwyn-Mayer epic of a nosebleed. This time they sent the ambulance straight away.

'You're doing it on purpose,' I said as my poor mother, face swollen, peered up at me from the pillows.

'That's what you get for having a Fire Horse for a mother,' she murmured, smiling wanly.

According to the more serious books on Chinese astrology, to be born in the Year of the Fire Horse is plain unlucky – so unlucky that once Chinese women actually tried to bring on an abortion to save their child from such a fate. That's the bad news. The good news is that they're only born every sixty years. Mrs P was born in 1906 (and so was that sad, brilliant man T. H. White), and she does seem to attract mishaps more than most and to do so at the most inconvenient moments. But she also had a greater dose of the 'Life Force' than anyone I know and has survived things that would send most people screaming into oblivion. It's something Fire Horses seem to have in common, and I've met quite a few, both the 1906 and 1966 vintages.

'Nothing to do with all that,' I said to my mother now. 'It's all because you will overdo things. I told you not to go rabbiting around in the kitchen.'

'I am not,' she said as fiercely as she could with her nose stuffed full of cotton wool, 'going to sit on a chair for the rest of my life.'

She'd lost so much blood they had to keep her in hospital for weeks to make it up again. Winston sat on the back of her armchair at home and howled, while I got on with the editing, dashed to the hospital every day and seriously considered suicide. Ray took me to Bristol, while Mandy minded the dogs. Ray was a rally driver and, if his car was a great deal older than Myrddin's, he knew just as many short cuts and went even faster.

The next Sunday there was a full colour picture in *The Observer* of my living room. Sitting in the big Windsor chair was a happy, relaxed-looking woman, cradling a cat, with adoring dogs round her feet. The room itself was bright and clean and cosy; a fire leapt, flowers spilled artistically out of vases. It was the sort of room I'd have loved to live in, and the woman they'd interviewed for the piece, efficient, 'with a bracing line in humour' (although you could see she had the odd sensitive thought), happy and content in her beautiful surroundings, was just the sort of person I'd have liked to have been.

'Well it *is* like that sometimes,' said Mrs P as she proudly displayed the article to the nurses.

'Not right at the moment, it isn't,' I muttered darkly.

But it was, by the time she came home again, and if the owner of the room was rather jaded she could at least put one foot in front of the other if she tried hard. Mrs P, of course, was bouncing with impatience.

'Why,' I cried, 'will you not just go to bed and rest?'

'I've got all my Christmas cooking to do,' she said, and nothing I could do would stop her trotting out to her lair to get on with it.

It snowed gently on Boxing Day and, as I came back from the yard that night, the cast-iron lantern on the side wall of the cottage gave it a quaintness it lacks during the day. The light underlined the great branches of the ash tree and sparkled off the snow under our feet as the dogs and I returned from checking the stock. As we passed the rose bush by the wall, it seemed as if one lone rose had lingered. It was a robin, head under its wing and pink breast plumped out. A dead leaf, clinging to a stem, acted as a tiny umbrella. It was a shame to disturb it, but the rose was well within cat height. I touched the side of its wing and the robin woke up, looked about, realized its awful mistake and flew off to its usual roost high in the thorn tree by the gate.

On New Year's Day it was crisp and cold and sunny, and the poultry looked like patchwork as they preened themselves against the green bank by the stream. I went for a walk on the meadow, the goats went mad with joy and the whippets chased Lily as she jinked and danced through the trees. By now Ike and Ginger Meggs were showing their breeding but, if over a short distance, they were faster than the big lurcher, she could give them best over the wide space of the meadow. For the moment, all this racing had taken her mind off squirrels. I sat up on the bank by the hollow ash tree and watched the goats shopping in the bramble bushes, and the dogs, tired at last, came to join me.

There are several big ash trees on the meadow and in the woods, but this one was on the edge of both, just high enough up the slope to give a long view of river and meadow, but not so high that it meant a steep climb to reach it. It stood quite alone and, from the meadow side, looked strong and whole. From behind, however, it was only half a tree. It was as if someone had taken a great sword and sliced the trunk from top to bottom, but so long ago that the wound was dark and weathered by time. It amazed me that the tree was so very much alive and could maintain its hold on the steep slope so well. Its roots formed a natural bank and there was room for the dogs and me to sit without the goats coming to disturb us, for very little grew under it. Over the years it had become one of our stopping places.

There was a heavy frost that night, but the sun came out the next day and played its magic game of perspectives with the valley, one moment making everything seem two-dimensional and then, with one twitch of the eye, deepening the shadows so that even the most distant outcrop of rock came alive, and sometimes the hills crowded in and sometimes they spread out to infinity. But the frost, when it took hold again, was heavier and it got heavier and heavier, until the ground began to crack and the sun was too weak to melt it.

'I heard a terrible noise last night,' said Mrs P one day.

'Probably Concorde,' I said absently.

'No, it was too late for that. And I don't think it was shooting either. There was this awful sharp crack and a kind of tearing noise. It seemed very close, too.'

I didn't pay much attention to this detailed description. Mrs P's sound effects, as I've said before, were a bit over the top sometimes. I checked the roofs, the buildings and the trees around the yard and on the immediate horizon, and forgot it.

It was quite a while before I went down to the meadow again. The snow came back and covered the frosty ground and the days were taken up with keeping the sheep and Doli and the goats fed and watered, and the house supplied with wood and coal, all of this taking so much more time because one false step and I was flat on my back. The birds came crowding onto the kitchen windowsills or stood in queues on the arms of the rotary clothes line, where I'd hung bags of Mrs P's special recipe of fat and raisins and peanuts – amongst other things. Behind the house, a big grey mountain fox stared at me insolently, peed against the telegraph pole and sauntered off casually, his brush flicking the snow as he went.

202

And still it froze and still the snow came and a truly awful blizzard was forecast. I rang Cardiff Weather Centre to check, and the man there was very sympathetic. 'You've got about eighteen hours to get ready and batten down the hatches,' he said, 'and I just wish you the best of luck. Where you live will be one of the worst-hit areas, I think.'

It didn't come (although by then I was a cot case anyway); instead there was the blessed sound of dripping. The thaw had set in. It dribbled and dropped; snow slid off the roof and took a few slates with it; the stream through the yard began rushing and tearing and the mud was almost knee deep.

At last, on a still day, with the water receding and the animals turned out to enjoy the weak, apologetic sun, the dogs and I escaped to the meadow once more – through the little wood, over to the pine tree to check on the owl, down the path and through the gate to look out on the broad grassland.

I couldn't make out what was wrong for a while. I followed the dogs, as they rushed ahead, and it appeared that there was a darkness over that usually clear, gently hollowed space. Something monstrous was destroying its symmetry.

It was the hollow ash tree. It had fallen, with some kind of almighty force, from its perch up on the slope, had wiped out the alder and hazel hedge below it and now lay across the meadow half buried in piles of smashed branches. It looked like an ocean-going liner stranded on a beach.

'I told you I heard a terrible noise,' said Mrs P smugly when I came home, still shocked by what I'd seen.

'It must have been that frost,' I said slowly. 'Cracked it like a twig. God knows how I'm going to get it shifted.'

'Why not leave it there,' shrugged Mrs P. 'It's not in the way, is it?'

'I can't do that. It's ruining the meadow. It's obscene, some-how.'

It took two men and a tractor four whole days to carve it up and carry the great logs up to the farmyard. They broke three chainsaw blades and had to give up on the iron-hard roots, which still lie at the foot of the slope like great smashed teeth. The rest of it provided me with firewood for the next two winters.

'There's tons of it,' said Arwyl Davies, whose tractor and chainsaws had been churning around between farmyard and meadow for ever, it seemed. He'd been persuaded into doing the job by his neighbour, Pete, who sometimes did odd jobs for me. I don't think Arwyl thanked him for it in the end. He'd thought it might take a day, maybe a day and a half, and instead he and Pete had sweated and cursed in the bitter easterly winds which now wracked the valley day after day. It cost me almost twice as much as the original estimate and Arwyl had been deeply apologetic about that.

'You've earned every penny of it,' I reassured him, and actually, by the time he'd paid for new chainsaw blades and extra diesel for the tractor and Pete's labour, I doubt if he broke even on the job.

'Well, I'll just bring up a few more of those thicker branches for you,' said Arwyl at last, 'and we'll call it a day.'

'Have some coffee first,' I said waving a big red thermos flask at him and Pete.

'I don't like coffee much,' said Arwyl.

'You'll like this coffee,' Pete told him.

Arwyl wrinkled his nose as he put his lips to the mug of coffee. His face lightened and then he smacked his lips and drank deeply.

'Some more?' I asked as he stared into the bottom of the mug regretfully.

'Yes please! Funny thing. I never liked coffee before, but that was really good. I might start drinking it now.'

'I said you'd like *this* coffee,' said Peter, and winked at me.

Arwyl, who'd been looking cold and tired and a bit worried before, drank his second mug and beamed rosily at his friend.

'You see,' said Pete, 'when it's cold, she always laces the coffee with whisky. You've probably just downed a couple of doubles.'

I heard them singing down in the wood as they demolished the last of the hollow ash tree.

Nothing has ever grown, except grass, on the great open bank where the tree once stood, but last summer the badger cubs used it for a slide and nothing could be more perfect for that.

As Mrs P said, when the first of the hard-won logs blazed on the fire, which had been kindled with the twigs the jackdaws had donated, 'It's an ill frost that does nobody any good.'

'I just hope,' I said, thinking of the devastation the tree had caused, 'that nothing ever brings down the ash tree by the house. It's even bigger and it would smash everything in its path – the barns, the house, the . . .'

'You worry too much,' said Mrs P firmly.

And she's quite right. I do.

Chapter 17

X—X—X—X—X—X—X—X—X

The crow sat in the ash tree and jeered at me.

'If I had a gun you'd smirk on the other side of your beak,' I shouted at it, and I flung another stick up into the branches. The crow looked bored to death. Finally it opened its wings and floated lazily down to the edge of the wood, where it settled in the goat willow and cawed derisively.

'I am definitely going to get a gun,' I told Mrs P when I stormed back into the house.

'Don't,' she said. 'The only thing you'll shoot is your foot. Get someone else to have a go at them.'

'I keep asking people and they promise and never come,' I said hopelessly.

'Probably because they know you'll suddenly feel sorry for the crows and start weeping and wailing.'

I ignored this hurtful barb and went back outside.

The winter had dragged on and on, with a blizzard at the back end of March, followed by more rain, which made the mud so deep now that my legs ached with the effort of dragging them through it. If the official time for spring had come, there was no joy in it. Even the gay birdsong of celebration faltered and only the mad, rollicking jackdaws and the crack-voiced crows shouted in the valley awash with gloom.

The crows, of course, were having a field day, with the ewes struggling to give birth with their wool clogged down by mud and their helpless lambs being born straight out into the cold muck. I had seen what crows can do to a helpless sheep, young or old, and, although my own were still tucked up in the hay-barn, the crows, emboldened by their success elsewhere, hopped in amongst them on the off chance of more pickings. And if they failed there, due to my constant diligence, they waited till the hens were let out and raided the nests of eggs. Meanwhile, their smaller cousins, the jackdaws, mobbed the feed troughs or stuffed sticks under the slates on the roof, down Mrs P's chimney and into the owl hole in the barn.

For a long time I'd thought that the wide rectangular slit high up in the gable end of the big barn was just another air vent. But then I learnt about the old practice of leaving an entrance for barn owls to keep rats and mice down. The idea that one day a barn owl might come back to live in my own barn was bewitching. It was even suggested to me that perhaps a pair could be released there from one of the breeding sanctuaries that are trying to repair some of the damage done to the barn owl population by modern farming. The jackdaws put paid to this idea by filling the owl hole with their dusty, musty thorn sticks, so that the hay below was a mess and I had at last to block the space up. The jackdaws retaliated by stuffing sticks round the hole where the electricity wires go into the barn, and almost caused a short circuit.

If the jackdaws were irritating and noisy, the crows were more lethal. Not content with raiding the eggs, they began to kill the smaller bantams and the young pigeon squabs. I had a nasty feeling they'd start on me next.

It was my own fault, as usual. I should have been destroying their nests, or making a real effort to find a good shot to come and clear them out. On the one hand my idiot sentimentality held me back and, on the other, crows are not easy to shoot. They seem to know when there's a gun about, and it would have needed someone with a lot of patience to catch this wily, sinful lot.

So, what with the rain, the mud, the jackdaws and the crows, lambing was more exhausting than usual. Added to which, the sheep ran through every variety of problem. There was no general illness, just a host of individual complications, which ranged from lambs that were too big, too many, too mixed up together, too soon or too late. The ewes had either no milk, too much milk, no mothering instinct, or so much that they wanted all the lambs belonging to everyone else as well. The lambs themselves, once born, were a fine bunch and, in spite of having to stay in out of the heavy rain and hail storms, made a race track of the barn for their games, using the recumbent ewes as hurdles.

At last it was all over and there was only one little soul for whom no willing udder could be found. Her own mother, Hetty, she of the golden face and much loved because of her own rather special birth,[1] washed her, suckled her and then gave birth to another, male, lamb which she adored to distraction. I found her trying to kill her first lamb a good twenty-four hours later, when I'd long since stopped worrying about that particular little family. After a week, during which my opinion of Hetty reached a very low ebb, I gave up trying to make her accept her lamb and began to bottle-feed it myself.

In between all the dramas in the sheep-shed, the goats had their own full-scale Techicolour production going on. One of them, Victoria, a wild little thing, had given birth to two males and, crying bitterly while I did it, I'd had them put down. Even the thought that their ultimate fate would be much worse, and that then they'd know all about it, whereas now they went from one contented sleep to another longer, more permanent one, never helps to make the decision easier.

In a normal year, I probably wouldn't have wheeled Hetty's unwanted lamb into Victoria. A lot of people do use goats to suckle spare lambs, but lambs can be pretty rough on the delicate udder of a finely bred goat. Neither have the few goats on whom I've half-heartedly tried the experiment in the past been too enthusiastic; rather, hysterically against the whole idea. So, on a morning of total chaos, when I took little Quilpa into the goat-shed to see if I could plug her into Victoria just this once, I wasn't too hopeful.

It was passionate, unquestioning love, on both sides, at first sight. Victoria washed the lamb, nudged it towards her udder and, for the first time since she'd given birth herself, cudded happily. As even the most obliging of foster mothers usually needs either the skin of her own dead offspring tied around the orphan or time for the smell of her own milk to penetrate it before she'll accept it completely, this instant success was remarkable. And so

[1]See *Wind in the Ash Tree*.

they remained, Victoria and her lamb, a blissfully contented pair, until Lulu gave birth.

She was, naturally, very late. Ever since her own mother had died as a result of bearing her and her two brothers, Lulu had been a nuisance. She is big and fat and loud and always where she shouldn't be. Now, when at last the rain had gone and the full glory of spring released the lambs and ewes from the shed, Lulu was still languishing in the lambing pens. I suspected that, back in the autumn, the ram had left her until he was without any other alternative. Mating with Lulu must have been a disturbing experience. She was named after the song 'Don't Bring Lulu', and I'll bet the ram found out why.

Lulu's udder grew and grew, and so did Lulu, until at last she gave birth to one enormous lamb, which was deformed and died almost at once.

'What are you going to do about milking her?' asked Gwynneth as we sat, exhausted, after delivering the lamb between us. 'Damn, that's a big udder. You'll have to strip her out.'

'I think I shall have to put that lamb Victoria's got onto Lulu,' I said slowly. I hated to do it, but milking Victoria was one thing, milking Lulu out was quite another. And although, at the moment, the lamb was young enough to live with the goats, she really needed to be out on the grass with the sheep. One day she'd have to live with the flock anyway; better she learnt to be a sheep now, rather than later.

This time I had the skin of Lulu's own dead lamb to put over little Quilpa, and Lulu was perfectly happy to adopt her at once. But the lamb herself was horrified. After its nice, elegant, smooth-haired goat, this great, slobbering, hairy monster with a voice like a fog-horn was a nightmare. Even when it had finally accepted Lulu and begun to enjoy the freedom of the fields and the frantic lamb races, if Victoria was outside and called to it the lamb rushed to her side and stayed there till Lulu came up in her big, bossy way and threatened to clobber the little goat. It was all for the best in the end, but at the time I felt awful.

'Well, what else could you do?' asked Mrs P, as I moped around. 'We needed the goat's milk, not the sheep's. And I'd really appreciate a few eggs too.'

209

'I can't keep the poor hens locked up all day now.' I said. 'They've hardly seen the sun for months. And if I let them out the crows pinch their eggs. As soon as they've had a few days of grass and grubs, I'll keep them in for a bit again.'

'Better to get rid of the crows,' said Mrs P darkly. 'Why don't you catch a couple of the horrible things and hang them up as a warning to others?'

I stared at her in disgust. 'Catch them? How do you catch a crow?' But Mrs P was suddenly very busy banging saucepans about and the conversation died there. I sighed and prayed for deliverance.

It came, quite unexpectedly, in a battered, orange car.

'Yes?' I demanded of the youth who crept out of it.

'Well, um, I was wondering if you wanted any odd jobs done,' he mumbled. 'My mother said you sometimes do.'

'And who,' I asked, 'is your mother?'

'She's the matron of the hospital. Mrs Carr. I'm James Carr.' He paused. 'I'm really looking for a job for the summer holidays.'

'It is not,' I pointed out unnecessarily, 'summer yet.'

'No, but all the others in my class at school have got their summer jobs all fixed up, so I thought I'd look about now. But I only want it part-time because I have to help my father on our farm.'

A crow began to squawk in the tree above us and was joined by another almost at once.

'Get out of it!' I yelled at them. They flew languidly into the next tree and stropped their beaks.

I turned back to my visitor. 'I don't suppose you ever see any dead crows about on the road do you? I'm looking for a couple to hang up as a warning. They're driving me mad at the moment. Anyway, I'm sorry, but I think I've got some help lined up for the summer.'

'I could come now, after school, and do a bit of wood-chopping or mucking out for you,' said James Carr, eagerly. 'Just to show you how I can work.'

'Sorry,' I said. 'I don't really need too much done at the moment. But if I hear of anyone who does, I'll let you know.'

He nodded resignedly, reversed his old car back down the lane, waved and was gone.

He came back three days later.

'I'm sorry,' I said, as he opened the car door, 'I still haven't heard of anyone looking for a worker.'

He didn't say anything, just reached into the back of the car and brought forth two very large, and very dead, crows.

'Where did you find them?' I cried.

'I shot them for you,' said James briefly, 'for you to hang up as a warning to the others.'

I looked at him thoughtfully as he stood there shyly, dangling the crows from his hands.

'Speaking of this job,' I said at last, 'how much to you want an hour?'

'Well, I thought I could come and do some work for you first and then you could decide how much I'm worth.'

'James Carr,' I said, 'you're on! First thing you can do is tie those crows up just above the hen house.'

I won't say that the sight of them diminished the crow numbers too much, but they did leave the hen house alone and stopped murdering the young pigeons. And James Carr was a great success. He walloped the nettles and docks down, weeded and trimmed the garden, carried buckets of water for me, mucked out sheds and made me laugh. For James didn't say a lot in his soft voice with the faint tinge of a Scottish accent, but he had a very dry wit and a quick ear for the ridiculous. But Mrs P found communicating with him a little difficult.

'You've got a voice like a silkworm, James Carr,' she said to him one day.

'And muscles like a chicken's instep?' said James, grinning at her and using one of her own expressions back. He never missed a trick.

One day he brought me a clutch of guinea-fowl eggs to hatch out under one of my broodies for his mother. When the tiny eggs cracked open and the chicks, with their big feet and creaky little chirps, came out, he handled them with great tenderness. If I could have, I'd have left James in charge of the whole farm. But James was still at school and, when the time came for me to get on the road again, I found myself in deep trouble.

Until she fell ill, Mrs P had always taken charge of the house, the dogs and the phone when I was away. Gwynneth, in spite of having a great deal to do on her own farm, had come over to feed the stock, milk the goats and bring in coal and wood for my mother. Now, although Gwynneth was still willing to care for the outside animals twice a day, I needed someone to look after Mrs P herself. Apart from the fact that I was terrified she'd have another of her massive nose bleeds when she was alone, she was also a lot weaker since her illness and, although she stoutly declared she was just as able to cope as before, I wasn't going to give her the chance.

At some time during March, when faint stirrings from Bristol reminded me of the summer ahead, I began to ask around for someone who wanted the job of house and mother sitting. I'd been about to advertise when a local woman asked if she could have the job. It seemed perfect because, before she'd married, she'd worked as a housekeeper for an elderly lady who was far less mobile than Mrs P, and rather senile with it. And so it was settled, although I had a nasty hunch that it had all seemed too easy somehow. There was her husband, for a start – a husband who liked his wife at his beck and call and his meals on time and hot.

I rang several times to check that this would not be a problem.

'Stop worrying! It was his idea anyway,' I was told sternly. 'He said we could do with the money. I'll leave him lots of meals in the freezer and he and my daughter can help themselves.'

Still not entirely reassured, I rang again several times. I also asked the husband if he was really happy about the whole plan and he was astounded that I had any doubts at all.

Now I must explain that setting up one of my safaris for *A Small Country Living* took an enormous amount of time. To begin with, I had to hunt down the stories and the people I was looking for. Mostly, I wasn't too sure what I was looking for anyway and sat for hours at the phone, making random stabs at an idea, until at last, in the midst of all the numbers I'd rung, I would find just who and what I wanted. Then there would be a long conversation to make sure I'd got the story right and to see if there were any sub-plots I could use as well. I would then start the whole procedure again, until I'd collected at least twenty interviews for, say, a five-day trip – often it was more like thirty. Once I knew where the people and the stories were located, I then had to plan the journey so that they were in geographical sequence, work out a possible schedule, and ring back to see if everyone could fit in with it. One hitch at this stage and the whole thing had to be worked out again from the start. The next step was to double-check all the detailed directions, spend a good day with maps to see if they tallied and then type up every single bump on the road, names, dates and phone numbers. Then it was a question of finding places to stay, making bookings, and so on.

The whole exercise took up time, patience and money for the phone. Added to which, by now a lot of people had agreed to rearrange their lives for me, often rushing back from shows or business trips or holidays and generally having to wipe out a day of their time. At my end, there was a major reorganization of the house and farm, to make things easier for Gwynneth or whoever was looking after them.

That year, my first sortie was to be made into West Sussex, Hampshire, Wiltshire and Somerset. It was well on into May and at last I'd put my fears to rest about whether the helper would come as promised. She and her husband had had plenty of time to change their minds by now.

Four days before I was due to leave, they rang to say she wasn't coming. They gave lots of reasons, but I was pretty sure that it had finally hit the husband that he'd have to do more than boil a kettle for the next week.

I rang the world over the next couple of days. I begged, I pleaded and I promised the earth, but most of the possibles had already taken up jobs for the coming summer. The only spark of hope came from Yorkshire, where Penny at Skipton Hill Farm said that Sue Wetherby, whom I'd met the previous year, might be interested in coming. I rang Sue and, indeed, she'd be delighted to help me out, but she couldn't just walk out on her present job in Northumberland. She could come in ten days' time, if that would help.

'That will cover the next two trips,' I told Mrs P, 'but I'll have to cancel all these other people and I won't have a chance to go back that way this year.'

'You go!' came the reply. 'Gwynneth and I will cope. Nurse Williams will come if I need her. I'm feeling so much better and, frankly, I'm glad that woman isn't coming. I knew she'd let you down.'

I wasn't happy about it, but as one voice they urged me to go, Mrs P and her back-ups, and so at last I went. I roamed around the country talking to strawberry and watercress growers; a former telephone engineer who created exquisite ceramic sculptures of every variety of fungi, some of them so delicate they seemed to be made of light; a bee-keeper who could make the old straw bee-skeps and 'drum' the bees from one to another; a man who ran a barn-owl rescue service; a lady who coppiced hazel in the woods to make the wooden spars which hold thatch in place on the roofs; a couple who restored old horse-drawn carriages and hired them out for special occasions; a wine grower who also made witty weather-vanes out of odds and ends; a breeder of Wiltshire Horn sheep (the ones with no wool); and a great many others. Finally, I met a delightful woman who was a saddler and could run you up harness for anything from a Shire horse to a goat.

She was my last call and, before I set off for home, I rang to say I was on my way. Nurse Williams answered the phone. My mother had been fine until that morning (when I'd spoken to her myself) but now her back was giving her trouble and she was in bed. The Beetle and I flew as never before.

'I'm fine,' said Mrs P, when I panted up to her bedroom. 'It's just my back. I'll be all right in a couple of days.'

'I knew I shouldn't have gone,' I moaned, again and again.

'Rubbish! You've got to earn our living, haven't you? And everything turned out all right in the end. Nurse Williams was here. I'll be up and about by the time you're off again, and that Sue will be here then.'

But Mrs P wasn't up and about when Sue came. In fact she was never to walk without a stick again. Osteoporosis had finally weakened her spine badly and, although I could get her downstairs for a while each day, she had to spend most of the next few months resting her back. But, for the moment, we thought it was just another attack of her old friend rheumatism, and I got Sue's room ready, fairly confident that, if Mrs P wasn't actually leaping about, she'd be mobile enough to keep them fed while I was away.

'I'd trust Sue to look after everything,' Penny had said when I'd first rung her. 'The only thing is, she can't so much as boil an egg – or, if she can, she'd rather not bother.'

So it had been arranged that Sue would look after the stock, Gwynneth would do the milking and act in an advisory capacity, Mrs P would cook the meals and Sue would make sure she did nothing else.

She arrived from the north in her little blue Citroën on a Sunday afternoon. She had a quick cup of tea and demanded to see the animals.

'No,' I said, 'put your feet up. You must be exhausted after that long drive in the heat.'

'I'd rather get on with things,' said Sue firmly. And so we went into the dreary business of explaining who was who, what was what, where they lived, what they ate and drank and all the signs of trouble to look out for.

Sue, who'd never been within stroking distance of a goat before, took it all calmly, checked the sheep with me, nodded when I told her the chickens and ducks had to be counted every night and only seemed dismayed when she saw Doli's empty stable.

'Doli,' I told her, 'is over with Bertie and Sara till she foals. The other person who was supposed to come didn't know anything about horses, so as Doli is always a bit unpredictable about her foaling dates, I thought it was best to send her where they could cope with any problems.'

'What a shame!' said Sue. 'I was looking forward to being here when she foaled.'

Horses were the centre of Sue's life. She was twenty-two, slim, neat as a pin, with her cropped hair, and stood absolutely no nonsense from man or beast. Before she came I was a bit worried about what she'd think of my untidy house, my unruly animals and the hysteria rampant about the place when I'm getting the series on the air. Now it was obvious that Mrs P wouldn't be up to cook her meals and there wasn't even a Doli about to make Sue feel at home.

'Have you heard anything about the foal yet?' she asked now.

'Not a thing. They say Doli's eating well and is looking happy. But of any foal there is no sign.'

Next morning, Sue did the rounds with me. By the time we'd finished she could give me chapter and verse of all the names, who had what and the various house rules. I've never known anyone, before or since, to get it all so quickly. She spent the morning cleaning Doli's stable out, exhausting the dogs with a long, hard run, and making the goat-shed so neat you could have eaten your meals off the floor.

We had just finished a scratch lunch when the phone rang. It was Sara Ellis.

'She's had it.' she announced. 'At five o'clock this morning, but I didn't ring before, because we've been trying to get near it ever since so that we could let you know what it is.'

'What do you mean, get near it?' I asked.

'Well, Doli was out in the field. It's better for them to foal out, as you know. But we'd have brought her in a bit closer to the house if she'd shown any signs last night. And now she won't let us near her.'

'But Doli's usually quite good about that,' I said.

'It's not so much Doli as the foal.' said Sara emphatically. It's off as soon as we come near, and Doli won't leave it. You'd never think it had just been born. Anyway, Doli's fine. She's shed the afterbirth, the foal's suckling and, from what we can see, it's a colt foal.'

'I knew it.' I said, trying to hide my disappointment. 'What colour is it?'

'It's a very dark bay with a white blaze, like Doli's. It's got the longest legs you've ever seen. A real little thoroughbred.' I'm just going out now to see if we can get them in and check them over.'

Sue's face was shining when I turned from the phone.

'So!' I grinned at her. 'One foal for you to look after! Shame it's a colt, but it seems to be OK. I'd like to get a foal slip on it as soon as possible.'

'Have you got one?' asked Sue.

'Yup. Brand-new. Soon as we can get it to lead the better!'

'Well, as soon as they've managed to get them in, let's go over,' said Sue. 'I'm really looking forward to getting it home.'

Sara rang early the next morning and her voice sounded most disgusted.

'It's a *silly* foal,' she said.

'Oh no!' I said, my mind flying over all the injuries a foal can do to itself. Doli's last foal had been brilliant at causing herself the maximum damage at all times. 'I'm sorry, Sara, has it meant you've all had a big crisis?'

'No.' She announced surprised. 'It's just that we couldn't see it properly across that big field, but now that we've got them in . . .'

'But what's that got to do with it being a silly foal?' I asked.

'Silly? It's not silly. It's absolutely beautiful.'

'You said it was a silly foal!'

'No, I said it was a *filly* foal. I'm the silly one for thinking it was a colt. Mind you, she's got a really wicked look in her eye. And we had to corner her in the angle of the fence before we could catch her. It took three of us to get her in. Doli, thank heaven, had decided she desperately needed a bucket of nuts.'

'Sue and I are on our way,' I cried and, before she could ring off, I let out a wild shriek of joy, which brought Sue hurrying in from the yard, and Mrs P to call out anxiously if we were all right.

The rain streamed down the windscreen and a fog was brewing on the Sugar Loaf Mountain as the Beetle climbed upwards, but, inside, the atmosphere was all sun. Doli's foal! Conceived with such difficulty, dreamt of for eleven months and now arrived, safe and sound and female.

'Colts are easier to deal with,' said Sue as we drove.

'Mmm. But if it was a colt I'd just have to have it gelded and sell it. My own riding days are over, I fear – certainly on something like that. But, now, maybe one day I can breed from the filly, if it's really good, and I'll always have something of Doli to remember her by.' I smiled at Sue. 'Anyway, with you here you can get this little terror off to a good start.'

The foal was exquisite – so dark she was almost black, a beautifully shaped head, a neat little body and legs that went on for ever. No one would have thought that the big draught mare, with the huge feathered feet, could have given birth to this dainty creature, which twitched its ridiculous fuzz of a tail irritably at her admirers.

'She's a little devil,' said Sara fondly.

'Yes,' said Sue, 'I can see that. She has got a bit of an eye. Come on, little one, we'll just put this foal slip over your head'– and she moved forward with the slip carefully held behind her back.

The foal moved like quicksilver and was on the other side of Doli immediately. Doli whickered anxiously as Sue followed the foal, which slipped back under her mother and stood ready to move again. There was no panic-stricken wobbly-legged baby terror about this; every move was carefully calculated. It took all three of us to outwit and capture her and she bit and kicked furiously.

'Good God!' I breathed. 'It's a monster! If she's like this when she's hardly been born, what's she going to be like when she's older?'

'We'll see about *that*!' declared Sue, as she buckled the foal slip into place. 'Just wait till you come home, little madam.' The foal glared at her and began pawing the straw with her foreleg.

'But she's wonderful,' I said happily to Sara. 'I'm glad you made the mistake this way round and not the other. But didn't Bertie tell you that it's one hole at the back for a boy and two for a girl?'

'I couldn't get near enough to see,' said Sara sourly.

'Neither could I, the time I rang him to see if there was a long-distance means of identification. But he thought it was hilarious.'

'I can imagine,' said Sara with some feeling. 'But have you noticed? The foal's got a clear round white circle on her rump. You'll always be able to identify her from that. I think we'll keep them in now. Don't leave it too long to come and get them, will you? Thought of a name for her yet?'

'No I haven't,' I sighed. 'I'm hopeless with names.'

'Stinker would be a good one!' said Sue. And Stinker she was for the first few months of her life.

Sue masterminded the collection of Doli and Stinker while I was away. By the time I went she had everything under control and the only thing she baulked at was the handling of the chickens and the geese.

'I've got this thing about feathers,' she confessed. 'I'll feed them and everything, but I won't be able to pick them up. And I honestly don't think I can cope with those geese.'

The two geese, Douglas and Daisy, lived in an enclosure by the gate, where they shrieked the alarm at visitors and thrust their necks through the wire of their pen so that strong men thought twice about passing them. Daisy was actually fairly amiable, but Douglas was a holy terror. I have a neat trick of catching him round the back of his neck just as he's about to strike and marching him into his house at night, but Sue, who would face up to a huge hunter and win, shook her head hopelessly at me when I demonstrated.

'Well, just get Gwynneth to put them in when she comes over to milk,' I said.

But that very evening Sue came inside glowing with satisfaction.

'I got Douglas in,' she said. 'I was standing there with him hissing at me and I just thought, "I'm not going to be seen off by a goose!" and it was easy after that.'

'Great,' I said. 'He's all bluff, really, but he's caught me a nasty nip a few times, so watch him.'

'But,' continued Sue, 'do we really have to have those two dead crows hanging up over the chicken house?'

'Oh, don't take them down,' I cried. 'James went to a lot of trouble to get them for me.'

And so Sue not only gritted her teeth and went amongst the chickens, she passed beneath the dead and extremely unsavoury crows without further complaint. Neither did she blench at the added job of looking after a virtually bedridden Mrs P, although that was something neither of us had expected.

I left her then, to take responsibility for everything and everyone with a confidence I've never felt before or since and set off for the north once more.

It was a varied and hectic trip. One day I was sauntering down the by-ways of seventeenth-century agriculture with a couple of academics from Hull University, and the next standing on a beach, not far from Alnwick in Northumberland, waiting for the fishing boats to come in. I went up to the Scottish border to wander amongst Border Leicester sheep (they of the outsize ears) and Longhorn cattle, and down again to the outskirts of Bedlington to see the terriers named after that town. There was another academic, this time talking about the modern smallholder, and one cold, clear day I sat by a blacksmith's forge in a remote village while the blacksmith himself played the Northumbrian pipes. I climbed over deserted fells which led down into Cumbria and haunted the lonely tracks to find pigs in fact and fancy and two delightful brothers who still farmed the old way and went everywhere about their farm on bicycles.

I drove into my own farm late one night a week later. Sue came out to help me unpack the car and then disappeared into her flat with a curt 'Goodnight.'

'Not so much as a cup of tea for a weary traveller,' I thought wistfully, as I settled the excited dogs down and climbed the stairs to see my mother.

Mrs P smiled at me ruefully.

'Sue's been wonderful,' she said. 'My back was so bad I couldn't even go downstairs to the bathroom and so she had to do everything for me.'

'Everything?' I asked, remembering what that meant to the full.

'Everything,' Mrs P nodded. 'And you know she organized Cynog and his lorry and went to get Doli and the foal back safely. Why don't you make us both a cup of tea and I'll tell you all the news.'

I went downstairs slowly, wondering what poor Sue had made of all the sickroom business. It was one thing for me to do those things for my mother, but this young girl had expected to look after horses and sheep and goats and have her meals cooked for her. Instead, she'd landed the job of nurse, cook and everything else, in a house that was already in chaos – certainly not what you'd call labour-saving, anyway.

I opened the door of the kitchen and got a great shock. It shone and sparkled like a detergent ad. And not just the surfaces either. Everything within and without had been washed and neatly reorganized. Even the slop bucket had been scoured out.

'Your blood's worth bottling!' I told her the next morning.

'Oh well,' said Sue briefly. 'I thought I'd wash about a bit. Now will you come and see if I've done the right thing with these goats.'

And what she'd done with those goats was something of a miracle. Instead of two wild, adolescent maniacs, I found Rebecca and Clare being led on a halter, made to stand quite still, beautifully groomed and models of good behaviour.

Rebecca was the kid which Adeline Shackles had tipped as a winner. Clare was the last of the kids I'd wrested from Gorgeous the year before. Both of them were due to be shown at the Royal Welsh Show, just a few weeks away.

Back in April, I'd had a call from a TV producer, Robin Rollinson of BBC Wales. Would I be prepared to present one of their half-hour round-ups of the Royal Welsh? Each year they did two programmes, both presented by different people. I did a quick calculation, realized that all this would be in the middle of the radio series, tried to back out of it, then thought 'Why not?'

'But how about making it a bit more interesting by having me take an animal to be judged?' I said. 'I've got a goat here which won't disgrace us and it might give people an idea of how it feels to be an exhibitor, rather than an amused bystander.'

And so it was arranged that I would take Rebecca to the Royal Welsh. So that she wouldn't feel too strange, I decided to take Clare along to keep her company, and enter her in another class.

Now, animals in their natural state do not walk about sedately at the end of a harness. To get them the way you see them in the show-ring requires a lot of hard work and time. When I'd left for the north, Rebecca and Clare had had neither expended on them. Now, in one short week, they were reformed characters.

'How on earth did you do that?' I asked Sue in awe.

'Oh, I remembered you mentioning something about it, so I rang your friend Christine, who's going to show them for you, and asked her what I could do.'

'And the foal?' I said.

'Ah, well! She's been a little more difficult,' said Sue grimly. 'But I am determined to win.'

And win she did, although young Stinker fought her every inch of the way. Sometimes, as they struggled out on the field, I would see Sue on top, and sometimes I would see the foal on top. From the stable I would hear a patient murmur, a great amount of scuffling, the sound of a firm smack and Sue's voice: '*Don't* be cross. Behave!'

Doli, whilst all this was going on, stood patiently by, as if knowing that her foal's future depended on the outcome of her initial training, and at last her daughter led without biting, allowed Sue to push her from behind and lifted her tiny hooves on command.

For much of her time in Wales, it rained steadily, but Sue's only concession to this was a limp tweed hat, perched on her short hair, and a neat, waxed riding jacket. Somehow, in spite of the rain, between all her work with the animals, she managed to quell the thistles, nettles and docks which had escaped James' brushcutter, drove to town to do the shopping, took a friend of mine off to a Hound Show, kept her flat impeccable and still had time to spare.

There was only one jarring note to her final days with us. She came back into the house one night with a look of juddering horror on her face.

'What on earth's happened?' I asked.

'Those dead crows,' she replied through clenched teeth. 'They fell on me and they were . . .' She began to shake at the memory.

'Oh no! They weren't . . . ?'

'Yes! It was dreadful!'

I was mortified. Although there have been a few people working here upon whom I would have dropped a couple of maggotty crows with pleasure, this girl who had worked so brilliantly, and without one word of complaint, deserved better thanks. Even so, when she did leave, to take up a job in charge of a Point-to-Point yard, she apologized for taking the money I'd agreed to pay her.

'I had a really good break,' she said, as she left in her little blue car.

'I wonder what she's like when she's *really* working, then,' said Mrs P.

Chapter 18

The Albertine roses flung themselves over the wall in a frenzy of pale pink and perfume; white pigeons cooed and bowed and looked a picture against the artistically lichened slates of the big barn; the hedge around the garden curved like a gentle wave; the green fields were starred with tiny white daisies; the cottage and buildings shone with whitewash; and around us the hills rolled benignly under a clear blue sky. It was a picture of rural bliss – the kind you see in glossy magazines.

There was little to see of the blind panic which had swept the farm for the last few days – James clipping and brushcutting till dark; Becky furiously whitewashing all the visible surfaces, or plunging into the kitchen to prepare quiches and salads as Mrs P sat in her armchair and egged her on, while I trimmed and groomed and mucked out, so that neat animals on beds of fresh golden straw would provide fetching interior shots if the weather turned difficult.

Now, with the troops still working away inside, I stood in immaculately clean jeans, a scarf carefully knotted into the neck of a freshly ironed shirt, brand-new wellies, and my hair tastefully arranged with just a hint of careless rapture about it.

'But I think you'd be better wearing those big driving glasses to hide your bags,' said Kathy, the make-up girl, with scathing honesty. Kathy had cut my hair and insisted that I wear clothes that didn't sag and made me feel a star, not allowing anything or anyone to ruffle my calm or my appearance.

To be honest, I hate them filming on the farm. Getting ready for the invasion, appearing after a sleepless night looking insanely cheerful amongst the animals, which are determined to play up as much as they can, or at least cough, limp, splutter and look like the walking dead as soon as the cameras are turned towards them, and making sure the dogs don't eat the crew, all add up to a special kind of nightmare.

It's not too bad when everyone is on your side, but the crew who'd come with Robin Rollinson were a stony-faced lot. Only Robin himself and little Kathy kept my spirits up. They'd all come to make a short film of the farm to play at the beginning of the Royal Welsh programme, but the crew had made it quite obvious that they'd rather be somewhere else.

'I can't spend two days with this lot,' I whispered to Robin. 'They'll make me freeze.'

'We might get another crew for the actual show,' said Robin, who was also beginning to feel the strain. If the crew isn't on your side, you might as well kiss goodbye to any hopes of making a decent programme.

The goats didn't help the general atmosphere by barging off to the other end of the field instead of cavorting merrily around their shed as I'd promised they would. Only dear old Dolores stayed close, so that I could speak to the camera with her, straining on her collar to get a closer look at everyone, beside me. The sheep did leap through their gate with dash and verve, except for the last two (who had obviously been put up to it by the others) who paused, coughed and limped pathetically until they were out of shot. Not wanting to take any chances, I led Doli out on her halter, hoping that Stinker would follow closely behind and give everyone a chance to say 'Ah' at her quaint baby ways. She followed in her own good time, but kept out of camera range until I was right in the middle of my carefully prepared 'ad-lib' piece to camera, when she raced up, barged into me, nearly knocked me over and disappeared again round the other side of Doli, with a contemptuous flick of her ludicrous tail.

'Rotten foal!' I said to her afterwards, but actually it worked rather well, I thought, when I saw the film. Two hooves up to the boss and the telly!

The crew packed up their equipment and departed silently, leaving me feeling like sixpenn'orth of dogsmeat, as Mrs P would say.

'Don't worry,' said Robin, 'I'm really very, very pleased.'

'You were lovely,' said Kathy soothingly. 'Now don't forget, wash your hair just before you come to meet us at the hotel the night before the show, and I'll be there to set it properly for you.'

'Just get there!' said Robin and he and Kathy left for Cardiff.

I put the show firmly out of my mind for the next few weeks. The radio programme got into full swing and, as I sat there editing furiously, the Albertine roses faded, the hedge began to leg it up into the skies again and the neat picture we'd filmed dissolved into reality once more. Becky came back for a bare twenty-four hours a week to let me get off to Bristol, but for the rest I was on my own. Even my trusty James had deserted me.

'I've decided to forget the rest of my A' levels,' he said one day, full of excitement. 'I'm going to agricultural college next year and I have to work on a proper farm till then. So I've taken a job on a place in Yorkshire. So I won't be here to do that summer job after all.'

'Never mind,' said Mrs P as I descended into gloom after wishing James a cheery farewell. 'I'm a bit better now, so at least I can sit downstairs and keep the dogs quiet for you.'

And at least she was there to sympathize and make decisive remarks about what was spinning through the editing machine. Having another pair of ears about the place does help. Always, when I'd finished putting the interviews together, Mrs P and Winston sat perched on the stairs outside the office (there's no room inside) and took up their roles as 'the Woman-and-Dog-in-the-Street.' I trusted their judgement far more than anyone else's. If Winston pricked his ears at the background noises, I knew they were clear enough, and if Mrs P, who knew nothing about the animals or crafts beforehand, couldn't get a clear mental picture of them, just by listening, I knew I'd blown it and would have to make some rapid adjustments.

Luckily, I had plenty of good material to play with that year. All the people I'd gone to see had that extra dimension I was always looking for, and my only problem was in deciding which part of their interviews I could bear to leave out. 'Cutting blood' we used to call it, and it really does hurt to dump good stuff on the floor. The only way I can finally stop dithering about it is to remember what one editor (who also said, if you brought him two minutes of tape, that it'd cut nicely to one minute forty-five seconds, so I always gave him three to keep him happy) told me: 'What people haven't heard, they won't miss.' I don't know if it's strictly true, but it does help to put the steel back into your editing blade.

There were two interviews in particular which caused me a lot of grief on this account that season. The funny thing was, I'd done both of them simply to keep the peace.

'You *must* go and see this *wonderful* tile-maker!' Mary Price had declaimed. 'I've ordered lots of his tiles for my bathroom.'

I was a little bored with Mary's home improvements. She and her husband, Hal, had bought a large run-down house in Bristol a couple of years before, and room by painful room they'd reclaimed it for gracious living. It seemed that during every single break in the studio Mary was ringing up plumbers, bricklayers, stonemasons, central-heating engineers, wallpaper shops, curtain makers and carpet layers – usually to inquire acidly why they hadn't done whatever it was they were supposed to have done, as promised. I was used by now to spending a great deal of our lunch hour enthusing or sympathizing over the latest developments, but I was not going to have them actually spill over into the programme itself. The thought of going to see Mary's bathroom-tile-maker, be he ever so rural, did not appeal. But Mary, rather like Mrs P, does not give up on any theme easily.

At last, I'd said wearily, 'Well, if I'm in that area I'll see him. But I won't go specially.'

As it happened, I did have to go within striking distance of Long Hamborough in Oxfordshire. I was not, however, greatly enthusiastic when I found that 'Badger Tiles' was situated behind some shops on a fairly busy road. I cheered up a bit when I saw that the place where they were made looked rather barn-like and there was nothing of the glittering showroom about it. Neither was there any sign of the proprietor.

An aged lavatory flush sounded loudly off-stage as I turned to leave. A very large man, looking as if he'd slept in his clothes for a week, emerged from behind a battered door, buttoning up his trousers and combing his hair with his fingers. At his feet, an ancient collie dog stumbled forward apologetically.

To describe Geoff Beaston as a mere maker of bathroom tiles was ridiculous. To begin with, he didn't actually make the tiles themselves; he decorated them and, given his background, his interests and his outrageous personality, the results were startling.

'I can do you anything from a sixty-foot swimming pool to a tiled cheeseboard,' he declared, waving his arms round the big untidy studio. 'The tiles you can see here are mostly of rare breeds of livestock, and wildlife. Over in that room I've got the big stuff, and there's a whole kiln full of mixed tiles waiting to come out when they've cooled properly. One of my best sellers is this set of six tiles that make up a Hereford bull.'

We rooted around in the stacked boxes of tiles, with their pigs and cattle, goats and horses, snakes and birds and badgers. All of them were stencilled onto a basic white tile and then fired again in the kiln. There was something vaguely familiar about the designs, but nothing I could put my finger on. Finally, Geoff stomped over to the kiln and opened it.

The first shelf yielded tiles painted like brickwork. I will not repeat what was scrawled on them.

'Graffiti tiles,' grinned Geoff. 'Pub owners like 'em for the loos. If you can't beat 'em, join 'em. Let me know if you see any good ones I can use. Always trying to improve my repertoire!'

The next shelf also had texts written on the tiles. But these were in plain blue and white and the quotations revealed a depth of interests ranging from Chaucer to Oscar Wilde and beyond.

The rest of the kiln was filled haphazardly with more pigs and goats and badgers. Some of the badgers were in their natural state, but most of them were dressed in seventeenth-century costume. Some were wielding swords and some were firing cannons.

'I'm a member of the Sealed Knot,' said Geoff Beaston with a bow. 'A Roundhead, of course!' The old dog, which had sat patiently beside us as we explored the kiln, now thumped his tail in agreement. And still the badgers, male, female, Roundhead and Cavalier, came forth.

'You're as bad with your badgers as I am with my unicorns,' I said at last.

'Unicorns? Oh, I've done a lot of those too. Come and I'll show you.'

He led me back to the boxes on the floor and hunted through them till he found what he was looking for.

'I'm a bit low on unicorns at the moment,' he said, 'I must get round to doing some more.'

'You!' I said in amazement. 'You made *my* unicorn tiles. I bought lots of them.

Geoff stared at me. 'You weren't the woman who went mad in that shop in London were you? They told me about the way you nearly cleared them out.'

'If it was a shop near the British Museum, yes,' I laughed.

'I suppose,' said Geoff, staring at me, 'that you've read Peter Beagle's book *The Last Unicorn.*'

'As if I wouldn't,' I said. 'Currently I have three copies in case one gets lost, and another one to lend to deserving friends.'

And so we sat, perched on packing cases, and drank surprisingly good coffee ('I can't stand the instant stuff,' said Geoff), while the old dog slumbered and twitched at our feet, and talked of Peter Beagle's book, of T. H. White and other unicorn lovers, mutual friends in the Sealed Knot (which goes around enacting Civil War battles, in case you haven't heard of them before), Mallory's *Morte d'Arthur*, the unicorn tapestries in the Cluny Museum in Paris and a hundred other things. The sun shone through the cobwebbed panes of the studio and danced amongst the dust, the dog snored and at last I remembered that I should have been miles away.

'But you can't go without seeing Graham Piggot,' cried Geoff as I began collecting my things together. 'He makes dragons.'

'Everyone makes dragons,' I said. 'Cute dragons, funny dragons, green dragons, red dragons, little dragons and big dragons – every craft shop's full of them.'

'Ah, but if you were to take, say, a scale of one to ten, most of those dragons would register at about three or four. Graham's dragons go all the way to ten. I'll just give them a ring and say you're on your way.'

'No! Please don't do that. I'm already late and I've got about twenty miles to go.'

It was no use. Geoff was calmly announcing into the phone that I would be with the Piggots in about ten minutes' time.

It took longer than that to parcel up the assorted blue-and-white tiles with quotations on them, the set of six tiles that made up a big Oxford Sandy and Black pig, the remainder of the unicorn tiles and a few other bits and pieces I'd been buying as we went along.

'I'll have to make some more unicorn tiles now,' said Geoff.

'Try and copy that lovely one Peter Beagle describes in his book,' I said. Geoff Beaston shook his head. 'I could try, but the best person to do that for you is Graham Piggot. Now, you turn left out of here, then right and when you get to the village of Bladon ask for the old Bakery shop.' And such was the force of his personality, this big, wild, highly intelligent man, that I stopped arguing and did as I was told.

'Old Bakery shop indeed,' I muttered, as I searched in vain for somewhere to park the Beetle in the steep, narrow streets of Bladon. 'I'll just take this road which looks as if it leads out of the village and forget it.'

I edged the Beetle round a sharp corner and something strange and wonderful flickered at me from the bow-fronted window of a tiny shop on the corner. Was it a *pig* with a battleaxe, a shield and a horned helmet? I stopped the car, got out and went back to have another look.

'You can park the Beetle by the side of the shop here,' cried a shrill voice, and a small woman, smiling broadly, rushed out from the bow-fronted shop, followed slowly by a quiet-looking man with long thin hair. Between them they edged me and the Beetle into a tiny parking bay.

'I haven't got long,' I muttered ungraciously as I got out of the car at last, wondering how on earth I'd extract the Beetle again, and followed the Piggots through the door, which jangled gaily. It clicked shut behind us and left outside the irritable, time-watching adult and the little shop opened its arms to a wonderstruck child. They were all there, her wildest fantasies, and all of them poised as if, a moment before, they'd been leaping about, chattering and laughing, and had frozen instantly as the bell on the door warned them we were coming. The pig must have been waving his battleaxe and singing something from Wagner; the old goat, reading in his armchair, carefully adjusting his spectacles; the icicle-men dancing; the hare winding his watch; the mermaid combing her hair; the old badger shuffling along in his slippers; the Red Queen shouting 'Off with her head' and all the card-men tumbling out of her way; the little lady centaur had just stopped galloping and the huge dragon had paused in mid-roar.

I couldn't take it all in at once. I rushed from figure to figure and it seemed as if each of them held its breath and watched me. At last I turned back to Corri and Graham Piggot, who'd been waiting, as they must always wait through that initial amazed reaction, for me to calm down.

'I might have known Geoff Beaston wouldn't send me on a wild-goose chase,' I said at last.

Even the arched cellars of what had once been the village bakery had their own atmosphere. It was here that the Piggots mixed their clay in the old dough mixer, which groaned and wheezed dramatically as they turned it. The great kiln, with its cargo of dragons and sea monsters, was cooling, but Corri described how it looked when it was firing: seen through the peep-hole, all the creatures glowed and breathed in the great heat. The dragons, in particular, seemed almost ready to burst forth and devour the world.

'They're not twee dragons,' I agreed.

'No,' said Graham, with a wry smile, 'you don't mess with my dragons. Sometimes, when I'm making them, they scare me to death.'

He didn't say a great deal, Graham Piggot. Corri, his wife, did most of the talking and that was completely taken up with the genuis of her husband, who'd started out as an ordinary potter, and then gone on to this extraordinary world of creatures out of his imagination and his reading. The dragons were pure Tolkien and the Alice figures were so vivid that at any moment I expected them all to whirl up into the air and hear Alice cry, 'You're nothing but a pack of cards!' As for the others, which had sprung from Graham's own thoughts, they were often fantastic, sometimes as wicked as Geoff Beaston's graffiti tiles and, above all stunningly alive. I wanted every single one of them.

'But at least I'm not leaving without that one,' I said, when finally, inch by inch, I'd come back into the real world.

It was the little female centaur, arms on hips, long hair flying backwards; imperious, beautiful and itching to be gone. She reminded me of Doli's foal.

Graham looked at me in dismay, but Corri said briskly, 'Now don't be silly. Someone will buy it eventually and Jeanine will give it a good home.'

Even so, her husband supervised the packing of the little figure, he insisted on the parcel being stowed in the car surrounded by coats and cushions, and he looked the picture of misery as I started the Beetle's engine.

'He's always like this,' said Corri. 'He wouldn't sell any of them if I wasn't about. Now stop fussing Graham. She'll ring us when she gets back to make sure it's arrived safely.'

'Meanwhile, why don't you get on with creating the Peter Beagle unicorn for me?' I said through the window of the grumbling car.

But I never did get it. The wrong author must have been standing over his shoulder, because when, a year later, Corri met me to deliver the unicorn, it was a perfect replica of the Tenniel one from *Alice*.

'You don't have to have it,' said Corri anxiously.

But how could I not have it? And, if there was a fire in the cottage, it would be one of the things I'd have to rescue, after I'd made sure of the little centaur, that is.

She sits on the windowsill and, as the light changes during the day, so her colour, expression and body angles seem to change too. Sometimes she is palest green like a warm sea, sometimes creamy white, and always she seems about to gallop to the end of the world. The unicorn sits on the table not far from the phone; sometimes it seems as if it's about to deliver a lecture, sometimes it seems to smile, and at all times it dominates everything else in the room. As one friend put it: 'If you were to tell me, as we spoke on the phone, that it had started to walk across the table towards you, I'd believe it.' But then he is a very perceptive man.

Long before the unicorn arrived, however, I had to cut the delights of the Piggots' little shop into pieces, along with nine other complicated interviews, get some sort of a script together and make it to the hotel, near the Royal Welsh showground, by Monday night. On Saturday evening it all seemed impossible, especially as I was expecting a visitor.

'Oh, don't worry about me,' cried Christine Palmer when she

arrived, still dazed from judging a goat show in Swansea all day. 'I'll just have a couple of boiled eggs and go to bed. Tomorrow I'll start putting the finishing touches to Rebecca and Clare.'

Although Sue had taught the two young goats to lead properly and stand still when they were told to, there was a lot more to be done before they were ready for the show-ring. There are tricks of the trade that experienced handlers know, such as inducing the goat to stand in such a way as to show off their best points and, with luck, draw attention away from their worst. Both goats needed a good manicure and their hooves oiled; they wanted their coats shampooed and groomed and 'polished' with a silk rag. In this case, they also needed handling by Christine, for it would be she who would actually take them into the ring to be judged.

Showing is very time-consuming, with a great deal of aimless hanging around. It also requires a certain expertise. Not only had I never shown a goat before, I would be needed by Robin and the crew from very early in the morning till the show closed at night. We had two days in which to cover a great number of events, breeds, crafts and 'bowler hat' interviews with the show officials. All this had to be edited, done again if necessary, and ready with graphics and music, for transmission on the Wednesday evening at six o'clock. The goat show would be just one tiny part of the whole programme – so tiny, in fact, that Robin was rather dismissive about it. I had hoped that the BBC would pay for Christine's travel from Pembrokeshire and the hire of a van to get the goats to Builth Wells and back.

'Sorry, Jeanine,' he said, 'but we'll only take about a minute, maybe two, for the goat sequence altogether. I think it's a great idea for you to have one in the show, but you'll have to organize that for yourself.'

And so Christine had arranged to stay at my place from Saturday night till Tuesday morning. Her husband, David, would hire a van to pick up her and the goats, and ferry them to the showground. And I would pick up the tab.

I didn't see a great deal of Christine for the next two days. While she worked with the goats, I stayed at my desk and wept, screamed and generally went on in my usual artistic frenzy. Christine was aghast.

232

Finally, late on the Monday afternoon, I emerged and smiled.

'Thank God,' breathed Christine. 'You look your normal self again. Are you always like that when you do the series?'

'Yes,' said Mrs P with feeling, 'she is!'

'But this time it was worse,' I said defensively, 'because I only had half the time to get it done in. Now all I've got to do is wash my hair, iron some clothes, make sure I've got everything with me and somehow drive to this hotel, a few miles from Builth, so that Robin can brief me about the show.'

'Well, the goats are as ready as I can make them,' said Christine. 'At least they won't disgrace you in front of the cameras. I hope!'

When I did get to the hotel at about ten that night, Robin Rollinson was very pleased to see me.

'Thank God you made it,' he kept repeating over and over again. Kathy picked up my limp hair in disgust, marched me up to my room to make sure I'd followed her wardrobe instructions to the letter, and left me downstairs with Robin again to work out our plans for the next day. By the time I crawled into my bed that night, I just wanted to die.

The crew was not the same one. This lot were enthusiastic, funny, protective and infinitely patient. But I did get one warning.

'Now don't worry,' said the sound engineer, as he wired up a neck mike, waited for me to thread it modestly down through my clothes, and connected the wire to a pack hidden under one of Shelagh Holmes's Manx Loghtan sleeveless jackets. 'When we're not actually recording, I switch it off. But it's just as well to remember that accidents can happen and that, as you're wired for sound, you shouldn't say anything you'd regret.'

The great thing about agricultural shows is the presentation of excellence – the best of so many of those worlds of enthusiasms, brought forth and shown with pride. To see the farm breeds in all their variety is wonderful enough (and to imagine the long, lonely hours spent back at the farm to produce the animals in such condition), and backing them up are the craft tents and their camaraderie, the stallholders who go from show to show with their wares, the associations trying to recruit interest, the crowds, the food of all kinds, the endless announcements, and the general air of holiday. Unfortunately, because the radio series went out in the summer, when most of the big shows were on, I seldom got a chance to see any of them, and this was my first time at the Royal Welsh. And now I was spoilt by having everything smoothed out for me by the crew and Kathy and Robin and his assistants. I had but to make a request and it was granted. And, in the few moments we had to rest, there was the BBC pavilion, where I was greeted by people I knew and given coffee and fussed over.

Because most of my professional life as a broadcaster is spent alone with a tape-recorder and only myself to arrange and organize everything, it was heaven for once to be able to concentrate on the job and leave the rest to other people – even when they dumped me in the crowd, set up their equipment on a roof far above and left me to walk along talking to myself, so that the rest of the people thought I was barmy; even when, whilst trying to enthuse about the judging of the Welsh Black cattle, half the show population kept pottering up to me to ask where the loos were, what time was the main event, and various other trifles. Kathy haunted my footsteps, just out of camera range, twitching my hair back into place, taking the shine off my face, making sure I had something to drink, rearranging my scarf and complaining that the neck mike was interfering with the general effect.

When we finally broke for lunch, the sound engineer joined us with his face a pale shade of grey.

'We've just had a report,' he announced. 'One of the radio stations picked up a transmission from somebody's mike and we think it was ours. It was a private conversation and it cut into the news bulletin just a while ago.'

'Oh dear!' breathed Kathy, turning towards me. 'That must have been when you were in the loo and I was talking to you through the door.'

'Yes,' I said, suddenly feeling not very well. 'I was moaning about the lack of space in there and what a nuisance it was trying to get my jeans down with that backpack wired up through my clothes. Remember? I nearly dropped the lot down the bowl.'

'I wonder if they heard you pull the flush,' shrieked Kathy. 'That'd be something in the middle of the news!' Ribald remarks began to fly up and down the lunch table and only the sound engineer and I sat in shocked silence.

As it turned out, the report had been grossly exaggerated and it wasn't our mike anyway, but string one of those things up on me to this day and, unless I'm on the air, I stay rigidly silent and try never to go to the loo.

After lunch we went to see how the goats in general, and Rebecca in particular, were getting on.

Although Robin had not been too wildly enthusiastic about the goats, once he and the crew got to that section they all went mad. The sight of the Anglo-Nubians with their long ears, aristocratic noses, and wonderful colours was enough.

'We must have an interview with one of those,' decided Robin, and we cornered a quiet little lady in a pink checked overall holding a big, beautifully behaved goat, which didn't move a muscle as I demonstrated how the ears should meet at the tip of the nose.

We had just finished when the British Toggenberg yearlings appeared. I saw Christine, all dressed up in her white show coat, looking very serious, but the goat she was leading – could that possibly be Rebecca, that calm, elegant, beautifully groomed creature standing like a queen? She bore absolutely no resemblance to the goat I knew at home. I glanced along the line to size up the opposition.

'I wouldn't get too excited,' I told Robin. 'There are some very good goats there. And she's never been in a show-ring in her life before; she's bound to blow it when the judge touches her. Let's just do our bit about the agony of waiting to know how your animal has done, and then forget it.'

And that's what we did – or almost, because just as the crew stood down, the judge was handing Christine the rosette for second place. The crew got their cameras rolling so fast they nearly fell over them and, for the moment forgetting they were there, I rushed towards Christine and almost hugged her and Rebecca. Almost, but not quite, because Christine was looking too official and smart to hug and probably Rebecca would have taken off skywards and ruined the whole thing. But it was hard to choke back the tears. It had been so long ago that I had bought Rebecca's great-grandmother, Dolores, from Christine, and had graded up the herd to breed status. Now here was the end result for all the world to see. To come second at a big show like that, never having been in a ring before, was a huge credit to both Christine and Rebecca.

'Why didn't that man make her first?' demanded Kathy loyally.

'Just as well he didn't,' I said. 'Everyone watching would have thought we rigged it. You know, though, that the judges have no idea whose goat is whose till they see it in front of them – in theory, anyway. And I didn't want this one to know Rebecca was of special interest because he might have made her last. They're very touchy about their integrity. Quite right , too! People say awful things if their animal doesn't win.'

'Oh!' said Kathy, to whom all this was pure Greek. 'I think your hair needs doing, by the way.' And there, in front of everyone, she brushed and combed me back into shape, to the huge amusement of Adeline Shackles, who appeared at my elbow and said, 'There, what did I tell you? I said she was a good goat.'

Poor little Clare, Rebecca's travelling companion, appeared in another class and came thirteenth. Although Christine felt she'd deserved a slightly better placing out of twenty-eight, I didn't blame the judge one bit. After all the fuss over Rebecca, I'd have put her last.

They spent a great deal longer than planned on the goats during the final programme. The crew all lined up for goats' milk ice-cream and kept coming back for more. They were already wearing Rare Breeds Survival Trust badges and getting totally carried away with all the less familiar breeds I'd insisted on us filming, such as the delightful little Dexter cow who mooed on cue, the huge Red Poll bull which was as gentle as a lamb, or the Torwen lamb with her black wool offset by her white belly, white 'tear drops' on her face and black ears lined with white. *Torwen* does in fact mean 'white belly', as the reverse, *torddu*, means 'black belly'. Both are Welsh Mountain sheep and both are more usually called Badger Faced sheep because of their markings. I already knew a lot about the breed because Myrddin Parry was one of the founder members of their Society. There was no way I would have left that showground without giving them a plug.

236

The next day, Mary Price and her secretary, Kate Chaney, joined us. 'To make sure you get to Bristol in one piece,' they said, eyeing my new friends suspiciously. Mary knew I'd be at breaking point by the end of the second day, and it's a long way from Builth to Bristol through the heavy Show traffic. So she and Kate tacked themselves onto the end of the cavalcade as we trotted from ring to ring, stand to stand, panoramic view to panoramic view. The climax was the showing and judging of the Welsh Cob stallions, with the crowd roaring and clapping and shouting as each horse was run across the main ring; high stepping, manes flying, nostrils flaring and their handlers racing along beside them for dear life.

There were so many TV and radio people in the centre of the ring to record this that someone suggested they should have a class for the best-turned-out crew. Mary went all Irish and began to show off her knowledge of horses, but Kathy and I watched anxiously to see which of the big stallions the judges would choose. It was the biggest, most touchy one, of course.

'You can't get Jeanine to interview that brute,' hissed Kathy to Robin. 'He'll kill her.' Everyone tucked in behind me as we ran to do our piece with the winner and his owner and, when we were in place, even the cameraman pointed his lens over my shoulder. Showing off, of course, I landed the stallion a wallop and told it to behave. There was no need, actually, because he stopped huffing and snorting and stamping quite soon. It's all a lot of hype anyway. The stallions are trained to show what spunky animals they are in front of the crowds. Once this one was on his own he was as good as gold.

'Oh, but you are brave,' breathed Kathy afterwards, and I felt a terrible fraud.

Several of the crew and little Kathy bought waxproofed coats, in case they had to do a bit more of this country filming. Kathy, who was dressed that day in bright yellow and looked like a well clad canary, disappeared inside her coat and had to be pulled forth and a really tiny one found for her. While everyone was admiring themselves in a long mirror, I slipped out to the next tent and bought a hat.

It was a floppy tweed affair, just like the one Sue used to wear in the rain. Since she'd left, the foal had been playing up quite

237

a lot, so I decided to try an experiment. If I wore Sue's type of hat and imitated her voice, perhaps young Stinker would toe the line again. It worked a treat and that hat is still known as the 'Foal's Hat.'

They got the programme edited and ready for transmission with a few minutes to spare. The best part of it was the goat sequence and, when it was all over and the final music had faded, the announcer in Cardiff said, with real excitement in his voice: 'And everyone here at the BBC would like to congratulate Rebecca on her success.'

I know it couldn't quite compare with winning the Derby, but at the time it felt just like that.

Mary and Kate shepherded me tenderly back to Bristol. The radio programme we put together the next day was one of our best. We ended it with the Piggots and a reading from Tolkien about the great dragon Smaug sleeping on his heap of treasure. We accompanied it with my recording of the old dough-mixer churning away at the clay. It sounded just like a dragon snoring.

Chapter 19

It was very quiet in the old cowshed. The great beams cast long, angular shadows along the walls and across the backs of the slumbering goats, each in its own place beside the iron stalls, where once the cows had sat cudding on the ends of their chains. Only one place, right at the end of the shed and directly under the swallows' nest, was empty.

I had been sitting on a bale of straw in what was once the feeding channel, with my feet up on the concrete barrier, for a long time – so long that the goats had finally turned their heads over their backs and slept. It was unusual for them not to pester me for more food, while the going was good. Tonight, all of them had eaten their hay, done a bit of ritual cudding and left me alone. Not one of them had gone near the empty stall.

For the whole of their lives that stall had been occupied. Each and every one of them owed her being to the goat who had made it her own, long before most of them were born. If one of them had ventured into that place, in search of the extra wisp of hay or the odd leavings in the feed bucket, a swift thump reminded them of their manners.

Dolores had ruled her herd implacably, and organized them in such a way that there was seldom any question of her authority. And if, sometimes, there had been a slight disagreement between us as to who was the real leader of the herd, let none of the others dare to presume upon it! In any rebellion, she was completely on my side.

It was a long time since she'd borne any kids – not since the time the time she'd broken her pelvis and the next year had to have a Caesarean to extract them.

'If they'd been pot-holers,' Bertie Ellis said, as he stitched her

239

rich, golden coat up again, 'they'd have been able to swim out past the kink, but I'm afraid the Great Controller didn't allow for that sort of thing in the birth plan, so we'll always have to get 'em out like this.' Rather than put Dolores through so much trauma again, I'd left her barren.

She continued to milk, year after year, in spite of this, and when at last the supply became a mere trickle, she and I went on with the daily routine, if only for the pleasure both of us got from the contact. She liked being milked, and I liked to lay my head against her side and talk to her. For this was no ordinary goat and to look into her eyes was to see a deep intelligence tinged with humour. I have never seen it in any other goat, although her granddaughter, Sophie, has a slight shadow of it. And, for those who think this is pure anthropomorphism, I suspect that Dolores was just as 'capropomorphic' (if there *is* such a word, and why not?) about me. Crippled and unproductive as she was now, I'd have given the whole herd for that one goat, but, just a few short weeks after her great-granddaughter had vindicated her breeding in public, Dolores had died.

She had been ill, in that odd, undefinable way that makes treating animals so difficult sometimes. Bertie had been to see her, had put her on all kinds of remedies, declared himself puzzled and left it to me to dose her and give her as much time as I could spare from the eternal editing. Slowly she began to improve.

On the morning after one of my weekly trips to Bristol, Dolores had seemed worse again. I ran to the house to ring Bertie and ask him to come, but by the time I had rushed back to her she was dead. She had gone so quickly and so peacefully that for a moment I thought she was merely asleep.

A friend helped me to bury her under the rowan tree at the end of the garden. That night I sat amongst the sleeping goats and thought about all the years we had shared, knowing that I would never see their like, or hers, again. I wondered, sorrowfully, who would take over the leadership of the herd, now that she was gone. I hoped it would be gentle Sophie, or even Minnie, but I knew that great big, gallumphing Gorgeous would have a darn good try.

An irritable chirping from the swallows' nest as the young birds, already too big for it, jostled each other for space broke the silence

and, as I sighed and rose to my feet, one or two of the goats began
to move. Gorgeous, who'd been sharing an uneasy bed with her
sister Minnie, stood up and stretched. She pottered over to the hay
and trod on Minnie's foot as she passed. Minnie jumped up in alarm
and soon the whole herd was on its feet and complaining.

'Gorgeous,' I said, 'you are a bloody pain in the neck!' and I
moved towards the light switch, hoping that in the darkness the
goats would settle down again. But it was too late, hay-racks were
being investigated and found wanting, heads were being banged,
water buckets rattled and Gorgeous bumbled about annoying
everybody. Frowning, I filled the hay-racks, read a few riot acts
at random and began to leave, but stopped again to watch sadly as
Gorgeous, suddenly realizing that the end stall was vacant, trotted
joyfully towards it. She was the last animal Dolores would have
bequeathed it to.

Gorgeous got to within about four feet of the empty stall and
stopped, as I'd seen her stop so often before when her mother
dared her to come any further.

'She's remembering,' I thought, but Gorgeous, still staring in
front of her, bent her head slightly as if to charge. Again she
stopped, and her ears waggled to and fro, as they do when a
goat is puzzled. Back she went, and again she moved forward.
This time she stopped, as if she'd been hit, and slowly a ridge of
hair rose up all along her back.

'Stupid goat,' I said, and glanced up at the walls. Perhaps there
was a shadow of a cobweb flickering about, or a cat had crept
through from the stable next door. There was nothing visible. The
rest of the goats, usually quick to respond to any alarm signals,
picked at their hay and ignored Gorgeous.

I watched her for a long time trying to get into that pen; watched
her go forward, retreat, advance and finally stand quite still staring
at something I couldn't see. At last, with the ridge of hair on her
back still erect, she began to shiver so badly that I had to lead her
away and settle her on her own with some fresh hay, which she
barely picked at.

I crept to the door and, when I'd switched the lights out, I
whispered back into the darkness, 'Welcome back, old friend.'

'The strange thing is,' I said to Mrs P later, 'that just for once

I wasn't consoling myself with anything like "the body may be gone but the spirit lingers on", and all that sort of thing. In fact, I was sure it was a trick of the light or something that had upset Gorgeous. But there was nothing. The rest of the goats would have reacted too, if there'd been anything of that kind. I have now come to the appalling conclusion that Gorgeous, as well as being a complete nuisance, is also psychic.'

'It's a pity,' said Mrs P, 'that goats can't become members of the Society for Psychical Research. I can just imagine Gorgeous conducting a seance.'

On that happy thought we went to bed and, if I still miss Dolores a great deal, the memory of that evening, when I'm absolutely sure that some part of her came back to cheer me up, helps a lot. Three days later Minnie casually walked into the empty pen without let or hindrance, Sophie quietly took over the leadership of the herd and, for a while at least, Gorgeous behaved impeccably.

Meanwhile, the series went on inexorably. When the Geoff Beaston interview came up, Mary was ecstatic.

'I knew you'd get on with him,' she cried. 'Why were you so difficult about going to see him?'

'Bathroom tiles,' I muttered, 'didn't exactly inspire me.'

'Ah, but it was his personality and the rest of his work I wanted you to see,' said Mary smugly.

I shushed her and we listened as the interview came up on the loudspeakers. My voice was inquiring about the possibilities of having my bathroom decorated with every breed of farm livestock. Geoff's boomed in, assuring me that I could have any animal I wanted. 'You can even have rabid snails if you like.'

We ended the programme that week with a nightmare sequence. There was me, in the bath, singing 'Oh What a Beautiful Morning' as I scrubbed. I am interrupted by a goat bleating, donkeys braying, cows mooing, pigs grunting and sheep baaing as they take up the chorus, join me gleefully, with much splashing, in the bath, pinching the soap, and the sponge, and leaving me bellowing at them to get on out of it. We thought of adding the rabid snails but couldn't quite imagine how they'd sound; and visitors are quite disappointed to find that my bathroom walls are painted plain white. The only unusual thing about them is the unicorn in the plaster.

It was odd about that. Until that summer my bathroom had been papered but, as in the rest of the house, the damp and mould soon made their appearance and the paper was peeling in a limp, depressing sort of way, which was only appreciated by the spiders who hid behind it whenever anyone came in, leaping out to terrify them as soon as they were in the bath.

Now Becky, who was coming back again to look after Mrs P each week, fancied herself as a house painter and attacked the wallpaper furiously. I came home one week to find naked plaster walls and Becky limbering up to paint them. But in amongst the streaks and patches of paste still lingering I saw, as plain as anything, the perfect head of a unicorn.

'Could you,' I asked Becky, 'just paint round that and leave it as plain plaster?' And, when I came back next week, there it was, beautifully picked out from the white paint. When anyone has a bath, the steam turns the unicorn's head a deep rose colour, and it seems to breath. It's a great talking point and nobody ever believes that someone didn't actually draw it.

Over the weeks that followed the kitchen was also transformed with dazzling white paint and all the marks of Mrs P's adventures in there were erased for ever. Like the deep-purple explosion on the ceiling where she had opened a bottle of elderberry liqueur she'd made and stored away to mature. It had been maturing on the kitchen ceiling ever since and had none of the artistic merits of the plaster unicorn. Gone too were the remains of the wildly volatile curry a kindly friend had run up for us, mainly on the walls above the cooker. So, what with Sue's rearranging of the cupboards and Becky's energetic painting, the kitchen, for one brief period, looked hygienic, neat and rather alien.

Mrs P, who was actually getting up by now for longer and longer periods, chose Becky's twenty-four hours each week to stay in bed.

'I can hear her muttering and clanking away down there,' she said, 'and I feel safer out of the way. I hope you've moved the happy plants out of the way too, because all those paint fumes can't be doing them much good either.'

The happy plants are what Mrs P calls them. Their real name is *Portuccaca afra*, more commonly known as Jade Trees. They live in the warmth of the kitchen and fill the windowsills with green light. They were Mrs P's special responsibility and, to get them for her, I'd moved heaven and earth – or a lot of earth anyway.

She had seen them first in Australia and, apart from the truly jade green of the delicate leaves, their legend had fascinated her. They're supposed to be lucky, but only on certain conditions. You must have the plant *given* to you. If you buy them, or steal them, the luck is reversed.

Mrs P had begged a cutting from the plant she was admiring, but the Jade Trees are also called Money Trees (not to be confused with the coarser, more common Argentias) and some people are a bit funny about them, feeling that to give away a cutting might disturb their bank balance or something. The owner of this plant was rather like that, and coolly ignored Mrs P's request. I regret to say that my mother, incensed by this stinginess, stole a tiny piece of the plant and hid it in her handbag.

Now, in common with most of the succulents, *Portuccaca afra* needs little more than a leaf to produce another plant. The tiny stalk which Mrs P had stolen, however, just curled up and died and, according to her, there were a few minor mishaps in her life around that time.

Living, as she was then, in a small Australian country town, Mrs P looked around in vain for a Jade Tree to buy and gradually she forgot about it. And then one day she was invited to tea in a strange house. There, looking just like those artificial Chinese trees which are made of real jade, was a beautiful specimen of *Portuccaca afra*. This time her hostess was only too happy to give my mother a cutting. It thrived, it grew enough for Mrs P to take further cuttings, and soon she had all the Jade Trees she could want.

Far away in England I heard a lot about the Jade Trees, which I'd never seen, because Mrs P, adding to the legend, had named each of them after one of the family, so that I would get letters saying, 'I'm a little worried about you because your 'Happy Plant' [as, by now she'd renamed the trees] doesn't look too well.'

When my mother joined me in London, she mourned her Jade

Trees incessantly and, if our fortunes seemed a bit shaky at any time, she was sure that they were being neglected in Australia. I grew a little tired of this, so that when I was asked to do a piece about the Chelsea Flower Show for a Radio Two programme I looked everywhere for the Jade Trees. As I'd never seen them and, at that time, Mrs P didn't know their proper Latin names, it was hopeless. In desperation, I tacked the story of my search onto the radio piece and asked if any of the listeners could help. It brought in a large response, mainly from people who said that if I ever found one could I let them know. But there was one call from a nursery in Kent, which invited me to come and look for myself amongst their large collection of cacti and succulents from all over the world.

I went and they couldn't have been more patient. They gave me cuttings from anything that I thought remotely looked like Mrs P's description. Along the way I found my own 'Elephant Foot', or *Dioscorea elephantipes,* which does look just like an elephant's foot, but puts out the most lovely creeping vine of pale-green leaves and white flowers. It also lives on the kitchen windowsills, dies back every summer, but delights me all through autumn and winter by rioting everywhere, even grabbing hold of the Jade Trees if I'm not careful.

At last there was but one large, steaming greenhouse to investigate. In a corner, hidden by its more flamboyant neighbours, was a lonely little plant which looked as if it had been made out of best quality green jade.

'Oh,' said the owner of the nursery, 'that's *Portuccaca afra.* We never get asked for that. I just keep one specimen for the collection. I've never heard it called a Jade Tree or a Money Tree before.'

When I got back to London, I unpacked tray after tray of cuttings and as she scanned each one my mother's hopes rose and died again. At last I brought in the *Portuccaca afra* and it was worth all the trouble, just to see her face.

'That's it!' she cried. 'That's my Happy Plant!'

I rang the nurseryman and advised him to start taking cuttings. I had a lot of customers waiting for the Jade Tree.

A few months later, when Mrs P's cutting was flourishing happily under her tender care, there was a special delivery of three more plants. One was from the owner of the nursery, who had indeed done rather well with *Portuccaca africa*, now that everyone knew what it was, and there were two from listeners who swore that their Jade Trees had changed their luck and these were presents to thank me. I doubt if any of them brought us any better luck, but they are lovely plants and all of them came to Wales with us. If we liked someone very much, we gave them a cutting.

'I just wish you wouldn't name the Jade Trees after people,' I said now to Mrs P as she fussed over their toleration of Becky's paint pots. 'Every time one of them droops a bit, I imagine its namesake is wilting too.'

I didn't tell her that her own special plant was looking rather wan, in spite of all my efforts to revive it, in its new quarters in the warm sunshine of the flat, next door to the cottage. Being superstitious can be very wearing on the nerves and, in spite of Mrs P's growing strength, the state of her plant was worrying me, but the series was nearly over for the year and soon I could give my mother far more attention.

There were just two more programmes to go, when the phone rang as I was flinging the last bits of the script together and racing against time to get off to Bristol. It was Becky to say she had the flu and wouldn't be able to come and stay with my mother.

I spent the next couple of hours trying to replace her, and finally found someone who could come that night and another friend who could come first thing in the morning and stay till I got back.

It was a long time after midnight when I got to Bristol. The roads had been deserted: no late night lovers strolled across the old packbridge at Crickhowell where I take a short cut; no hopeful anglers lingered by the banks of the Usk as I passed it, first as a tiny trickle and later as a full-bodied river; the pubs were dark and silent and only one or two people hurried down the bright streets of Bristol itself, as the Beetle ground down Whiteladies Road and round the corner to the Alandale Hotel, right opposite the BBC.

The next day ws a good one in the studio, with lots of laughter and very few dramas. Kate Chaney and I got the information sheets ready and the letters answered in record time, and I managed to catch the shops for once. I bought a large box of Thornton's chocolates for the friend who was looking after Mrs P, flew around Sainsbury's, and was on the road once more.

That night there was no queue over the Severn Bridge; the sunset was soft enough to cut out the glare of the sun as it beamed low from the west; the dusk was clear and full of cool sweet smells; no hay lorries lurched and blundered in front of me; and a bright moon lit the final miles as I crossed the mountain. Everything was perfect, and ahead of me lay not a house in chaos and smelling of paint, but a kindly friend, a cheerful mother and peace.

The yard lights were on, the little cottage looked quiet and welcoming and I came through the pink door, holding out my chocolates to our friend. She ignored them.

'Mrs P gone to bed?' I asked, smiling.

'Your mother's not here, Jeanine. She had one of those awful nosebleeds. The ambulance took her to hospital about an hour ago.'

I felt as if I'd been sandbagged.

Chapter 20

⚜⚜⚜⚜⚜⚜⚜⚜⚜⚜

The atmosphere on the yard was extremely tense. I paced up and down, went into the barn once more to see if everything was quite tidy, shifted a bin fractionally, shooed a cat away, and went back to stand at the main gate and stare at the stretch of lane disappearing upwards, shielded by the hedge.

Finally I opened the wide gate and climbed the hill to the top, where I found Hugh Morgan and his brother Wyn, sitting by the road, gazing silently out at the view. It is a spectacular view and normally I would have turned to admire it – the valley dropping down sharply below; the sharp peaks of the Fans towering mightily over the green fields, which looked so much steeper from this angle; the gentler hills around, with their ever-changing perspectives of depth and distance. Today, however, I merely glanced at it impatiently.

'Any sign?' I asked Hugh.

'Nothing,' he said. 'I did take a walk along the road to see if I could spot him.'

'I hope,' I said fervently, 'that he doesn't get stuck on these narrow lanes with that load. God, I hope it's good.'

Hugh shrugged. 'You'll find out soon enough anyway, if he gets here.'

I went back down the hill to the farm, to man the phone in case there was a hitch and we needed to mount a rescue operation.

This was the final piece of a jigsaw I'd been putting together for the past week. I was waiting for hay to be delivered; hay I'd never seen and had bought from someone I didn't know.

It was the largest amount of hay I'd ever invested in. Normally I bought it in small loads throughout the winter and each load, what with finding decent hay, negotiating a price for it and then arranging transport, nearly drove me insane; for, while it is difficult enough to find good hay and have a full load delivered, nobody wants to bring you a couple of tons.

Apart from the cost, my main trouble was that to get a big, loaded, hay lorry through my gate and into my narrow yard was not to be contemplated. Usually, therefore, Myrddin Parry had gone to collect the hay for me on his trailer, so it had to be fairly local. But Myrddin has a hay allergy and it was only as a last resort that I would ask him to spend a day spitting and coughing over my load. But I'm afraid, in the absence of any other means, that's what it usually meant. This year there was another problem.

It had been a wet, sodden summer, the odd days apart, and already the forecast price of the hay which had been made was reaching the sky. Canny farmers and dealers were hanging onto their stocks anyway, hoping the price would go even higher as the winter bit. I was in despair of getting anything reasonable either as to quality or price and was beginning to investigate other alternatives, when Penny in Yorkshire suggested that a friend of hers might be able to help. He had managed to make all of his hay in a brief period of fine weather in June and, although he usually only sold it after Christmas, it was worth asking him if he'd let me have a load now. The only trouble would be that, as he lived in Oxfordshire, I'd have to get it to Wales somehow.

Mike let me have the hay very reasonably. It was guaranteed best meadow hay and suitable for all my stock. I made more phone calls and found a reliable firm which would collect the hay – all seven tons of it. Even after I'd paid for the transport and the driver, the hay would still be cheaper than any I'd been quoted for locally.

The last problem was to get it down the hill and into my yard. Myrddin was busy that day, but he offered to lend me his tractor and trailer if I could find someone competent to drive them. I found Hugh Morgan and his brother Wyn, who could spare a day from their work in the forestry. That just left the weather (seven tons of wet hay was not what I wanted), which had not been kind of late.

It was a brilliant autumn day. Hugh and Wyn arrived in good time and went up to wait for the lorry. The barn had been cleared, the cheque made out for the transport, the driver's tip was in my pocket and there was nothing else I could organize. I began to go quietly and steadfastly mad.

What if the hay was no good? When you buy from a dealer, the theory is (although I've never been brave enough to try it) that if you are not satisfied you can send the load back. But I didn't have that option. I had bought the hay direct from the farmer and the lorry driver was simply delivering my goods. There was no way I could send it back to Oxfordshire.

What if the lorry didn't make it and Hugh and Wyn had to go home and could not spare another day? What if the lorry tipped its load out on the narrow lane and blocked if for ages? What if Myrddin's tractor broke down (as it had once before, bringing my hay up a steep hill) and we couldn't get the hay into my yard? What if I sold the animals and never bought hay ever, ever again?

I looked in on the goats and observed them picking disdainfully at the remains of last year's hay. They're fussy things, goats. If the hay was no good they'd starve rather than eat it. Besides which, bad hay is worse than useless. If it has mould or poisonous weeds in it, it's a killer.

A loud neighing from Doli and an excited squealing from the foal, both grazing on the top field, sounded on the still air, and a faint, lovely perfume wafted down the hill towards me. It was a smell more wonderful than any you'll find in a bottle; it was the smell of really well-made, sun-ripened hay.

The tractor and trailer appeared almost at once and Hugh was punching the air and grinning broadly. 'It's good,' he cried. 'It's the *best*!'

And it was – such hay as I've never had before or since. The smell of it made us all a little drunk and, as Hugh and I unloaded it and Wyn (who's an ace hay-stacker) packed it in the barn, we laughed and joked and kept sniffing like addicts. Good hay has that effect on anyone who's been through the worry of making it themselves.

Hugh and Wyn made several trips up the hill; Myrddin joined them at the last and, with the lorry on its way again, my barn full to the raftered beams with hay and one of the loose-boxes taking up the overflow, I felt incredibly rich. Wyn had even left me proper steps up into the stack, so that this year there would be none of the terror of heavy falling bales as I hoisted them down.

I still dream of that hay and its smell, which it kept right through till the next spring. I rang Mike in Oxfordshire to tell him how delighted I was, but he was not pleased.

'That wasn't the *really* good stuff I meant you to have,' he said. 'I had to go out, but I told the men it was the next bay in the shed you were to have. I was really angry when I found they'd made a mistake and given you the hay out of the wrong one.'

The thought of what the *'really* good hay' must have been like has haunted me ever since.

If the sight and smell of my hay filled me with joy, the quantity inspired awe. I'd never bought so much in one lot before. The only reason I'd been able to do so this year was that my book had been taken by Norton's in New York. They in turn had sold the paperback rights, and a lovely big cheque came my way. Not, you understand, the sort that best-sellers can expect, but respectable enough to give me ideas above my station. I had the living room painted and I bought the hay. And a brand-new car, the first (and, I suspect the last) I'd ever owned.

Mrs P was still in hospital. Once again, they'd needed to make sure she replaced the blood she'd lost, and also Dr Williams wanted her to have physiotherapy for her back. While she was away seemed a good time to repot the Happy Plants, which perked up at once, and to tackle the rest of the painting.

I am not the world's best painter. No matter how much I try, there is always more paint on everything except where it's supposed to be; paint tins develop arcane lives of their own and decant their contents wilfully and maliciously; brushes (no matter how expensive) leave their bristles on walls and doors; fingers stick together like a superglue ad. The overall effect is ghastly, with bubbles, bald patches and long streaks of paint. I therefore decided to engage yet another Rebecca (it was my year for Rebeccas) to paint the living room for me.

By now, after years and years of woodsmoke, the walls had kippered nicely and, although the more artistically inclined visitors loved them for their old-master patina, the room was getting darker and darker, like a well frequented pub.

'It should take about two days,' said Rebecca, who had once painted an entire power station in Australia with her boyfriend. 'Three at the most. One day to clear everything out and wash the walls and ceiling, one to paint it and another to do any extra coats, and tidy up.'

It took us two weeks – two weeks I don't ever want to go through again. Even Rebecca got rather hysterical about it.

The charming, cosy woodsmoke look did not give up in a hurry. It absolutely refused to be covered. No matter that Rebecca and I scrubbed and scrubbed, as soon as we put the white paint on the walls a nasty seeping yellow came through. Coat after coat after coat of emulsion and still it was there, looking like a disease. It was something similar to those bloodstains in ancestral homes which will not go away.

Rebecca and I found out a lot about woodsmoke stains. We discovered, at last, that there was a product which costs the earth and is sold mainly to those well frequented pubs when they want to freshen up their image. You put this product on before you paint the walls and it stops the woodsmoke stains coming through. There were other methods which were either much messier, much more expensive or much more dangerous, but by then, with Rebecca threatening to desert and me sobbing quietly, we opted for a couple of coats of oil-based paints – white eggshell finish on the walls and thick gloss on the woodwork. It looked all right, but it took me half a year to move all the books back into the room and now the walls are almost as bad as ever. I've decided to go permanently for the well-frequented-pub look after all.

The new car was also white, with jazzy red lines painted on the sides and a scribble, which looked like Dracula's signature, on front and back. It was a Fiat Panda four-wheel drive – a 'special edition', with a roo-bar on the front, called a Madagascar. It was also on special offer, although I didn't know at the time that this was because they were trying to clear the old models out before introducing one with a more powerful engine. This one did not have a very big engine and its bodywork was so light, after the Beetle, that I called it The Tonka Toy.

The dear old Beetle had, for some long while, spent almost as much time in the garage getting repaired as it had on the road. Just about everyting in it had been replaced, but still something would go wrong. It was in a moment of complete frustration with it that I thought of buying another car. The cheque from America came just as that thought occurred. I bought the Panda, regretted it at once, left it in the carriage shed by the barn and went on using my limping Beetle.

Myrddin had a new car too. His had cost twice as much as the Panda. It was a four-wheel-drive estate. It had all the latest technology, including electric windows and automatic locking devices. The panel by the steering wheel was a wonder of coloured buttons which worked everything. Myrddin was still trying to figure out which button worked what when he decided to give the new car a good run by taking me to North Wales to look for Whistle Sticks.

We found them in a little cottage where everything was going on at once: bread being made, children coming and going, sticks being polished and lots of conversation and laughter. It was Simon Pendrell who was making the bread and Maggie, his wife, who was polishing the sticks. The Pendrells took it in turn to keep house or make sticks.

The sticks had a whistle cut into their handles, so that if you got lost on the hills you could simply blow for help. Some of them even had deep hollow handles, which had tablets of glucose and a measure of brandy inside. Myrddin, who said he never bothered with a stick, was deeply sceptical about these sticks, probably because he can do a very piercing whistle using his own two fingers. Nevertheless, he didn't mind demonstrating their range for the recording I wanted to do, so we sent him off down a rocky slope with a Whistle Stick. The Pendrells didn't know, and I'd forgotten, how fast and far Myrddin can walk in a short space of time. If you tell Myrddin to demonstrate something, he demonstrates it good and proper. The Pendrells and I waited and waited, until Maggie was all for sending out a search party and Simon was wondering how to make the whistles stronger. At last the sound of laughter and three shrill blasts came floating up the hill towards us.

As a matter of fact Myrddin did buy a stick. This one not only had a whistle in the top but something else in the bottom. One way of getting sheep to move along is to bang a stick on the ground at them, which isn't much use if the ground is soft and muddy, so the Pendrells had created a stick with a noisy rattle in the bottom to make a loud clacking noise.

It was hard to leave the Pendrells; they were so full of bright ideas. Maggie had a little sideline too. All his life her father had smoked a pipe and, for some reason, had kept all the tobacco tins. His daughter, being a thrifty Welsh girl, used the vast collection to make up little emergency kits for walkers, which would fit in a pocket. Each tin contained a plastic bag for collecting dew, a rubber band with a bead on it to clang onto the top of the tin to attract attention, a small candle and some matches (there was a strip on the side of the tin for striking them on), glucose tablets, a length of twine and a fishing hook, a tiny list of helpful hints and miniature slabs of dark chocolate.

We left, rather full of fresh bread, and called at Cae Dafydd again to see Tina and Frank, at their wood-turning this time. They were frantically busy making up a huge order for Christmas – Victorian needle cases, spinning tops, spindles, darning mushrooms and lots of other lovely old-fashioned things.

When Gert and I had gleaned what we wanted from the workshop we all went back into the house for coffee and there, in a special room, was a collection of Graham Piggot's sculptures – mostly the naughty ones.

'Every time we've got a few pounds to spare I rush off to Bladon to see what's new,' said Tina when I exclaimed over this coincidence. 'He's just made me this wonderful little goat.'

I recognized it at once. It had been in the Piggots' shop when I was there and Graham had said it was for a lady in North Wales. Tina, as ever was!

I had also, since last I'd been to Cae Dafydd, got to know a little more about Modern Game Bantams.

'Have you still got any of those stilt-walkers for sale?' I asked.

'I'm actually looking for a good home for a little trio.' said Tina. 'and I have a spare Silver Sebright too, if you're interested.'

So one gap in the Silver Sebright family was plugged with a small lady called Isabella, and the stilt-walkers came into our lives.

Modern Game Bantams are very tiny, perhaps not much bigger than a blackbird, but they have incredibly long legs. They were really bred for exhibition, particularly suitable for children to handle and, although their breeding has some Old English Game in it, they are the tamest, most delightful of birds. They don't stand any nonsense, though, and the cocks will front up to birds vastly bigger than themselves, but once they know you they'll perch on your hands and sing to you in that odd little chortling voice they have. They do have rather particular ideas about where they want to roost, and one of mine had always to be collected from the goat-shed, where she roosted on the kids' backs. The birds I had from Tina Holly were black with a pale gold ruff round their necks, but later I had some from another breeder which were white and gold. I called the cockerel Mr Damart, because he looked as if he was wearing long white underpants.

My only regret is that I hadn't taken up Tina's offer of some stilt-walkers the year before, but now they were safely tucked up in their box in the back of Myrddin's new car as we set off, far too late, for the south.

It had begun to rain, and soon the wind rose and dashed it against the windscreen, just as the wipers faltered, dragged their blades helplessly and died. One button on the panel, which was now lit up like a fairground, went out. And, one by one, most of the others went out too. Myrddin got out and tried to find the fuse box. A few more buttons on the panel blinked out. I think we finally had dipped headlights left, and every mile expected them to fail too. Only Myrddin, with his eagle eyes, could have seen where we were going through that blinding rain.

'If you need to sound the horn,' I said, 'I can always blow the Whistle Stick. And are you sure these doors will still open by hand?'

The windows, of course were firmly and electrically closed. Their buttons had been amongst the first to go off. If they'd been open at the time, we'd have had a very wet journey. As we drove, I stopped envying all those marvels of modern technology and thought lovingly of the dear old Beetle and wished I hadn't invested my windfall in the Panda. But Mrs P had fallen in love with it.

'It's warm and I can get into it without hurting my back,' she said, when I finally picked her up from the hospital. So for her sake I began to drive the Panda and finally appreciated the way it could nip round the lanes without pulling my arm practically out of its socket. And I must admit that it got up the truly awful track which led to the Shackles' farm without too much trouble, after I remembered to engage its four-wheel drive.

Although I had Gert tucked up in the back of the Panda, this visit to the Shackles' was, as much as anything, a sentimental journey. At the end of it, I hoped to find a portrait of Dolores, a portrait painted not on paper or canvas, but knitted into a sweater. Frankly, I couldn't really believe it was possible – a picture of a goat, yes, but not a really lifelike portrait of Dolores.

Knitting sweaters had become something of a commonplace as a cottage industry, with all the new machines available, but Margaret and Adeline had come up with a novel idea. They would guarantee to reproduce your favourite animal, to the life, so that you could wear it. Adeline would do the original drawing, and transfer it to graph paper so that Margaret could make a pattern out of it. They'd told me about this new enterprise, and shown me a couple of sweaters, when they'd brought the current male over to serve the goats that season. These days they no longer arrived in a little yellow three-wheeler, but came in state in a redundant ambulance. In spite of the goat graphics on the side, it was a bit alarming to see that big white vehicle (which still looked just like an ambulance) turning into our yard. Mrs P and I had seen enough ambulances over the past year. But it was a giggle to decant their goat from the back section, which was still lit dramatically by a red light.

The new sweaters were quite impressive. Enough, anyway, for me to bring forth a colour photo of Dolores and ask if the Shackles' could reproduce that in wool. We had spent some time choosing the colour of the actual sweater, and decided on forest green to make a good background for the rich red-gold of Dolores's coat. Now, some weeks later, they'd phoned to tell me it was ready.

When Margaret Shackles opened the door of their cottage, it reminded me a little of Mrs Tiggywinkle's abode – paraffin lamps, an ironing board and a rather portly lady bustling around with an old flat iron. The Shackles' had no electricity at that farm, and pressing my sweater meant heating up the iron on top of the Rayburn.

I sat down and waited. The door clicked open and I turned, expecting it to be Adeline coming home from school, but it was a young collie bitch who entered. Margaret frowned at her and said sternly, 'Shut the door behind you.'

The Collie wagged her tail, turned, and did as she was told.

'Well,' said Margaret, pressing on the damp cloth over the sweater so that steam rose, 'she taught herself to open the door and we had to get up and shut it to keep out the draughts. So Adeline taught the dog to close it herself.'

She set the flat iron aside on a stand and surveyed her work carefully.

'Now, I'll just hang this over a chair for a moment to air and then you can try it on.'

'Before I do that, I'd like to get the sound of the hissing iron, the dog doing her party trick, and record the interview about the sweater,' I said. 'You can surprise me with your handiwork for real, then.' For I'd carefully avoided looking at the portrait until it was ready to try on.

It all worked very well. Outside, there were pigs squealing as Mr Shackles did the feeding. Inside, the iron hissed, the fire spat, the dog opened the door and shut it, and Margaret told me how many different colours of wool she'd used for Dolores' portrait. And then, with a flourish, she presented it to me.

It was no fake, my cry of surprise. There was Dolores to the life, including that very special look in her eyes. Underneath, it said 'The Unicorn Herd' (for Unicorn is our prefix).

'And as an extra surprise,' said Margaret triumphantly, 'look on the back.'

On the back was a unicorn, its mane and horn flecked with pale blue to give them a mother-of-pearl look.

I don't wear the sweater much, afraid of something happening to it, but when I do Dolores seems to come to life. Her and me against the world. Just the way it used to be.

'One day,' I said to Margaret and Adeline (who had eventually come home from school), 'I'll get you to do Doli, and you can put the foal on the back. Did I tell you that she's had her horoscope done?'

They looked at each other and raised their eyebrows. Smiling politely, they waved me off down their pot-holed track once more. Even in their rather individualistic world, people don't go having their horse's horoscope done.

They don't usually in mine either. Not that is, until I'd told my listeners about her birth, and a letter had come at once asking if the writer could cast the foal's horoscope. All I had to do was supply the exact date and if possible, time, of the birth.

Unable to resist the offer, I provided the information, and back came a proper astrological chart and two foolscap pages of detailed predictions as to the foal's character and preferences, which ended with the remarks:

> This foal is a real individualist. She will at times be moody and difficult but just when you begin to despair she will change and be sweetness itself. She may be one step ahead of all your actions so often you may think she can read your mind . . . .
>
> One thing she will not be is dull . . . Even if she lives to be 40 years old, she will always look youthful and take pleasure in life.

At the time, of course, all I knew was the foal's difficult side, although her carefully timed appearance in front of the television cameras did make me suspect her of that 'mind reading' business. Realizing, too, that I may have given away a few hints as to her forthcoming personality on the air, I decided to test Jan Shaw, the equine astrologer (although the foal was only the second horse she'd cast a horoscope for), properly. I sent her the birth dates and times of two unnamed goats and asked her to cast their horoscopes and come and meet them afterwards.

Jan Shaw didn't do too badly on the caprine character forecasts and, if Minnie did take the opportunity to relieve her of a few minor articles of clothing, and Gorgeous stood raising her lip suspiciously, and Clare tried to eat the horoscope itself, the visit

258

was a success. And, although I didn't know it at the time, she was absolutely spot on about the foal. Then I thought it was all a rather dotty but charming idea to have her horoscope cast, and I certainly batted off any suggestions that I have my own done. I didn't need the stars to tell me that my own future was likely to be very difficult.

Mrs P and I hadn't said much about it. She came home and did her 'Woman-and-Dog-in-the-Street' act with Winston for the Christmas programme. What with the Whistle Sticks, spinning tops, goat sweaters, horse horoscopes and much more, it was a cheerful programme. I got them to make a special cassette of the recording and handed it to my mother, saying, 'You'll be able to play it to the family on Christmas Day.'

She nodded sadly. We both knew that the damp Welsh air was not going to do her back any good. It was far too long since she'd seen my brother and his family, and the time had at last come for her to go home to Australia.

I booked her a flight on the 10th of December and arranged for Colin Newman to drive her to Heathrow in his hire car and for a friend to meet her there.

Both of us were determined not to go through the awful airport farewell scene. Neither are we ever happy if I'm driving the car. Mrs P has never really come to terms with the fact that her infant daughter is grown up enough to see the other cars on the road and notice things like red lights. Her constant cries of alarm have a shattering effect on my nerves and accidents are narrowly avoided.

'Let's just say goodbye here,' she said, 'so I can think of you with the animals. Besides which, Winston is going to be a problem.'

The night before she was due to leave, we had a minor crisis because the lock I'd bought for her big suitcase went missing completely. Its own keys had been missing for a long time before that. I stayed up all night turning the place upside down, but had to ring Colin to buy us one and bring it with him.

Colin, who runs a small local garage, had polished his car till it shone, placed cushions and rugs inside it, and looked a different man himself, all smartened up and out of his overalls.

It was raining and, thinking to save my mother the muddy walk to the main gate, he reversed the car through the garden and down the grassy path to the front door.

Mrs P and I were both outwardly calm and cheerful. Only when Winston suddenly burst out of the door and tried pathetically to get in the car with her did both of us gulp a bit. Colin packed my mother gently into her seat, got into the car himself and tried to drive off.

The wheels span, the mud flew, Colin gave me a sick smile and Mrs P, encased in her rugs, stared rigidly ahead. Behind them, I heaved and pushed and panicked and the rain fell steadily from above.

The car dug itself deeper and deeper into the lawn, until ruts were halfway up its wheels, and long streaks of mud covered all Colin's careful polishing. Somewhere, behind us in the house, Winston was howling piteously.

At last, panting and weeping, I told Colin it was useless. He'd have to take the Panda or the Beetle to get Mrs P to Heathrow. At the speed they went, I doubted if he'd make it.

'No,' said Colin. 'Go and get the Panda. Put her in four-wheel drive and I'll hitch this one to the roo-bar. You'll have to reverse out.'

So that's what we did and, at last, Colin's car came up out of the lawn with a great sploshing sound. There was no time for last-minute farewells and the journey ahead would be fast and furious for my mother, instead of the quiet, unfussed and leisurely one I'd planned.

As the mud-spattered car paused by the gate, Mrs P put her head through the window and cried, ' I didn't have time to make your Christmas cake.'

I stood gazing up at the empty lane for a long while after the car had disappeared. Finally, I collected the shovel and, in the pouring rain, began to fill in the deep, muddy spaces in the lawn.

Chapter 21

Kathleen Griffiths, Cliff's wife, made me a Christmas cake, the nearest to one of Mrs P's I've ever had. In amongst the cards, the postman brought a pudding, made to a sixteenth-century recipe, from Christine Palmer. Gwynneth delivered a tree and Myrddin arrived with the holly. One way and another, they all made sure I celebrated as usual. Mrs P rang me from the middle of the family party 12,000 miles away and, not long after that, she had her own little flat in Canberra, an electric invalid bike to charge around on, and a couple of weekly fixtures to play cards, at which she won frequently.

Lily and the whippets still scan the trees for likely squirrels and Winston, fat and rebellious as ever, still sits on the stairs and plays his 'Dog-In-The-Street' role when I'm editing, or keeps my feet warm when I'm writing. Mary Price has gone on to greater and grander things at the BBC. Gwynneth and her family, to my sorrow, have left the valley to farm somewhere else; and a few weeks ago I attended Myrddin's wedding. Never was a wedding attended by more good will from his friends, for, as one guest said, 'People use the word "neighbour" lightly, but Myrddin, means it. And when you need him, he is *there*.' And we all agreed with that completely.

I seldom see Bertie Ellis these days. His assistant, Kate Hovers, comes out to deal with all the mysterious ailments my animals still entertain me with. Rebecca the goat is a grandmother, her own mother Sophie never changes, and Gorgeous has quietened down a bit, but not much. Doli's foal is a great big horse now. She has also completely changed her colour. She has a silver mane and tail and her body is dappled grey like a rocking horse. She still has a clear white circle on her rump and I still haven't found a name for her. She is just 'The Filly', but her ears have curious white markings on them, like stitches, as if someone had sewn them on as an afterthought. 'Frankenstein's Filly,' someone suggested, but her character is far too beautiful for that.

It is true that we went through the first eighteen months of her life with difficulty together. In fact I almost sold her three times. But now it is as if she has absorbed into her being all the other loved animals who are no longer here. I can see Merlin, Blossom, Dolores and, somewhere in there, though they are poles apart in looks, there is dear old Doli herself. She, by the way, is just beginning to show her age, although to see her galloping along with her daughter you might not think so, and certainly she looks a lot brighter than she did when the Lloyds first knew her, long, long before she spent the summer with Tapanui.

Before I came to live in the valley the Lloyds farmed next to a forestry, several miles away. There was a poor, tired horse working in that forestry and the Lloyds, feeling sorry for her, allowed her handler to let her out to graze on one of their fields every Sunday. When they moved, they often wondered what had happened to the poor 'old' horse and never once suspected it was Doli – she of the gleaming coat and hedge-hopping habits, who waggled her left leg at her lover. It wasn't till two years later, when I told them how I'd bought Doli, that it all came together. And, if I'm correct in my calculations that Doli was born in 1966, it all goes to prove that Fire Horses *do* usually land neatly on all four hooves.

It is spring again in the valley. The tiny, petulant cries of lambs, and the crowding hum of their mothers gathering to be fed, echo round the hills. The garden is full of sprays of golden forsythia, the flowering currant is covered in bright pink bells and the Minack violets send their perfume up to my open window.

At last the winter mud has given way to rich grass once more and last night, as the dogs and I came back from checking the stock, I looked up at the great branches of the ash tree spreading out against a brilliant sky. It was as if Tolly himself had said, 'Abracadabra! Let that tree burst into stars!'